BULLYING
NO MORE

UNDERSTANDING AND PREVENTING BULLYING

Kimberly L. Mason, Ph.D., LPC, NCC

BARRON'S

Disclaimer: The information provided in this book is designed to provide helpful information about bullying. Every reasonable effort has been made to ensure that the material in this book is accurate, true, complete, and appropriate at the time of writing. The information, strategies, and techniques contained herein may not be suitable for every person or situation. You should consult with a licensed professional where appropriate. The author and publisher shall not be liable for any omission, error, or injury, damage, loss or financial consequences arising from the use of the book. The decision of whether to use or not use the information, strategies, and techniques contained in this book is solely up to you.

Note: All names used throughout this book have been changed to protect the identities of the original people involved.

All inquiries should be addressed to:
Barron's Educational Series, Inc.
250 Wireless Boulevard
Hauppauge, New York 11788
www.barronseduc.com

ISBN: 978-1-4380-0209-5

Library of Congress Control Number: 2013012500

Library of Congress Cataloging-in-Publication Data

Mason, Kimberly L.
  Bullying no more : understanding and preventing bullying / Kimberly L. Mason, Ph.D., LPC, NCC.
    pages cm
  Includes bibliographical references and index.
  ISBN 978-1-4380-0209-5
1. Bullying.   2. Child rearing.   I. Title.
BF637.B85M2685   2013
302.34'3—dc23   2013012500

Printed in the United States of America
9 8 7 6 5 4 3 2 1

Contents

Acknowledgments

Special gratitude goes to my wonderful husband, Todd, for his patience, encouragement, and support given to me during this project. Thank you for believing in me, lifting my spirits, and reminding me to eat and sleep. Thanks for picking up the slack and riding the roller coaster with me. I am so grateful that you are always there for our children, family, and me. After 20 years of marriage, you are still the one I laugh with, live for, dream with, and love.

To my sons, Zachary and Jordan, you are my inspiration. Thank you for your encouragement and support, without complaint, as I sat at my computer day after day. Zach, I appreciated that you made me laugh when I was down. Jordan, I am grateful for your hugs and kisses that re-energized me when I was exhausted. I am blessed to have you as my children.

To my sisters, Tracy and Shawn, thanks for encouraging and supporting me throughout my whole life.

To my mom, Cynthia, thank you for loving me, guiding me, and teaching me that I can do all things through Christ, who strengthens me. Always remember, you are the suitcase, and I am the tag.

To the family members that I have lost during the course of writing this book, I am so grateful that you were a part of my life. You are my angels in heaven. I miss and love you.

Many thanks to Sara Albert for being my sounding board as I formulated the ideas for this book. I appreciate the time taken out of your busy schedule to read my chapters and give me feedback.

To all of the counselors, teachers, parents, and students, thank you for sharing your experiences with me.

Lastly, a special thanks to Wayne Barr, Anthony Regolino, and Barron's Educational Series, Inc., for giving me the opportunity to write this book.

Why This Book?

Bullying is an age-old problem that is widespread in our schools and communities. It is frequently misunderstood by adults who consider it to be an unavoidable part of growing up. For many children who are bullied, these negative behaviors often continue because adults fail to respond to their need for help, peers are too scared to get involved, and the children themselves are too anxious, afraid, and exhausted to try anything else. Being bullied causes enormous stress for many children and their families. Bullying also has long term effects. Bullying keeps thousands of children from attending school because they feel unsafe at school. It undermines the quality of the school environment; adversely affects students' academic and social outcomes; causes victims physical, emotional, and psychological trauma; and in extreme cases, leads to serious violence and suicide.

Although the problem of bullying is longstanding, the methods used by aggressors have become more covert and difficult for parents and educators to detect. With the advent and popularity of the Internet and social media, bullying has taken on a new form called cyberbullying. Aided by new social media tools, youth cultures are developing alternative notions and practices of appropriate, responsible behavior in both their online and offline worlds. Thus, adults must take an active role in identifying bullying behaviors and working with youth by empowering them with the values, skills, and motivation to make safe and responsible choices in both words. Adults have a responsibility to intervene in issues dealing with bullying in order to create and maintain safe and peaceful school, home, and community environments. A relationship is a give and take partnership where two or more parties come together and compromise for the good of maintaining a healthy relationship. Because relationship difficulties emerge in a large number of bullying incidents, restorative approaches help enhance children's interpersonal competence in order to promote healthy relationships now and throughout their lives by restoring positive relationships between all parties involved in the bullying.

When most people talk about "bullying," they instinctually feel sorry for the victim, want to get that person help, and become adamant that justice be served. In contrast, when it comes to dealing with the bully, most people feel disgust and immediately think of ways of how the bully should be punished and "get what he or she deserves." Then there are the bystanders, the peers who defend, stand by, or join in the bullying. Most people show disdain for the bystanders for either participating in or not becoming involved. By holding the bully accountable, most adults typically employ a retributive justice approach. The goal of this rigid system of rewards and sanctions is to punish or reprimand (i.e., revoke privileges from) the bully, to deter and correct the bully's cruel behavior, to prevent future transgressions, and to teach self-control. However, these punishment tactics rarely work or last. They also do little to promote ethical character. On the other hand, restorative interventions assist in restoring positive relationships and build communities that emphasize repairing harm over violation of rules and authority.

Many times I've been asked by parents, "Is it possible to bully-proof my child?" "Can my child's behavior be changed without being punished?" My answer is always a resounding "Yes. It's possible." However, it will take a shift in your mindset from a punitive approach to a restorative one where misconduct is viewed as a violation of relationships rather than rule breaking. In restorative approaches, all parties equally experience some form of harm, whether hurt, humiliation, guilt, or shame. Everyone involved in the bullying is affected along some continuum. It is also important that we place repairing the harm done to relationships and people over and above the need for assigning blame and dispensing punishment. Now, that may be difficult for some of you to hear, especially if you were bullied and still have residual feelings as a result of it. That is a normal reaction. As an overweight kid, I was the target of verbal ridicule by an older sibling and by peers at school. Taunts such as "Thunder Thighs" and "Bertha Butt" were a common occurrence. Therefore, I understand firsthand what it means to be hurt or embarrassed. This is why I believe a restorative approach (which builds up relationships) is a good fit for remedying the issue of bullying (which tears down relationships).

As a parent, I have two sons, ages 20 and 14, who were involved in bullying. One was the victim, and the other was the bystander/defender. In both situations, I was confronted with the same questions and helpless feelings that many other parents and adults experience when their child is involved in bullying. "How do I know?" "What do I do now?" "How can I help my child through this?" "How can I repair the hurt? "What is the school's role?" "How can I get the school to intervene?" "What if the school does not help?" Fortunately, because of my knowledge, I was able to intervene on my sons' behalf immediately and get the bullying stopped. However, I know that many parents and most adults are not equipped with the knowledge and skills to intervene or help advocate for and protect their child from further harm.

Hence, you know the reason for this book. This book provides you with answers to your questions so you can recognize and respond quickly and appropriately to intervene and prevent bullying from occurring. For example, a curious parent told me:

> *I've read a lot of bullying problems...mostly from the victim's point. I'd like to know if there are ways to recognize if one's own child is a bully. Are there ways to help bring the child out of the bully mode? I am not saying or concluding that my child is a bully. We want to be responsible parents, and see that the children are neither victims nor bullies. Sometimes parents worry that their children may be victims and don't see the other side. I want to check on both extremes, that's all.*
>
> Tina, a Curious Parent of an 11 Year Old

This book provides both Tina and you with the answer to your questions: what signs to look out for, the do's and don'ts of responding to bullying, ways to help children cope, ways to hold children accountable, when to get the school and authorities involved, and the legal issues surrounding bullying, just to name a few. Parents are vital in teaching their children how to build positive relationships and challenge their positive attitudes toward the use of bullying to resolve conflicts. This book furnishes you and other adults who work with children with the knowledge and skills to help children develop prosocial behaviors and attitudes in order to improve and/or strengthen their friendships that are central to their success in school and life. All adults are encouraged to teach children ways to repair, restore, and reinforce relationships in prosocial ways that build buddies and not bullies.

You will notice that I use the terms "bully" and "victim" (also known as target) throughout the book. This is used for easier reading and writing and doesn't mean that we should label a child as either a "bully" or a "victim." Remember, we need to separate the act (or behavior) from the person. So I use these two terms to avoid saying "children who bully" and "children who are targeted."

Finally, it is my goal that this book guides parents, educators, community leaders, family members, youth, and anyone who works with youths to teach children to become competent, caring, confident, compassionate, considerate, courageous, and resilient individuals. The goal is to help children become capable of building, developing, and sustaining positive relationships as well as teach them to resolve interpersonal conflicts positively. Adults play an essential role in promoting children's positive development by directly teaching them social-emotional skills, such as listening when others are talking, developing empathy, recognizing and managing emotions, disagreeing respectfully, and resolving conflicts through nonviolent means that respect the needs of all parties involved in bullying.

The book is divided into four sections. "Part I: Understanding Parent and Child Interactions" provides information about how parents and adults can learn to communicate with their children so the children will listen and vice versa. It covers the generation gap between parents and children, parenting styles, children's response styles, and goodness of fit. "Part II: Understanding Bullying" educates parents on face-to-face bullying and cyberbullying. It covers topics such as what constitutes bullying and cyberbully behavior and what is not considered bullying, how cyberbullying differs from face-to-face bullying, who's involved in bullying and cyberbullying, ways kids use technology to cyberbully, why some kids bully and use social media to cyberbully, consequences of bullying, warning signs, and why kids don't tell. "Part III: Responding to Bullying" provides parents with a restorative approach to intervention, the do's and don'ts of responding to bullying, ways to help children cope, ways to hold their child accountable, when to get the school and authorities involved, and an update on the laws and legal issues surrounding bullying. Finally, "Part IV: Preventing Bullying Behaviors" provides a prevention model that parents can use to help eliminate bully behaviors by teaching their children the personal, social, and life skills needed to become competent, caring, compassionate, considerate, and confident young people in their school, community, and home so they can be a buddy and not a bully.

The tactics I recommend in each chapter are simple to follow and easy to understand. Yet they are often challenging at first to implement. They must be practiced with patience and practiced some more, until the new skill becomes automatic. At first, you and/or your child may want to give up. Resist the urge and don't. Perseverance is the key. If you first don't succeed then try, try, try again. Learning a new skill and demonstrating a new behavior takes time. So keep up with the routine. Although the process might be unpleasant in the beginning, the end result (new behavior, new confidence) will be worth it. So don't give up. Use the time to develop, build, and sustain a healthy relationship with your children. Be their role model. I know practicing new skills is not always that easy. With repetition, though, it will become effortless over time. Good luck in your journey.

Sincerely,
Kim

Map Key for Text Boxes

The following map key provides you with information on what the symbols mean when navigating through the book.

 Point to Ponder: These are questions for you and your children to consider.

 Tip: These are facts or important snippets of information to note.

 Toolbox Tactic: These are strategies you can use with your children, teacher, or school.

 Case Study: The case studies provide you with an example of how you can translate the information being covered into practical skills to use with your children.

Part I

Understanding Parent and Child Interactions

Chapter 1

Relating to Your Child

This chapter provides information about how parents and adults can learn to communicate with their children so the children will listen and vice versa. It covers the generation gap between parents and children, parenting styles, children's response style, and goodness of fit.

> *If a child lives with criticism, He learns to condemn.*
> *If a child lives with hostility, He learns to fight.*
> *If a child lives with ridicule, He learns to be shy.*
> *If a child lives with shame, He learns to feel guilty.*
> *If a child lives with tolerance, He learns to be patient.*
> *If a child lives with encouragement, He learns confidence.*
> *If a child lives with praise, He learns to appreciate.*
> *If a child lives with fairness, He learns justice.*
> *If a child lives with security, He learns to have faith.*
> *If a child lives with approval, He learns to like himself.*
> *If a child lives with acceptance and friendship, He learns to find love in the world.*
>
> "Children Learn What They Live"
> by Dorothy Law Nolte

Communicating with Children

> *If I am in the game, I need a game plan. I could grow into a tyrant (ouch!), or I could grow into a friend to my child (oops!). I don't want either of those roles. I want to be a loving and predictable parent—predictably there, predictably dealing with problems as I find ways to support my budding teenagers' exploration of responsibility.*
>
> Janie, Mother of Two Boys

Raising a child is no easy task; raising a child in the 21st century is even more daunting. As a parent of two boys, ages 20 and 14, I often find myself being pulled into two different worlds like Janie does—wanting to protect them from being hurt yet understanding that they need to learn from their mistakes, wanting them to succeed in life yet knowing I must allow them to fail; wanting to be supportive of them yet holding them accountable for their actions. On the other hand as a counselor, I recognize that parental practices such as harsh and inconsistent punishment, too little or too much involvement (overprotection), being overly responsive (which hampers the relationship), and permissiveness for aggression at home are connected to bullying and victimization experiences at school.[1] For example, having a highly responsive mother places a child at risk for becoming one of millions of "teacup" children, made fragile by overprotection and overinvolvement. Sadly, this leads the child to be further victimized. However, having a responsive mother protects the child from being aggressive toward others.

As 21st-century parents, we face a unique set of challenges with the rise of technology. Put simply, you and I have many more things to consider as we decide how to parent and educate our children than our parents probably did. Our 21st-century children are growing up in a different world and are far ahead of us than we were their age. The way our children think is often not the way we think, and their brain processes information very differently than ours. Consequently, it is essential that we understand the world in which our children are growing up. This chapter will help you understand the generation gap between you and your children, your parenting style, your children's temperament, how you could respond to your children based on "goodness of fit," and tips for socially relating to your children.

TIP

Children with involved parents, no matter what income or background, are more likely to:
- Earn higher grades and test scores, and enroll in higher-level programs
- Be promoted, pass their classes, and earn credits
- Attend school regularly
- Have better social skills, show improved behavior, and adapt well to school
- Graduate and go on to postsecondary education

National Coalition for Parent Involvement in Education[2]

Parent Says This, Child Says That

My children don't do what they are supposed to do. I have to tell them over and over and over again. What I was doing wasn't working and yet I was doing the same thing over and over again and expecting my child to do something different. Before, I was upset that my child wouldn't change. It hadn't occurred to me that I hadn't changed either. Why did I expect a different result?

A Frustrated Parent

"You're ruining my life." "You never let me do anything." "You're mean." "You don't love me." "You're right, I suck!" Do any of these sound familiar? How many times have you heard your children respond in these ways? What emotions did they stir within you? Did you feel angry, defensive, disrespected, guilty, sad, or manipulated? Did these feelings cause you to confront your children and respond with comments such as "You never clean your room." "You're not going to amount to anything if you don't study." "You are so irresponsible." "Won't you be more like your sister?" Do you want to stop playing the game of "Who will win the argument"? If so, then it is important that you understand how we as adults see and perceive things are not how our children see and perceive things. For example, after learning that your child has bullied, you may blame him/her and yell, "You're always getting in trouble." "You're a bad person." "You're such a holy terror." These comments may lead your child to respond, "Like you're so perfect in handling problems." "You never hear my side." "You're mean too, so I'm just like you."

WE SEE AND SAY THINGS DIFFERENTLY	
Parent's Say This	Kids Say That
• "They don't listen to me." • "I love their confidence, but I see little humility." • "They think they know everything." • "They get distracted all the time; they can't focus."	• "They are so 'old school.' They don't understand me." • "I bring my laptop to class, but I am on Facebook there." • "I don't know why they won't let us text. They insist on talking." • "They are boring and irrelevant."

Why is there a disconnect between children and their parents? After asking several parents and kids this question, the bottom line is each group sees things very differently except for one thing: respect. The kids feel the adults are irrelevant and disrespectful. The adults feel the kids are inexperienced and disrespectful. Hmm. It is curious that both groups feel disrespect. Let's explore how you can feel more respected so your children can feel more respected.

As noted previously, you and your children see things very differently and perceive confrontation differently. Parents are usually concerned with the outcome (e.g., that the child followed the rules—doesn't bully others). Children are generally concerned with the process (e.g., controlling the mood or the direction of the argument itself).[3] Often, children know what buttons to push in order to get what they want, that is, for you to lose your temper/lose control over your emotions and lose your ability to enforce the rules. For example, 14-year-old Rebecca would yell and scream in a sarcastic tone each time her mom would enforce the rule of not using the computer past 10:00 P.M. for social use. Mom got so upset she began to get defensive and started yelling back, stating that Rebecca is "ungrateful" and "lucky even to have a computer." As a result, a bitter argument occurred between the two. Eventually, mom became so frustrated that she gave in and let Rebecca stay on the computer saying, "I'm tired of fighting with you. Do whatever you think is best. I don't care."

If you ever felt like Rebecca's mom and wanted to throw your hands up and give up, don't. There is hope that you can learn how to communicate with your children so they will listen, and vice versa. Like the frustrated parent noted above, not only do your children need to change their attitude and the way they respond to you, you are encouraged to alter how you respond to them. When your children begin to push your buttons, you must remind yourself that you are responsible for whether or not you become angry. Are you being critical or blaming your children? Are you not paying attention, expecting unattainable performance, using a tone of voice that accuses your children of being stupid or incompetent, and coming across as having the only right answers?

In cases such as these, we can expect others to protect their position by fighting back. We need to remind ourselves that we have a choice about how we feel about a situation and how we respond to people. So when we feel we are "put on the spot" we need to say different phrases that are emotionally neutral and will calm the situation. Let's practice.

Pretend that your child, Emma, is angry at you and begins to yell and scream in front of other people. She calls you an "S.O.B." and says, "You're unfair." "You're always on my case." Write down as many things as you can think of that would be emotionally neutral or calm the situation. For example, you could say, "There's probably some truth to that. Thanks for letting me know."

TIP

According to the JWT Intelligence (*www.jwtintelligence.com*) report, "Gen Z: Digital in Their DNA," this generation prefers to socialize digitally. Around 4 in 10 youths indicated that it is easier, more convenient, and more comfortable talking to people online than in real life.

Generation Gap

Parents want their kids' approval, a reversal of the past ideal of children striving for their parents' approval.

Jean Twenge
Author of *Generation Me*

Each generation is defined by its life experiences, giving rise to different attitudes, beliefs, and sensitivities. Studying general similarities and differences can be tricky. No individual completely fits the profile of a particular generation. However, research suggests that the majority of people born between a rough set of dates actually do share many characteristics and are classified according to key historical events that occurred during the particular timeframe.[4,5,6] They are also characterized by four distinct types: idealist, reactive, civic, and adaptive.[6] The following chart provides a description of the different generations.

GENERATION TABLE	
Generation Alpha	Born 2010 and later. This generation will likely be the most formally educated in history. They will begin schooling earlier and study for longer. Brought up in an era of information overload, they are expected to be even more tech savvy and materialistic than their predecessors, Gen Z.[6] Defining event is probably the Sandy Hook shootings.
Generation Z (Gen Z), iYGeneration, Generation Now, Gen iY	Born 1991–2009. A **civic** generation, inner driven within the information revolution, striving to get ahead. Described as tech savvy, creative, confident, and with a strong work ethic.
Generation Y, Millennial Generation, Net Generation, Generation Next, Gen Y	Born 1981–1990. A **civic** generation, inner driven within the information revolution, striving to get ahead. They saw the birth of the World Wide Web. They build parallel careers (i.e., believe that they will be able to pursue more than one line of work at the same time). Their defining event was the Columbine shootings and September 11, 2001. Described as flighty, transient, optimistic, cooperative team players, rule followers, and racially and ethnically diverse.
Generation X, 13th Generation, Gen X	Born 1961–1981. A **reactive** generation, street wise. They build a portable career (i.e., intent on looking for career security rather than job security). They saw the fall of the Berlin Wall, *Challenger* explosion, the first computer floppy disk sold, and AIDS. Described as lost, cynical, and wasted.
Baby Boomers	Born 1943–1960. An **idealist** generation, often stressed out. They tend to be optimistic, communicative, and value education and consumer goods. They share the Kennedy assassination. They build a stellar career (i.e., listening to the tick of the career clock, they find themselves questioning where they've been and where they're going). Described as smug, hippies, and then yuppies.
Silent Generation	Born 1925–1942, 95% of this generation is retired. They are an **adaptive** generation because they lived through the Great Depression. They are characterized by a belief in common goals and **respect for authority**. They build a legacy (i.e., build a lifetime career with one employer to make a lasting contribution). Described as withdrawn, cautious, unimaginative, indifferent, and unadventurous.

Which generation do you fall into? What about your children? My husband and I are Gen X parents and our sons are Gen iY kids. I approach tasks very differently than my oldest son, Zach, which quite often leads to tension in my house. For example, I usually engage in one or two tasks at a time, while he is a multitasker (an aspect of his generation). One day, I noticed he was talking on his cell phone while browsing the Internet on his laptop and looking at his Facebook page on my iPad all at the same time. (He was supposed to be doing his homework. He wasn't.) I could not believe what I was seeing. I wondered how he was attending to any of the information he was receiving. In my opinion, he wasn't. However, he didn't see it that way. This disagreement led to an argument, which caused both of us to stop listening since we were trying to convince each other we were right and the other person was wrong. Sadly, the conflict was not resolved. One parent stated it best. Our children "don't think about turning things off to engage in discussions. In their minds, they can do it all at the same time."

 TOOLBOX TACTIC

Which Generation Do You Fit Into?

Take the following fun quizzes and pick which fashion trends, news events, movies, TV shows, or toys you remember from your formative years. Your answers will indicate your generation type. By completing this quiz you will probably be able to reflect on your own generation and interpersonal relationships.

http://projects.usatoday.com/news/generations/quiz
or
http://www.quibblo.com/quiz/8tdrRNK/Generational-Quiz

Parenting in a Technological World: Bridging the Digital Divide

Today's parents face a generation gap with their children since their life experiences differ from those of previous generations. As noted previously, the way we communicate with our children and how we deal with confronting displeasing behaviors differ in the way we and our children meet specific goals. Likewise, the way we communicate with our children through technology differs and serves a different purpose.

Although learning the latest technology is second nature for our kids, we often find it difficult to keep up. One parent noted, "They speak different languages, and they have different sets of beliefs and suspicions."

The digital divide between generations is one of the most debatable topics of modern-day life. Each generation defines the purpose and function of technology differently. Digital natives use social media platforms effortlessly to stay connected with friends, for entertainment, to complete tasks, and for fun. Texting is normal and is the standard way they communicate with one another. In contrast, for digital immigrants, those of us who grew up in a predigital world, communicating with our friends means calling them on the home phone. Seeing them means physically walking over to their house. Digital immigrants may or may not use the Internet as a tool to perform tasks such as paying bills, shopping, booking airline tickets, or setting up a face-to-face meeting. Digital communication is just as real to natives as face-to-face meetings are to immigrants. In other words, natives (our children) take away the same meaning and feeling that immigrants (we parents) experience from a face-to-face meeting. Two students commented:

> *It's great being able to automatically know how to use technology—we don't have to ask anybody for help. We already know what to do, so that saves time. I really love technology.*
>
> 14-Year-Old Girl

> *It's a way of life. Adults need to just deal with it. I can't help it if they don't know how to work the computer.*
>
> 14-Year-Old Girl

Whether you are a digital immigrant who has chosen to avoid or limit technology, one who has reluctantly adopted some technologies, or one who has enthusiastically embraced technology and has immersed yourself in the online culture, one thing is for sure: Social media is here to stay. We have to work with it, not against it. The Internet, texting, social networking, video chatting—these are the realities of our children's lives. We cannot expect our children to go backward; we have to meet them where they are. In other words, we must learn to communicate in the language and style of our children. Doing so will let us communicate with them regarding their real and virtual worlds so we can comfortably and confidently parent in the real world. For most of our children (and for many adults), social lives and relationships are changing because the lines between the digital (i.e., virtual) and real worlds are blurring. Social media holds tremendous promise for creating a better world—a more peaceful and respectful world where we can build connections and practice prosocial behaviors. Social media can either isolate us or bring us closer together. Either way, it affects relationships with peers and the relationship between us and our children. So, do you speak the same language as your children?

TOOLBOX TACTIC

Are You an Immigrant or a Native?

As you get older (as an adult), you may feel the "gap" between you and your children (i.e., Generation iY) in a more distinct way. Typically, the wider the age gap, the more you will feel like an immigrant in a land of natives. This means you will have to work harder to speak their language and know their customs and values. Take the following quiz to see if you are an immigrant or native. Visit *www.savetheirfuturenow.com/immigrantornative*

What Language Do You Speak?

Are you a NOOB? Are you a POS? Will you BRB? Will I CUL8R? CTN? Do you know what MMA and SCNR means? Your children do. If you answered no to any of these questions, you are not alone. A survey commissioned by the National Center for Missing & Exploited Children and by Cox Communications (*cox.mediaroom.com*) revealed many parents do not know what LOL (laughing out loud—57%), BRB (be right back—68%), POS (parents over shoulder—95%), and A/S/L (age, sex, location—92%) mean. One parent commented, "I don't know what kind of ride I have been on. I think you need an advanced degree to keep up with what our children are doing with all the coding they are using to keep what they are doing from their parents." Does that sound familiar? Do you share the sentiment? Do you ask yourself, "What purpose does a text serve?" If so, you're not alone. One of the challenges we have as parents is deciphering what our children's texts mean. Acronyms, text shorthand, and emoticons all serve a different purpose. Several years ago, I came across a fantastic cartoon designed by Clive Goddard (*www.CartoonStock.com*) that sums up what most parents feel like when they try to read a text. A message resembling an archaeology finding is written on a stone tablet. It states, "But this is fantastic, professor! It's like no language I've seen before!" So are you becoming obsolete in the language you use and the way you communicate with your children? If, so read on to learn how you can speak through texts so your children will respond and listen.

TIP

According to the media and marketing information company, Nielsen, in 2011, teenagers aged 13–17 sent an average of 3,364 mobile texts per month, or 114 per day. Girls sent and received 3,952 messages per month, compared to 2,815 for boys.

POINT TO PONDER

Do you text? If so, what language do you use in your text? Do you speak by typing out text messages with full words ("oh my goodness" or "you are my best friend forever!") rather than the standard abbreviations ("OMG" or "ur my bff!")? How tech savvy are you? How many texts do you send per month? How does that compare with the number of texts your child sends each month?

Chat Translators and Digital Dictionaries

If you come across terms that are unfamiliar to you like NOOB, POS, GRIEFER, BRB, MMA, and SCNR, you can go to one of several translators and dictionaries that will help you decipher the terms your kids use in chat rooms, in text messages, and on instant messaging boards. To help bridge the digital divide, you should understand at least a fraction of the "codes" they use as they text. A fantastic translator is *www.Lingo2Word.com*. You can use this online searchable text messaging dictionary for words and phrases used in e-mails, chat rooms, and ICQ (instant messaging). It will translate your text messages from text lingo to plain English or from plain English to text lingo. *Lingo2word.com* is a great translating tool because acronyms are continually being added. It lists the most popular emoticons, text messaging words, and acronyms to help enhance your texting vocabulary. Other text lingo translators are *noslang.com, teenchatdecoder.com, netsmartz411*.org, and *1337Talk.com*.

What's Your Parenting Style?

What do your parenting decisions say about you and about how you deal with your children in challenging situations? How would you classify your parenting style? You may have heard about the recent buzz surrounding a new book titled *Battle Hymn of the Tiger Mother* by Amy Chua. The author offers a controversial account of raising her children as a Chinese mother. As a result of her book, the term "tiger mom" is now being used to describe overly protective, hyperinvolved, strict mothers.

As I noted earlier, there is a link between different parenting styles and the impact they can have on children. The phrase "parental style" describes parental behavior as perceived by the child. It has two dimensions: The first, responsive, means being responsive to a child's needs, showing parental love, providing warmth, being supportive, and maintaining warm communication with the child. The second, being demanding, means controlling the child's behavior, setting limits and expectations for the child, and being willing to confront the child who disobeys.[7,8]

In his book *Generation iY: Our Last Chance to Save Their Future*, Tim Elmore, the founder and president of Growing Leaders, suggests there are eight harmful parenting styles that developed out of parenting the new generation of children.[9] Despite these eight harmful parenting styles, a ninth parenting style offers you a healthy approach to parenting your Generation iY kids.[10] Each of these parenting styles reflects different patterns of parental values, practices, and behaviors and a different balance between responsiveness and demandingness.[7] Let's explore these parenting styles and see how they are impacting our culture and contributing to the rising generation of adults.

Nine Parenting Styles

Type 1: Helicopter (Responsive and Demanding)

Helicopter parents tend to hover over their kids, keeping them from normal life difficulties. They side with the children over authority. These parents are involved in every aspect of their children's lives, often attempting to solve all of the children's problems. These people feel it is up to them to insure that life turns out well for their kids.

Result. Parents who struggle with feeling out of control or find it difficult to trust others tend to hover and use micromanagement as a parenting style. This style of parenting prevents children from learning from normal failures. So these children do not learn how to persevere. Children of overprotective parents are more likely to be bullied.[11]

Solution—Land the helicopter. When your children come to you with a problem or you see that they are struggling, do not fix it right away. Allow them the opportunity to discuss with you various options so they can solve the problem. Teach them this five-step problem-solving strategy:

1. Ask yourself, "What is the problem?"
2. Think up three possible solutions (options) to the problem.
3. Look at each option for a minute. Ask yourself, "What are the pros and cons of each?"
4. Pick the best option/solution.
5. Try out the solution, and see if it works.

Type 2: Karaoke (Responsive but Not Demanding)

Karaoke parents work hard at emulating their kids' generation (i.e., sound and look just like children). This permissive parenting style is often evidenced by individuals who try to be more of a friend than a parent, are afraid of being unpopular with their children, and are afraid to seem "uncool" and make their children unhappy. They are generally nurturing and communicative rather than the authority figure of parents. These "indulgent" parents make very few demands of their children, avoid confrontation, and rarely discipline. They fail to earn respect and to demand obedience.

Result. Parents often assume the karaoke style because of their own emotional insecurities wihle growing older. Children of permissive parents are impulsive. As a result, these children often exhibit riskier behaviors as teenagers, such as misconduct and drug use. These kids are less likely to respect authority and often perform poorly in school.

Solution—Be parents first, friends later. You need to relate to your children in an appropriate manner. Focus more on their needs than on your own. Remember that your children need boundaries and limits. They see these limits as a reassuring sign that you care about them. Boundaries are also a sign of ongoing parental protection. They need a parent who they can look up to and respect.

Type 3: Dry Cleaner (Neither Demanding nor Responsive)

Dry cleaner parents are always dropping their kids off for others to raise or for experts to fix because the parents often feel ill equipped. Frequently, these parents will be from a dual-income home where both parents are either too busy to spend time with their kids or believe parenting or connecting with their kids is not their specialty. They demonstrate a parenting style that damages their children's ability to bond with them. Consequently, these parents hope the school, a counselor, or a church youth group can fix any damage the children's home environment may have caused. Plus, if something goes wrong, they have someone to blame.

Result. These neglectful parents fail to mentor their kids and provide any authentic face-to-face time the children require. They prefer to abdicate and pass the buck of responsibility.

Solution—Balance child time and parent time. Our children benefit from affection and time with us. Research indicates adolescents who have regular contact with their parents in pleasant circumstances are much less involved in high-risk actions and are more successful academically. So you need to examine your schedule and your priorities to make room for actually relating to your children. Children need to be reassured that you feel they are important and are a priority. Your contacts do not have to be elaborate in order to foster mutual respect and affection. Talking with your children—particularly about their interests—playing games with them, or enjoying entertainment together helps build the relationship.

Type 4: Volcano (Responsive but Not Demanding)

Volcano parents, a variation of overinvolved parents, tend to "erupt" suddenly over relatively minor issues. Many of them still have some unrealized dreams from their past—sometimes an unhealthy past— and try to fulfill them through their children (i.e., live out their life through their children). So without warning, these parents may erupt all over school authorities when they become frustrated over something that happens to their child. For example, volcano parents will write papers or do homework for their children and then storm into the teacher's office when they receive a poor grade.

Result. Because these parents have unrealized dreams, their children represent the best way for them to accomplish the dreams they gave up on years earlier, even if it is vicariously done. Given that they have "baggage" that they never really dealt with in a healthy way, the parents want and need their children to be successful and "make it." They see their children as their last hope of leaving some sort of name or legacy for themselves. Therefore, volcano parents will do whatever it takes for them to succeed. They are usually infuriated and short-tempered because the boundaries between them and their children have become blurred. All too often, children of volcano parents develop their own volcanic tendencies.

Solution—Engage in self-care. First, you must address your own emotional health and deal with your own issues so you won't further teach your children inappropriate ways of handling failure and frustration. Talk to a friend, spouse, or counselor regarding these issues. Second, don't complete your children's tasks or schoolwork. It prevents them from learning. Third, by showing interest and encouraging your children to express their opinion, they will think more critically about their own beliefs and the value of completing a task on their own. Choose a topic that interests them and explore it thoroughly. Discuss it over dinner by asking "thinking questions" that begin with:

- Why do you believe...?
- What effect do you think this has...?
- How can we get more involved, make a change, and so on...?
- How can we learn more...?

Type 5: Dropout (Neither Demanding nor Responsive)

Dropout parents (also known as slacker parents) give up. They do this either emotionally by "checking out" from being a parent or literally by leaving the family to fend for themselves. These parents may be self-centered, be overwhelmed by their circumstances, be tired, be frustrated, or have simply given up trying to maintain parental authority. These parents fail to provide a healthy role model: parents who finish what they start.

Result. This style of rejecting parenting produces children who show similar parenting patterns since they were raised in uninvolved homes. These children tend to be interested in their own lives and less likely to invest much time in parenting their own children. They are generally less competent and confident than their peers. These children may demonstrate impulsive behaviors due to issues with self-regulation, may lack self-control, and may have low self-esteem.

Solution—Show you're not perfect. First, parents should seek out counseling to understand the issues that prevent them from being involved in their children's lives and to discover ways to help them cope with life's ups and downs. Afterward, they should reengage as a parent. They should begin with an apology for being physically and/or emotionally unavailable for their children.

Type 6: Bullied (Neither Responsive nor Demanding)

Bullied parents are beaten down by their strong-willed kids and are intimidated by their threats. These parents have surrendered their authority to the children, who are in control. They lack the courage and strength to lead their demanding children and prepare them for a potentially harsh adult world.

Result. This style of parenting leads to children who are controlling, aggressive, and less empathetic.

Solution—Be the parent, not the doormat. Determine what values will govern your family, and fight for those values. "Choose your battles" is a phrase often used to refer to times when we choose not to fight over a trivial matter. However, it also means that sometimes we do choose to fight worthwhile battles to uphold what is important. Furthermore, because bowing down to every whim teaches your children to take others for granted or, worse, to feel entitled to special treatment, it is never too early to engage them in charitable activities to develop altruism—a selfless concern for the welfare of others. For example, your children can shovel snow off your elderly neighbor's driveway, escort you when bringing home-baked cookies to a new neighbor, serve food at a homeless shelter during the holidays, and volunteer in an after-school program. All of these activities allow children to appreciate what they have and to understand their value as a person. They give children a sense of their ability to contribute to the good of the world. Likewise, recharge your "batteries" by taking care of at least some of your own needs in order to avoid resenting your children. Balancing your child's needs with your own needs teaches children self-respect.

Type 7: Groupie (Responsive but Not Demanding)

Groupie parents idolize their children, make celebrities of their glorious offspring, lavish gifts on them, and deny their children nothing. These parents are very involved with their children but place few demands or controls on them. They do not require their children to regulate themselves or to behave appropriately. In other words, their children can do no wrong.

Result. Due to the absence or neglect of their own parents, these parents may swing the pendulum to the other extreme, never missing any milestone their children experience. Thus groupie parents can increase their children's self-image to unhealthy levels. Additionally, this parenting style leads to children who learn that there are very few boundaries and rules and that consequences are not likely to be very serious. Consequently, they never learn to control their own behavior. As a result, these children may have difficulty with self-control. They may demonstrate egocentric tendencies that can interfere with proper development of peer relationships.

Solution—Avoid the pedestal. Loving your children means treating them as people, not idols. It means learning to say no when appropriate and requiring them to think of others. Today, competition is key. We want our children to be all A's: attractive, academic, artistic, and athletic. Sometimes it's hard for us to accept that our children might just be average and that average is just fine.

Type 8: Commando (Demanding but Not Responsive)

Commando parents establish rules and guidelines. They expect their children to follow the rules. These parents tend to rely heavily on the use of "coercion" to force the children's compliance. Coercion includes the use of threat, intimidation, physical punishment, fear, and love withdrawal. This authoritarian style of parenting is all about respecting those in a position of authority. These parents, when questioned, will offer no explanation behind their decision. They may simply reply, "You live under my roof, you follow my rules! What I say goes." They insist there is only one right way but do this with little love. They let the "rules" trump their relationship.

Result. These parents may feel their own reputations depend on their children's performance. If the children do poorly in school, it makes the parents look bad. This style of parenting leads to obedient children. However, the kids learn that following parental rules and adherence to strict discipline is valued over independent behavior. As a result, they may become either rebellious or dependent and become less spontaneous and curious. Children of these parents tend to be more anxious, withdrawn, and unhappy. They also tend to have more difficulty with peer relationships (hostility and aggression) and bully others, which often results in problems in school.[1]

Solution—Avoid control. If you depend on control and force to get your children to cooperate, you may quickly notice that this is a losing proposition. It may work when children are younger. What happens, though, when the children get older or bigger than you? They can defy your orders and walk out. You need to think of different ways that you can encourage your children to cooperate without coercion. You can no longer tell your children, "Because I said so," or "Do as I tell you to do." They see this as hypocritical. The way you relate to your children speaks louder than words. For example, a parent says "don't smoke," yet he or she smokes. All too often, parents do not follow their own rules or advice. Subsequently, they need to model the behaviors they want their children to follow. Respect and appreciation are best taught by example and experience. If you want your children to be kind, you must be kind, respectful to others, respectful of your children. You set the foundation your children will follow. Children do best when they live in a home where each individual's contribution to the well-being of the family and functioning of the home is honored.

Type 9: Authoritative (Equally Demanding and Responsive)

Authoritative parents, also known as "balanced" parents, establish clear rules and guidelines, monitor the limits they set, and allow children to develop autonomy. These parents encourage children to be independent but still place controls and limits on their actions. They talk, discuss, provide feedback, allow for cooperation and collaboration. Their disciplinary methods are supportive rather than punitive. They reason with their children and consider their children's point of view even though they might not agree. They understand how their children are feeling. These parents teach their children how to regulate feelings and often help their children find appropriate outlets to solve problems.

Result. This style of parenting leads to the happiest, most adjusted, most capable, and most successful children. They learn how to negotiate and engage in discussions. The children understand that their opinions are valued. As a result, they are more likely to be socially competent, responsible, and autonomous.

Solution—Keep up the good work. Keep doing what you are doing. Authoritative parenting involves a combination of affection and attentive responsiveness to individual needs. You encourage responsible, prosocial behavior by reinforcing children's independence, autonomy, self-confidence, and self-esteem.

POINT TO PONDER

Now that you've read the nine different parenting styles, which of them do you see as most harmful and/or prevalent? As a parent, do you struggle with one or more of these? How did your parents parent you? What parenting style did they use?

Parenting can be tricky. Finding the right balance is difficult. Are you parenting too little or too much? Are you a parent who hovers or a parent who's distant? Are you too slow or too fast? No one parenting style is "right" while all other ones are "wrong." Most of the time, parenting children is done by trial and error. How we were raised, when we were raised, and where we were raised are all factors that play an important role in how we parent our children. All parents must decide for themselves how to raise their children. There are no fixed rules, no written instructions, and no operator's manual. Given the fact that no two kids are alike, what works for one child may not work for another. One thing is for sure. The optimal parent is one who is involved, closely monitors and supervises the child's online and offline life, is responsive, sets high expectations, and simultaneously respects their children's autonomy. When these conditions are met, children are less likely to engage in bullying behaviors.[1]

TOOLBOX TACTIC

Parenting Style Quiz[9]

What is your parenting style? Rate yourself against the following statements to find out. Remember, provide the most honest answers to each one.

IS THIS YOU?	NOT TRUE					VERY TRUE		
	1	2	3	4	5	6	7	8
1. I have a difficult time letting my child fail at a project.	O	O	O	O	O	O	O	O
2. I worry that my child will not like me one day .	O	O	O	O	O	O	O	O
3. I feel dependent on professionals to help me lead my child.	O	O	O	O	O	O	O	O
4. When I see my child struggle, I want to step in and take over.	O	O	O	O	O	O	O	O
5. I tend to want to stay in constant touch with my child.	O	O	O	O	O	O	O	O
6. I love relating to my child and his/her peers as a friend.	O	O	O	O	O	O	O	O
7. I don't feel I'm able to handle the pressures of raising my child.	O	O	O	O	O	O	O	O
8. I often get very angry when my child doesn't perform well.	O	O	O	O	O	O	O	O
9. I have a hard time if I don't know what my child is doing 24/7.	O	O	O	O	O	O	O	O
10. I spend lots of time thinking how I can remain "cool" to my kid.	O	O	O	O	O	O	O	O
11. I rely heavily on my child's teachers or coaches.	O	O	O	O	O	O	O	O
12. I get very upset if someone judges my or my child's conduct.	O	O	O	O	O	O	O	O

Scoring Key (Place your scores on the lines provided):

- If you scored between 15–24 on questions 1, 5, and 9, you might be a helicopter parent. You scored _____ .
- If you scored between 15–24 on Questions 2, 6, and 10, you might be a karaoke parent. You scored _____ .
- If you scored between 15–24 on Questions 3, 7, and 11, you might be a dry cleaner parent. You scored _____ .
- If you scored between 15–24 on Questions 4, 8, and 12, you might be a volcano parent. You scored _____ .

How Does Your Child Respond to You?

Parenting doesn't happen in a vacuum. The way you communicate with your children affects the way they communicate with you and vice versa. Like you, your children also have styles, which may or may not mesh with your parenting style. Children are born with a tendency toward reacting to people and events in specific ways, a preferred way of responding called temperament. These traits are not meant to label, just to describe general tendencies. Each temperament has its own strengths and challenges; one isn't better than another. Working with temperament, rather than denying or ignoring it, is a constructive, respectful way to guide children's development.

The ease with which your children adjust to their environment is strongly influenced by their temperament, particularly adaptability, sensitivity, and emotionality. Adaptability means adjustment to new situations or length of time needed to accept changes in plan or routine. Sensitivity means sensory threshold or how easily your children are bothered by changes in the environment. Emotionality means emotional regulation or their tendency to experience and express emotions.[12,13] Children in the same family often have different temperaments. Parents who have several children are likely to recognize the differences and react differently to each child. For example, a parent would probably respond quite differently to an overly active, impulsive child than to a shy, timid child. The parent would probably discourage impulsive behavior in the overly active child but encourage assertive behavior in the shy child. Five ways children react to people and to their environment are listed below.

Type 1: Easy/Flexible

Easy children are calm, happy, extremely adaptable, predictable, regular in sleeping and eating habits, positive in mood, average in intensity, and interested in new experiences.[12] The easy child can fit into almost all environments and can meet most demands.

Word of caution: A parent may overlook easy children's needs because these children are so "good" and accommodating.

Type 2: Spirited (Difficult/Challenging)

Spirited children seem to be born more curious, adventurous, powerful, persistent, sensitive, energetic, perceptive, and serious and have high needs.[14] Spirited children can be loud and dramatic if they are focused outward. They can be quiet and intently observant if focused inward. They can be easily overstimulated by their environment, "lock in" to important ideas, and love to debate. These children are goal oriented and easily distracted; they notice everything going on all the time. Taming spirited children is not about using coercive and harsh discipline to teach them who's boss or have them yield to authority.[15] Rather, it is about helping them channel their energy into something productive, teaching them to calm themselves, and helping them use their resources constructively.

Word of caution: Many parents find themselves angry, frustrated, and often exhausted as a result of having children who live life with more vigor and enthusiasm than most of us. (I know. I have a spirited child.) Spirited children can drive us crazy with their energy and antics. Once tamed, they have the stuff to succeed. For further information on raising a highly spirited child check out, *Raising Your Spirited Child: A Guide For Parents Whose Child Is More Intense, Sensitive, Perceptive, Persistent, and Energetic* by Mary Sheedy Kurcinka.

Type 3: Explosive (Difficult/Challenging)

Explosive children are difficult, unpredictable, withdrawing, nonadaptable to change, extremely negative, very intense, often fussy, irregular in feeding and sleeping habits, unable to concentrate and pay attention, restless, fidgety, unwilling to be confined, always moving, fearful of new people and situations, easily upset, high strung, and intense in their reactions.[11,16] Explosive children can be loud and forceful whether miserable, angry, or happy. Nothing seems to work with difficult children. Gradual and repeated demands presented with patience, consistency, and objectivity are required. Flexibility is the key attitude in coping with an explosive child.

Word of caution: Without assistance, explosive children will receive nothing but negative feedback from their environment. Adults often communicate a host of negative feelings to these children such as hostility, impatience, or bewilderment. Sometimes parents must spend time away from explosive children to maintain sanity and perspective. For further information on raising explosive children, check out *The Explosive Child: A New Approach For Understanding and Parenting Easily Frustrated, "Chronically Inflexible" Children* by Ross W. Greene.

Type 4: Sensitive (Slow to Warm Up)

Highly sensitive children (HSC) are described as passive, easily overwhelmed, and startled by stimuli. They are deeply reflective, mild mannered, affected by other people's moods, and slow to adapt. These children tend to withdraw or to react negatively to novelty.[17] They are shy and reserved with new people and situations. Gradually, they adjust to new circumstances or routines. HSCs are distinguished by their cautious nature and wait-and-see attitude. However, their reactions gradually become more positive with experience.[11,17] The above qualities can make for smart, conscientious, creative children. With the incorrect parenting or schooling, though, HSCs can become unusually shy or timid or can begin acting out. HSCs are often mislabeled as overly inhibited, fearful, or "fussy." If raised with proper understanding and care, HSCs are no more prone to these problems than are nonsensitive children. HSCs can grow up to be happy, healthy, well-adjusted adults.[17] HSCs need an environment where stimuli are presented gradually and repeatedly, in a positive manner, over and over and over and over.

Word of caution: Too much pressure will increase the negativism. These children must be encouraged, never forced. Instead, sticking to a routine and your word, along with allowing ample time to establish relationships in new situations, are necessary to allow independence to unfold. For further information on raising highly sensitive children, check out *The Highly Sensitive Child: Helping Our Children Thrive When the World Overwhelms Them* by Elaine N. Aron.

Type 5: Intuitive

Highly intuitive children often are unusually aware of the needs and feelings of friends, parents, and siblings.[18] They can finish your sentence, sense danger before it happens, "catch" other people's moods, and even tell you what's wrong with the family pet. They may tune into an unspoken family conflict or tell someone to "be careful" before stumbling into an unknown situation. Do you have a highly intuitive child? Read the following 10 traits and check those that apply to your child.[18]

1. My child has a way of finishing my sentences and reading my thoughts.
2. My child has an ability to "see" things before they happen and is surprised that other people respond to his or her predictions with amazement.
3. My child frequently translates the needs of younger siblings and pets for me and is surprisingly perceptive.
4. Noisy, crowded events agitate my child. He or she takes a long time to bounce back after such disruptions.
5. My child "catches" others' emotions or upset moods almost like a cold.

6. My child is prone to headaches and stomachaches related to other people's stress.
7. My child feels tension during traumatic world events, maybe even drawing pictures of them or spontaneously talking about them with no knowledge of the events.
8. It is hard to keep a secret or surprise from my child. He or she routinely guesses what the birthday presents are, for example.
9. My child has a tendency to have insights about other people and the world that outpace developmental norms.
10. My child reports feeling different from his or her peers.

If most of these qualities ring true for your child, your child may be an intuitive empath or a highly intuitive child.[18] For further information on raising highly intuitive children, check out, *The Highly Intuitive Child: A Guide to Understanding and Parenting Unusually Sensitive and Empathic Children* by Catherine Crawford.

Word of caution: These highly intuitive children have a special gift. However, their heightened abilities also come with special health challenges such as headaches and stomachaches as a result of feeling others' stress.[18] Listed below are ways you can help and support intuitive children.

- Stay open to their perceptions without judgment.
- Try not to inflate or deflate their intuitive experience when you respond to it.
- Realize that they may need your help in learning how to manage the stressors associated with this trait.
- Help them see that their way of feeling and seeing life is an important part of who they are, just like any other gift or talent.
- Remember that these abilities are fundamental to their natural intelligence.
- Let them know they are never alone and that you are available to help them problem solve their intuitive and empathic stressors.
- If they have empathically taken on someone else's mood, aches, pains, or worries, help them to practice asking "Is this feeling mine?" Remind them they are not responsible for someone else's feelings.
- If they are stuck in a pattern of being very in tune to others or to the pain of the world, help them switch to being on the "self-channel." You can do this with exercise, by encouraging them to express their feelings in art, or even by taking a couple of slow, deep breaths with them.

TIP

Here are some quick tips to follow when working with your children or any children.[9]

They need to hear the word *watch*.

> They need an example from you more than they need entertainment from you. When kids lack direction or discipline, they don't need more diversion. What they need is an example that demonstrates how to grow wise as they grow up.

They need to hear the word *practice*.

> They need long-term preparation more than short-term happiness. Kids have plenty of amusements that offer pleasure; they need help getting ready for a not-so-pleasurable future where they'll need to pay their dues on a job for a while.

They need to hear the word *no*.

> They need a mentor more than a buddy. I decided a long time ago that my children have a lot of buddies, but they have only one mom—me. So sometimes I have to be the bad guy and say "no," which is not always fun. However, I know it will earn their love and respect in the future.

They need to hear the word *wait*.

> Most things happen quickly, with little wait time. We want instant gratification, which means our ability to delay gratification has shrunk. Consequently, you, teachers, coaches, employers, youth pastors, or anyone who works with children must build wait time into the game plan when working with youths as a rehearsal for adult life.

Matching Your Style to Your Child's Style

Goodness of Fit

Matching your parenting style to your children's style matters the most. Goodness of fit is a term used to describe how well or how poorly the parent's temperament meshes with their children's characteristics.[12] A good fit means parents match their demands or expectations with what their children are able to do, given the children's temperaments, ages, and abilities. A poor fit leads to stress in the parent-child relationship, and parents feel less happy and less capable in their parenting. Research shows that children who experience a poor fit are more likely to develop behavior problems.[12] The match or mismatch between children and parents determines the harmony between them. For example, a child with ADHD or a very hyperimpulsive child (like my son Zach) who has a passive, depressed, lethargic mom would not be a good fit. The child in that situation would be allowed to do anything he or she likes because the mom is not going to have the energy level to set down any type of structure.

TOOLBOX TACTIC

Get acquainted with your child's preferences, temperament, and type. Take the free age-appropriate sorter for your child, either the Early Child Sorter (ages 4–8) or the Middle Child Sorter (ages 9–12). These ask questions about your child's typical behaviors, feelings, and likes and dislikes.

- The Early Childhood Temperament Sorter (ages 4–8)
  http://www.parentingbytemperament.com/earlychildsort.php
- The Middle Childhood Temperament Sorter (Ages 9–12)
  http://www.parentingbytemperament.com/MidChildSort.php

Get acquainted with your own preferences, temperament, and type by taking the Adult Temperament Sorter Quiz. This asks about your typical behaviors, likes, and dislikes.

http://www.parentingbytemperament.com/AdultTemperamentSorter.php

TIP

Strategies for Positive and Effective Discipline

Remember to C.A.R.E. when working with your children in redirecting their behavior[19]

Calm—take a breath, approach the situation calmly
Acknowledge the behavior/emotion—always begin with "I"
- "I see you're throwing rocks."
- "I hear yelling."
- "I see you are feeling really mad."

Remind and **r**e-direct —remind about the rule, re-direct the energy positively
- "Remember, rocks are not for throwing. Let's find a ball."
- "Remember, we use our inside voices in the car. Let's sing a song!"
- "Remember, hitting hurts my body. Let's find a pillow to hit."

Engage—get involved, get connected
- "I see the purple ball by the swings; can you throw it to me?"
- "Which song should we sing first? How about Itsy Bitsy Spider?"
- "Show me how mad you are. Squeeze that pillow as HARD as you can."

Creating a Good Fit with Your Children

By understanding your children and their temperament and by accepting them the way they are, you can plan ahead (i.e., be proactive). You can prevent problems by structuring their environment so as to enhance the positive traits and subdue the negative traits. This also means that rather than just reacting to your children's behavior, you can plan where your children might have specific needs or difficulties and use parenting strategies that make it easier for your children to behave.

My older son, who has been diagnosed with ADHD, is highly active, distractible, inattentive, impulsive, and talkative. Most of the time, he is restless, can't sit still, and is a bundle of energy. He is my Energizer bunny whose batteries never seem to quit. Instead of using a commando parenting style, I use an authoritative one. Since I know my son, it is unrealistic and unreasonable for me to demand or expect him to sit still or remain quiet for a long period of time. I know he needs to take short breaks while doing his homework and avoid events that require him to sit quietly for a long time. I provide ways for him to release his energy, such as going to the gym or running in the park. On the other hand, my younger son is a highly sensitive child who adapts slowly to changes and is shy, passive, and mild mannered. Instead of using a dropout parenting style, I use the helicopter one. Since I know about him, I must be patient with my son and avoid hurrying him up in trying to get him to socialize or interact quickly with others. Although, I know he needs time to feel out people before he will open up and respond to them, I continue to encourage him to initiate or join in conversations.

Here are some tips to keep in mind when matching your style to your children's style as you strive to achieve this fit.

- Be aware of your children's temperament. Respect their individual strengths and uniqueness without comparing them to others or trying to change their basic temperament.
- Be attuned to your children's temperament. Encourage them to accomplish tasks at their own pace.
- Be aware of your own temperament. Adjust your natural responses when they clash with your children's responses.
- Think about how your own temperament style meshes with your children's temperament style.
- Make communication a priority. Be open to discussion. Take time to explain your decisions and motives. Listen to your children's point of view, and encourage teamwork to generate solutions.
- Make your children aware that their opinions are respected. However, remain firm in your decisions.
- Set limits to help your children develop self-control. Respect their opinions, but remain firm on important limits.
- Be a good role model because children learn by imitation.
- Enjoy your children.

 TIP

When asked about problems facing their generation, many millennials responded that the biggest complaint they have about adults in general is the poor example that adults set for kids.[5]

Appreciate your children. No matter what your children's temperament may be, show respect and understanding. Let them know you accept them the way they are—no matter what happens. Reinforce that their temperament traits combine to make them a very unique and special individual. Remember that some traits seen as challenging in children now can be valued later. Extremely open and approaching children become adventurous and exploring adults who make new discoveries. A child with high energy and persistence could become the next U.S. Open Championship (golf) winner. Here are some tips for helping your children modify the traits that might be problematic for them:

For children with very high energy

Heed the signals that indicate it's time for your children to blow off steam, and find a way to let them do so. Incorporate some active time during the day. Walk to school instead of driving, or stop at the park on the way to the grocery. Avoid using confinement as a method of discipline.

For children with very low energy

Allow enough time for tasks and activities. Use a timer to set a goal for when a chore should be finished. Reward your children for sticking with a project and completing it in a timely fashion.

For children who show high sensitivity

Acknowledge your children's feelings, and provide ways for them to make themselves more comfortable. Layer clothes to allow for adjustments on days that are too warm or too cold. Avoid overstimulation, e.g., loud music, strobe lights, and noisy groups of people.

For children who show low sensitivity

Help them notice external cues by pointing out sounds in the environment, odors, and changes in the colors of stoplights. Explain interpersonal cues, such as facial expressions, body language, and personal space.

For children who demonstrate high predictability

Provide advance warning of changes in their routines. Help them learn to handle changes now to develop flexibility as they grow older.

For children who show low predictability

Create routines, even if they seem odd. Ask the children to sit down with the family for dinner even if they are not hungry or to go to bed at a regular time even if they are not sleepy. Reward successes, such as turning in a paper on time.

For children who approach new situations easily

Provide firm rules and close supervision. These children are curious! Teach them to use reasonable caution with new people or in new situations.

For children who withdraw

Allow them time to adjust to new situations; let them set the pace. Quietly encourage them, without pushing, to try new activities and make new friends.

For children who are slow to adapt

Give plenty of warning about transitions. Role play or practice expected behaviors before going into new situations. Acknowledge the stress they feel in new situations, and encourage them to talk about it. Alert them to predictable sensitivities.

For children who adapt too easily

Teach them to make their own decisions rather than just go along with the peer group. Encourage them to find out all they can about an activity before signing up and committing their time.

For children who tend to be negative

Try to ignore their general negative mood, but tune in to real distress. Encourage them to recognize and talk about the things that make them happy. Act as a role model for positive social interactions.

For children who are always positive

Be sensitive to subtle signs of unhappiness that they may be bottling up inside. Teach appropriate ways to express feelings of sadness, anger, fear, and frustration.

For children who are less responsive

Don't equate a lack of intensity with a lack of feelings. Watch and listen carefully to pick up more subtle clues to problems.

For children who are overly responsive

Teach them to control their emotional responses through anger management, self-talk, or calming strategies.

For children who show low persistence

Break tasks into small steps, and acknowledge small successes. Try timed work periods followed by short breaks. Reward them for making sustained efforts and finishing assignments.

For children who are overly persistent

Provide lots of warning before transitions. Remind them that they cannot always be perfect.

For children who are highly distractible

Reduce external distractions as much as possible. Keep instructions short. Use a special cue—gesture or word—to get them back on task.

For children who show low distractibility

Cue them when it's time to move on to something new. For example, say their name or touch their arm. Alternatively, set a timer to remind them when to move on to the next task or activity.

Parenting Tips for Success

Avoid the Common Mistakes While Listening to Your Child

- Denial of feelings—"There's no reason to be upset. It's foolish to feel that way."
- The philosophical response—"Life is like that. That's just the way things are. You have to learn to take things in stride."
- Advice—"You know what you should do? Try..."
- Questions—"What were those emergencies you had that caused you to miss this test?"
- Defense of the other person—"Your teacher was not completely in the wrong here. I can see why he or she would be really troubled by this behavior."
- Pity—"Oh you poor thing. How terrible for you."
- Amateur psychoanalysis—"Maybe what's really causing you to act this way is that you have a lot of unresolved anger about this."[20]

What to Do Instead?

Give an empathic response

It is important to validate your children's feelings. "You must have felt very upset about that. To be treated like that in front of my friends would be hard to take."

Use Praise and Raise Self-Esteem

When children feel good about themselves, they are more likely to behave well and want to be productive. Unfortunately, many "difficult" kids feel most adults don't like them, don't see their positive qualities, and don't want to change their minds.[20]

- Notice and describe the good things you see in your children.
- Describe the positive feelings you have about your children and their behavior.
- Sum up your children's praiseworthy behaviors in a single word.

Use Encouragement

Children need to have their feelings accepted and respected. They do better when they feel better. A misbehaving child is a discouraged child. Therefore, encouragement is the best way to deal with misbehavior. There are four methods of encouragement:[21]

1. Encourage Acceptable Actions

This allows children to learn and practice more appropriate action.

- "How are you supposed to ask? Right now, please try again."
- "What have I asked you to do when I'm talking and you need something? Right now, please try again."

2. Encourage Cooperation

Whenever a child helps out, cooperates, or makes a contribution, there is an opportunity to use encouragement. Remember that the child could have made a different choice.

- "I like the way you handled that."
- "Your room looks great."
- "I knew I could count on you."

3. Encourage Independence

Adults need to teach conflict management skills (see chapter 8) and then limit their own involvement so children have an opportunity to practice these skills independently.

- "How would you like to handle this?"
- "What have you tried already?"
- "I think you can work this out."

4. Encourage Improvement

Most interpersonal skills require a great deal of motivation, effort, and practice before they can be mastered.

- "It seemed much easier for you this time."
- "I know you are not happy with it, but you did do better than last time."
- "You did better today."

Use Discipline, Not Punishment

Punishment and discipline are different in what they do and how they are accomplished. Punishment involves a sanction or penalty as a consequence of a child's unacceptable behavior. It usually includes control, force, and pain to get children to behave in an acceptable way. Punishment often results from a parent's feelings of anger and frustration. It sends a message to children that they are bad. Punishment focuses on past misbehavior and offers little or nothing to help children behave better in the future. In other words, it doesn't help them learn how to behave in an acceptable way. For example, if a child hits his brother and then receives a spanking, he is not taught what to do the next time he feels angry with his brother. Parents who use physical punishment are setting an example of using violence to settle problems or solve conflicts. Remember, children imitate their parents' behavior.[20] There are two common problems with punishment (other than that it often doesn't work).

1. Punishment is a distraction

Kids become preoccupied with being punished. Instead of thinking about what they need to do to make the behavior better, the children focus on anger and revenge for being punished.

2. Punishment is confusing and ineffective

Since most punishments are inconsistent and not logically connected to the behavior being corrected, they are even more confusing and ineffective. Children do not learn what to do instead.

In contrast, discipline is a positive method of teaching children self-control. It teaches children how to control their behavior so they can act in a socially acceptable way, and not because they fear punishment. Discipline focuses on how children are behaving in the present and how parents want their children to behave in the future. It is consistent. Discipline imposes logical or natural consequences that embody the reality of a social order (i.e., norms set by society). It must logically follow the child's behavior. When using consequences as a form of discipline, the consequences should include the following four components.[21]

1. Relatedness

This discipline must be logically related to the behavior. Usually adults apply the same consequences for different behaviors.

2. Duration

The discipline should be short term and should fit the way your children think. Shorter consequences give them more opportunity to collect information and demonstrate behavior. Just because a little is good does not necessarily mean that a lot is better.

3. Respect

Consequences must be delivered without attacking, insulting, or humiliating your children.

4. Clean slate

Once the consequence has been applied, resist the urge to keep reminding your children of the past offense. They now have more information and fresh opportunities to learn.

Six-Step Process to Formulating Consequences

1. Point out a way to be helpful.
   Instead of saying "Sit down or you will lose your privileges."
   State "Can you get the erasers for me?"
2. Express strong disapproval (without attacking character).
   State "I am very disappointed that you would mark that book."
3. State your expectations.
   State "I expect that when you get a book from the library, you will take care of it like it was your own. That means not writing on it or hurting it in any way."
4. Show your children how to make amends.
   State "If you get some scotch tape, you can tape up the page you cut with the scissors."
5. Give a choice.
   State "You can erase the marks out of the book, or you can lose library privileges."

6. Take action.

>   Revoke the children's privileges without threatening them. Wait for them to notice and perhaps ask about it.

7. Solve the problem.

>   State "What can you do to make this situation better?"

Encourage Cooperation

Children need to have a role in partnering for cooperation. To engage cooperation from children, do the following:[21]

- Describe what you see, or describe the problem. Instead of blaming or accusing the children, make a descriptive statement.

>   Instead of "You can't seem to keep things neat."
>
>   State "Your books are out of order in your desk."

- Give information instead of making a demand.

>   Instead of saying "Straighten your desk."
>
>   State "If you have a neater desk, you will get your work done faster."

- Say it with a word.

>   Instead of "You have several books on the floor and a lot of papers that are falling out of your desk. Plus your pencils are all over the desktop."
>
>   State "Desk."

- Talk about your feelings.

>   Instead of saying "You never clean your desk."
>
>   State "I feel concerned when I see your desk unorganized."

- Write a note.

>   Do not yell.
>
>   Just put a nice note onto the desk.

TIP

Parental involvement is a major influence in helping teens avoid risks such as smoking, drinking, drug use, sexual activity, violence, and suicide attempts, while increasing educational achievement and expected attainment. Parental participation in children's lives is central and critical to the successful development of children and adolescents.

Council of Economic Advisers[22]

Concluding Words for Parental Success

Parenting in the 21st century is no easy task. As such, we need multiple tools and approaches to help us meet the needs of our unique children. Parenting isn't only a collection of skills, rules, and tricks of the trade. It also encompasses who you are, what your family culture and beliefs are, and how you transmit the most personal and cherished aspects of your values to your children. To help you accomplish this task, I leave you with the following tips to help you to relate to your children so they will be able to relate to you, while earning respect for each other.

Set Goals

It is difficult to gauge how well you are doing as a parent if you don't set goals. Evaluate your needs as a family as well as your children's needs. Create a list of yearly, monthly, and weekly goals. The goals should revolve around the values and life lessons that you want to teach your children. Begin with small goals, such as setting aside a few hours each day to read to your children or work on a project together. Consider setting the type of goals that will help you become a better parent, such as taking a parenting class or reading a parenting book. Discuss these goals with your children. Come up with realistic goals to avoid setting yourself up for failure.

Manage your Stress

Growing demands at work cause a lot of stress for some parents. This affects their ability to handle their parenting responsibilities. Keep in mind that your children will also learn how to deal with stress, anger, and difficult situations by observing the way you handle them. Be conscious of your daily activities and behavior. Recognize when you are stressed. Find positive ways to deal with the stress such as exercising or meditating. Focus on your home life when you are not working, and avoid allowing work issues to interfere with family time.

Schedule Regular Family Time

The time that parents and their children spend watching television, playing video games, or using the Internet can interfere with the amount of time they spend together as a family. Make it a priority to spend at least four hours of quiet time together with your children a few times a week. This will give you an opportunity to talk to them, give them your undivided attention, and discuss important issues. Use a calendar to keep track of your planned outings or family time. Be creative. Think of activities that you can enjoy together, such as family game night, picnics, or family dinners.

Encourage Open Communication

Parents can provide the guidance and support that their children need to make good decisions by having open communication with them. Children should feel comfortable talking to their parents about their concerns. Promote open communication in your home by talking to your children about issues related to drugs, sex, and violence. Provide them with age-appropriate information. Answer their questions. Allow them to express their own opinions about these issues.

Part II

Understanding Bullying

Chapter 2

Recognizing Face-to Face Bullying

This chapter provides answers to some frequently asked questions about bullying. What is it and what isn't it? How common is bullying? When and where does bullying occur? How does bullying differ among youths? Is it the same as conflict? What's the difference between teasing, rough play, and bullying? What are the warning signs of bullying?

What Constitutes Bullying?

I was bullied quite badly when I was in 5th grade, but no one knows why, not even me! At first it started off with just name calling, but one day it got a bit more serious. I nearly had my shin broken and nearly had to go to hospital when the bully kicked me. The school did nothing about it! I hate bullies; I think more can be done to stop them.

15-Year-Old Boy

Bullying is a systematic form of violence that is cruel, devious, and harmful. Most kids have a good idea of what bullying is because they see it every day. It is everywhere and knows no boundaries. It occurs at school among peers and at home among siblings. With the advent of technology, it occurs through social media platforms. For many kids, there is no reprieve from bullying. Because of the many faces of bullying, understanding what it looks like and its dynamics will help you recognize and stop it before it escalates. However, before we look at issues surrounding bullying, I want you to think about what you consider to be bullying.

TOOLBOX TACTIC

What Do You Consider to be Bullying?

Circle the items that you consider to be bullying.

1. Making fun of the way somebody looks
2. Chasing away younger kids when they want to play on the swings
3. Accidentally bumping into someone in the hall
4. Calling people names because of the color of their skin
5. Making other kids play a game your way
6. Teasing someone about the clothes he/she wears
7. Telling someone that the shirt he/she is wearing doesn't look good
8. A group of kids won't let you sit with them at lunch even though there's room
9. Telling someone that he/she is not being nice
10. Joking with people by "putting them down"

Now give the same items to your children to see what they consider to be bullying. Discuss how their responses are the same or different from yours. Which were the three most common behaviors or characteristics? Why do you and your children think people choose to engage in these behaviors? Discuss some ways they could handle the situations noted above.

Using one of the bullying situations listed above, role play to act out effective ways to handle the situation.

Now that you have examined how you define bullying, let us take a look at how researchers and practitioners define bullying. Bullying is defined by three characteristics.

1. **Repeated:** The bully continues harassing the target over and over again. It is not a one-time incident.
2. **Intentional:** The bully intends to cause fear, distress, and/or harm to the target's body, feelings, self-esteem, or reputation. The behavior does not occur by accident or mistake. The bully takes pleasure in witnessing the hurt and pain.
3. **Power imbalance:** The bully's power can come from his or her physical size, strength, age, social status, popularity, wealth, race, technology skills, access to embarrassing information, or knowledge

of another child's limitations. Bullying does not occur between kids who are equally matched.

Bullying is a form of aggression where the bully willfully and deliberately intimidates and humiliates the target to induce fear through threat of further aggression. Bullies feed on fear. Once fear is created, the targeted child feels powerless, guilty, and embarrassed to tell an adult or to fight back. Bullies also feed on attention. They count on bystanders to participate actively, to support their behavior, or to sit back and do nothing. Once fear and attention have been gained, the bully can act without the dread of retaliation or incrimination. Consequently, the cycle of violence begins.

Kids who bully are excellent observers of human behavior. Kids who target others are constantly testing other kids around them. If a kid passes the bully's test, he or she is usually left alone. However, if the kid fails the test, the bully continues to target the kid and others begin to target that child too. So what does the test look like? Bullies often shop around to find a kid they know they can win against. This child is less likely to retaliate or report them but is more likely to show fear and/or give up material goods (e.g., money, shoes, iPods, and so on.) without a fight. Generally, a child's initial reaction to the bully will confirm or refute a bully's assumption that the child is a person whom the bully can take advantage of. This explains why some kids who are targeted usually find themselves in the same situation over and over again. For example, Sara writes, "Bullying is still going on. Even though my parents moved me to another school, I am still being picked on. It's not any better over here." Remember, bullies thrive on fear. Thus if a target does not validate the bully by showing fear, the bully will more than likely move on. On the other hand, if a target validates the bully by backing down or crying (i.e., showing fear), the bully will more than likely exploit and capitalize on that fear.

Over the years while working with kids who bully and those who are bullied I have learned one thing—kids will be tested and must control how they respond. Kids can't control being tested, but they can determine whether or not they will be continually picked on. A bully will not continue to target another kid unless that kid and others give the bully the power and reaction he or she is seeking. Kids with disabilities and shortcomings may be tested more often than other kids (more on this topic later in the chapter). However, once kids learn to pass the bully's test, they will no longer be picked on. It does not matter how many flaws or shortcomings kids think they have. Once they learn and master the techniques discussed in chapters 6 and 8, they will be left alone.

TIP

Bullies are opportunists. They know who, when, where, and how to harass their target without being seen and without retribution.

Four Types of Bullying

Children bully each other in many ways, even if the bullies do not realize it at the time. Bullying behaviors generally fall into four categories. However, bullies sometimes combine several tactics in order to intimidate and isolate their targets. Whichever form of bullying a child uses, its effects have serious social, emotional, and health-related issues long after the bullying has been stopped. Be on the lookout for the four main types of bullying:

Type 1: Physical Bullying

This type involves hitting, kicking, shoving, stealing, or damaging property.

Type 2: Verbal Bullying

This type involves taunting, teasing, name calling, mocking, or making degrading, sexist, racist, or homophobic comments.

Type 3: Relational Bullying (Psychological Bullying)

This type involves:

- Excluding an individual or a group of people from a group
- Being purposefully frightening
- Starting, perpetuating, or spreading rumors
- Intentionally excluding someone from conversations or social gatherings
- Using stern looks or other means to make a child feel unsafe.

Although no physical contact has actually been made, relational aggression is a form of both psychological and emotional abuse that uses relationships as a way to inflict injury upon others.

Type 4: Electronic Bullying (Cyberbullying)

This type uses electronic devices, the Internet, mobile phones, or other social media platforms to intimidate, threaten, or humiliate another individual or a group of individuals.

Two General Categories

Bullying falls into two general categories. The first is overt, direct, and detectable—such as a physical or verbal assault. The second is covert, indirect, and more difficult to spot—such as the spreading of rumors or deliberate social exclusion. Boys usually bully through overt, physical attacks or face-to-face bullying. Girls usually use more subtle, covert, or behind the back bullying. Because indirect bullying is harder to detect, many schools underestimate the extent of this subtle form of bullying. Research indicates that more direct physical forms of bullying tend to escalate in elementary school, peak in middle school or between the ages of nine through fifteen, and decline as children reach high school. In contrast, verbal and indirect bullying, particularly cyberbullying, increases in high school (*http://nces.ed.gov*). The reason we see an increase in cyberbullying among adolescents is due to their having greater access to, proficiency with, and freedom in using technology. I discuss adolescents' use of cyberbullying to harass in chapter 5. Whichever form the bully uses, it must be taken seriously. Both forms meet the bullying criteria—behavior is repeated, intentional, and power based.

TIP

We now know that:

- Bullying is NOT prewired, harmless, or inevitable.
- Bullying IS learned, harmful, and controllable.
- Bullying SPREADS if supported or left unchecked.
- Bullying INVOLVES everyone—bullies, targets, and bystanders.
- Bullying CAN BE effectively stopped or entirely prevented.

TIP

The National Center for Education Statistics (NCES) (*http://nces.ed.gov*) survey of youths ages 12 through 18 indicated that over 7 million children reported being bullied at school and over 1.5 million children reported being cyberbullied on or off school grounds. Bullying kept over 141,300 children from attending school because they felt unsafe at school or on their way to or from school.

How Prevalent Is the Problem?

If your child has been involved in bullying he or she is not alone. Children are involved in bullying about once every 7 minutes.[1] Bullying statistics vary greatly depending on a number of factors, including how bullying is defined, how data is collected, and the willingness of those involved to report incidents. Estimates of the number of children who experience bullying vary widely (ranging from 10% to 70%), depending on the age of the group studied and how bullying was formally defined (*www.cdc.gov; http://nces.ed.gov; www.stopbullying.gov*).

The National Center for Education Statistics reported three out of ten youths in grades 6–12 are involved in bullying, as perpetrators, targets, or both (*http://nces.ed.gov*). In a national sample of 16,410 youths in grades 9–12, the Centers for Disease Control (*www.cdc.gov*) found one in five youths (over 20%) reported that they experienced bullying at school during the past year and approximately 8 percent admitted to bullying others. Some kids—6.5%—had both bullied others and been bullied themselves. Unfortunately, some kids have resorted to violent means to protect themselves from being a target of bullying. These include engaging in physical fights (11.1%), bringing a weapon to school (5.6%), or threatening or injuring others with a weapon at school (7.7%) (*http://nces.ed.gov*). These sobering statistics illustrate why we need to take bullying seriously since the consequences of bullying behaviors can lead to violence in our schools and our children's engagement in at-risk behaviors.

 TIP

"It is important to remember that bullying is not about anger or conflict; it's about contempt—a powerful feeling of dislike toward someone considered to be worthless, inferior, and undeserving of respect."

Barbara Coloroso
Author of *The Bully, the Bullied, and the Bystander*

According to findings from the School Survey on Crime and Safety (*http://nces.ed.gov*) during the 2009–10 school year, about 39% of middle school administrators and 20% of administrators at the elementary and high school levels reported that bullying took place on a daily or weekly basis. Additionally, 19% of middle schools and 18% of high schools reported daily or weekly problems with cyberbullying, either at school or away from school. A majority of the time, kids who are bullied attend school with kids who bully them. In fact, 33–35% of bullying takes place in the classroom at the elementary, middle, and high school levels. Targets of cyberbullying were more likely to get into a physical fight (15.6%) at school, to be the target of a crime (12.8%), and bring a weapon to school (7.4%) than kids who were not cyberbullied (5.1%, 3.3%, and 2.4%, respectively) according to *http://nces.ed.gov*. As a result, how can kids who are bullied concentrate, focus, and remember things they have learned if they are constantly anxious and stressed out of fear of further torment and humiliation? Simply put, they can't. In one survey, Hoover and colleagues[2] indicated that 14% of youths in grades 8–12 reported, "Bullying diminished their ability to learn in school." A 15-year-old girl commented:

> *One of my friends started hassling me on MSN messenger; she was sending me nasty messages and text messages and this carried on at school. This really affected me at home and at school; I couldn't concentrate on school work, my grades dropped, and I was always upset and down.*

The prevalence of bullying in schools is almost certainly higher than what is reported to teachers, school administrators, or parents because many bullying incidents occur out of view of adults and often go unreported. In fact, 80% of the time, school staff do not know that bullying has occurred because many of the incidents are verbal, brief, and occur when monitoring is low. Only 36% of students who were bullied notified a teacher at school about the bullying incident (*http://nces.ed.gov*).

TOOLBOX TACTIC

"Youth Online" lets you analyze national, state, and local Youth Risk Behavior Surveillance System (YRBSS) data from 1991-2009. Visit the website listed below to compare how frequently youth are involved in bullying as offenders, targets, or both in your state and local community. Available at *http://apps.nccd.cdc.gov/youthonline*

TIP

Bullying tends to happen most often in and around schools—specifically in those areas where there is little or no adult supervision (e.g., playground, hallways, cafeteria, locker rooms, restrooms, and bus stops) although the classroom is not immune (before the lesson begins). There is a correlation between increased supervision and decreased bullying. Bullies stop when adults are around.

(*http://nces.ed.gov*)

How Does Bullying Differ Among Youth?

Boys vs. Girls

According to the *School Crime Supplement to the National Crime Victimization Survey* (*http://nces.ed.gov*), a higher percentage of females (20%) than males (13%) ages 12–18 reported being the subject of rumors. Simultaneously, a lower percentage of females (8%) than males (10%) reported being pushed, shoved, tripped, or spit on. In addition, a higher percentage of females (6%) than males (4%) also reported being excluded from activities on purpose. In other words, boys have higher rates of using physical contact such as tripping someone in the hallway or pushing a peer on the playground to inflict harm. Girls have higher rates of using their relationships to inflict harm, manipulate peers, and injure others' feelings of social acceptance. These findings are consistent with other research. Girls rarely report physical abuse (6.7%). Boys (15.1%) mainly report physical bullying like getting in a physical fight on school property (*www.cdc.gov*).

Why do we see this difference? Bullying differences based on sex may stem from being socialized into traditional male and female roles. For instance, many males are socialized to be macho—to be strong and tough. On the other hand, girls may have been socialized to act feminine, not be aggressive or fight physically, and not engage in open conflict. Therefore, they engage in relational aggression because it is under the radar and protects them. To some extent, the rise of female aggression is related to the increased use of social media platforms to bully. Girls are twice as likely to cyberbully, which is a covert form of relational aggression, than are boys (*www.cdc.gov*). If you would like to read more about bullying girls, see James

Garbarino's book *Jane Hit: Why Girls Are Growing More Violent* and Deborah Prothow-Sith and Howard R. Spivak's book *What We Can Do About It and Sugar and Spice and No Longer Nice: How We Can Stop Girls' Violence.*

TIP

According to the Office of Juvenile Justice and Delinquency Prevention, when girls physically bully or fight in schools, they may do so as a result of teacher labeling, in self-defense, or out of a general sense of hopelessness.

(www.ojp.usdoj.gov/ojjdp)

As children we come to appraise ourselves as we are appraised by others.
Dr. Harry Stack Sullivan
Psychiatrist

Age/Grade

Research indicates that bullying behaviors decline with age and with increasing grade level. In general, the risk for being bullied increases in childhood beginning with preschool children, peaks during early adolescences (or middle school), and begins to decline during high school. For instance, 39.4% of 6th graders reported being bullied at school compared with 20.6% of 12th graders (*nces.ed.gov*).

Why does bullying peak in middle school? Middle school can be a tough, competitive world where kids are increasingly sensitive to social pressures and norms. Children in middle school experience new levels of self-consciousness and new anxieties about fitting in. Social dominance theory focuses on the maintenance and stability of group-based social hierarchies. It explains prejudice and aggression among members of larger societies. According to this theory, children use bullying as a strategy for moving higher in the social pecking order. They attempt to define their place in the new social structure. This occurs particularly during the transition from elementary to middle school when patterns of social hierarchy are being established. According to the Centers for Disease Control, 36.8% of middle school students reported being targets of bullying, 7.5% acknowledged being bullies, and 9.6% reported being victims of bullies (*www.cdc.gov/mmwr*).

During early adolescence, kids begin to identify strongly with their peers, value being a part of a group, and evaluate who they are and what they are good at. In accordance with homophily theory, kids tend to form friendships and spend time with those who are similar to them in certain key ways. Thus peer groups become stratified (grouped based on shared characteristics). Issues of acceptance and popularity become increasingly important. Consistent with attraction theory, as children enter middle school, their attraction to aggressive peers increases. The social striving for acceptance can make humiliating or demeaning others an attractive option if the outcome is perceived as possibly achieving greater popularity or status. For example, being tough, strong, and aggressive are important status considerations for boys. Appearance is the leading determinant of social status for girls. Consequently, some kids may bully to achieve acceptance and status. A 12-year-old boy commented:

> I have been bullied since 2nd grade and since then I have never been happy or had a good time at school. In elementary school it wasn't as bad. Then I thought ok I can handle this until middle school. Middle school came, and the bullying got worse. I skipped school a couple of times to escape the bullies, and my work decreased dramatically. I dumbed down so I would fit in with the bullies. I tried and failed. And the only reason that I skipped a grade was because I'm intelligent.

Race

Racist bullying is a cross-cultural phenomenon and transcends ethnicity. However, children of nonwhite ethnic origin experience more racist name calling than white children of the same age and gender. In contrast, white and black children are more likely to report bullying than other ethnic groups (*http://nces.ed.gov* and *www.cdc.gov*). A 15-year-old boy commented:

> My friend's friend started to make fun of my ethnic background, so I told him to stop disrespecting me. He ignored my pleas and started to get even more verbally abusive. I ignored him, but he started talking to me saying that I shouldn't f**k with him because he would beat my a** down in front of his friends.

Disability

Children with learning disabilities, specific language impairments, social-emotional disorders, and physical disabilities are three times more likely to be targets of bullying and are ostracized or purposely ignored more often than their nondisabled peers.[3,4,5] In many cases, children with behavioral difficulties may trigger peer victimization and social exclusion. The bullying occurs due to nonconforming behaviors and/or interests as well as intense emotional and/or behavioral reactions to victimization that encourage the child who is bullying.[3,6] Obese adolescents are at risk of victimization because their peers view them as different and undesirable.[7] A 13-year-old girl commented:

> *I've been bullied quite a few times about my weight. I hated it. I try to deal with it the best I can, but if I can't, I tell my parents. Trust me it does help.*

Sexual Orientation

Results from the *2009 National School Climate Survey* indicated that lesbian, gay, bisexual, and transgender (LGBT) youth are at risk for being targets of severe bullying. Nearly 9 out of 10 are harassed at school, and 8.8% are physically assaulted at school because of their sexual orientation (*www.glsen.org*). Nearly two-thirds (61.1%) of LGBT youths felt unsafe in school because of their sexual orientation. They were four times more likely (30.0%) to miss at least one day of school in the past month because of safety concerns. Despite these findings, a large percentage of LGBT youths (62.4%) fail to report the incident to school staff, believing little to no action would be taken or the situation could become worse if reported. A 17-year-old girl commented:

> *I have been bullied since I was in middle school. I am now a senior in high school, and I still get bullied. I don't understand it. They make fun of me and tormented me and my friends for being gay. They threw things and hit us when we walked by. They also told me I was ugly. I don't think I'm ugly. Why do people choose to be so cruel?*

 TIP

Severe school bullying that targets a victim specifically because of race or sexual identity can be considered a hate crime in some states.

Reporting Bullying

The majority (57%) of kids who experience harassment in school, regardless of demographics or reasons for the harassment, never report these incidents to school staff. The kids who are bullied believe that little to no action would be taken or the situation would become worse if reported (*www.glsen.org*). When surveyed about their response to bullying, 70% of teachers believed that educators usually intervened when they observed bullying. However, one out of four targets felt school staff did not respond well. One out of three students believed teachers were interested in stopping bullying behaviors (*www.nea.org; nces.ed.gov*).

TIP

Two-thirds (65%) of high school students reported that they have been verbally or physically harassed or assaulted during the past year because of their perceived or actual appearance, sexual orientation, gender expression, race/ethnicity, disability, or religion (*www.glsen.org*).

Indeed, there is an urgent need to take action and protect children who are bullied based on their differences. Bullies use differences to make targets feel bad about themselves. Bullies use verbal taunts such as "you're ugly," "you're stupid," or "you're fat" as an excuse for their bad behavior. Remember, our differences make us special and unique. No one deserves to be bullied, and no one makes someone bully them. We have the right to be ourselves, to wear what we want, to form our own opinions, and to be who we want to be. Life would be dull if everyone was the same. Differences make life interesting, and these differences should be respected. We cannot stand by and watch or allow bullies to take that away from us. Therefore, bullies need to be taught to celebrate our differences. Targets need to take back their power by not feeding into a bully's hunger for fear, attention, and things. In Chapters 6, 7, and 8, I provide you with strategies and tools you can use to empower your child to stop the cycle of bullying.

TIP

> Kids who bully attack a target's unique attributes in contempt of the target's existence.

What Bullying Is Not

Bullying Is Not the Same As Conflict

Conflict and bullying are two different things. Conflict involves a struggle between two people. Bullying is about one person unfairly misusing strength or power. Conflict is a normal, natural, and necessary part of life. Normal conflict implies that each person is responsible for part of the problem, is on an equal footing, and has an equal chance of resolving the issue. Conflict provides children with the opportunity to think of creative and innovative ways to handle situations and solve their problems. The problem arises when normal conflict is altered by the three things that characterize bullying—imbalance of power, repeated behaviors, and intent to harm. At this point, conflict is transformed into bullying behavior.

Keep in mind that bullying is an aggressive act where the child who bullies wins and the target loses. With each incident, the bully progressively becomes more powerful. Simultaneously, the target increasingly becomes more powerless. The message that both children are partly right and partly wrong and that they should work toward a compromise is inappropriate for kids involved in a bullying situation (or in any situation where someone is being victimized). Targets of bullying do not ask to be harassed and tormented. They do not have anything to give up. This is one reason why it is not appropriate to use conflict resolution or meditation strategies for bullying situations. These strategies assume shared responsibility between the involved parties. In fact, bullying is about one person intentionally misusing power to harm another.

Bullying should be addressed in a way that sends the message that no one deserves to be bullied, assigns fault only to the one who is bullying, and ensures that the bullying is stopped. Bullies need to be told their behavior is wrong and will not be tolerated. Bullies must be told they will be held accountable and responsible for the harm they do to others. On the other hand, targets need to be told that they do not deserve to be bullied and that the adults around them will do everything possible to stop the bullying. Teaching your children how to handle normal disagreements will help prepare them for life. (Chapters 5, 6, and 8 provide you with ways you can do this.)

TIP

Conflict is a normal, healthy part of life. It can help children gain confidence in their ability to make positive decisions. On the other hand, bullying breaks down children's self-esteem and undermines their confidence.

TOOLBOX TACTIC

How do you handle conflict?

- Do you hit, push, call someone a name, or spread rumors to handle a disagreement?
- Do you fight to handle your problems?

To help your children explore issues around fighting, give them the Why Fight questions listed below.

Why Fight?

Answer these questions to think about fighting.

1. What good comes from fighting?
2. What harm comes from fighting?
3. Think of students who don't get into fights. How do they avoid fights?
4. Why do you get into trouble?
5. Who is usually with you when you get into trouble?
6. Where are you when trouble starts?
7. How do you get yourself out of trouble?
8. What are some ways to keep yourself out of trouble?
9. If someone wants to fight you, what choices do you have?
10. How could you get help if you needed it?

Bullying Is Not Teasing and Rough Play

He used to laugh about it when people mocked him over his dress sense and music taste, so we didn't realize it was anything serious.

A High School Parent

It can be difficult to tell the difference between teasing, rough play, and bullying. What may seem like bullying behaviors may just be two children learning how to interact. Friendly teasing such as "You are a klutz" or "You are weird" is normal for kids. When the teasing is mutual, it is harmless and healthy since it helps kids build relationships, form bonds, navigate social situations, and develop a sense of humor. Friendly teasing communicates affection, since you would tease only someone with whom you are familiar and to whom you feel close. The person being teased should not look distressed. For example, with friendly teasing, Carl may notice James's nonverbal clues—a joking tone of voice, a relaxed body posture, a friendly facial expression such as a smile, and a friendly gesture like a mild slap on the back or push. In this instance, both Carl and James are smiling and laughing. When I was a kid, I used to get teased because of my last name, Leiter (which sounds like "lighter"). My friends used to joke around and make comments like "Come flick my Bic" or "Come light my fire." I even had a middle school teacher tease me by calling me "cigarette lighter." I laughed right along with them because I knew their intentions were not hurtful but playful. It was good-natured ribbing among friends.

On the other hand, teasing isn't only about the content of the comment or nonverbal cues. Teasing also involves the intent of the message and how it is delivered. For example, with unfriendly teasing, Carl may notice James's aggressive nonverbal cues—mocking tone of voice, threatening body posture, and mean facial expression. Examples of unfriendly teasing are when James talks about Carl's looks ("pimple face"), culture ("rag head"), or how well he does in school ("geek" or "nerd"). When this happens, James's intention and motivation are to make fun of Carl and James doesn't care that his comments hurt Carl's feelings.

TIP

Friendly teasing is always seen as an experience that strengthens a social bond, not one that is meant to be painful. It has a positive impact whereas bullying has a negative impact.

TOOLBOX TACTIC

How could you help a child like Carl manage being teased? Help your children manage teasing.

1. Talk about it. Initiate a conversation about the teasing. For example, you could say, "I noticed that you got really mad at James when he called you a klutz. Can we talk about it?"

2. While your children are telling you their stories, try to determine if the teasing was playful or if it was more damaging, like bullying. Listen, not react, to how your children are being teased. Listen without disagreement. If your children tell you their classmates called them ugly, don't just jump in to reassure them that they're beautiful. As soon as you do that, you've let your children be victimized. Instead, listen to what they say, and then help them come up with a plan to address it the next time it happens.

3. Define the terms. When both people are equal in size, intelligence, and age and both are having fun, it's friendly teasing. However, when the two are not equal—one is more popular, bigger, or powerful—and the exchange is out of balance, it's not friendly teasing but bullying.

4. Teach friendly versus unfriendly teasing context clues. Teach the context clues that surround playful teasing (e.g., body language, laughter, smiling, or sarcasm) so your children can see the difference between serious and joking comments. Then use those tools to joke back.

5. Look at the intention behind the teaser's comments (see chapter 3).

6. Teach your children not to react to the teaser's comments by crying in front of the teaser. Rather, state that it is OK to cry at home where they are safe. Teach them to stay calm, take deep breaths, or count to 10 forward and backward. They should also avoid any cross-teasing or hurtful comments.

7. If your children are resistant to talking about the teasing, do some investigating by using the back door approach. The following questions can also be used to open up a discussion to find out if your children have been teased.

Ask them the following:

- How do kids joke around these days?
- What is teasing like for kids today?
- What kinds of teases are fun?
- What kinds of teases are bullying behaviors?
- What is the fine line between teasing that is fun and the teasing that is bullying?
- How can teasing quickly turn into bullying?
- Why do kids who are teased sometimes not show their distress?
- How can kids determine whether another child is upset?

Remember that the goal of friendly teasing is to make connections and form closer relationships with others, whereas the goal of bullying is to isolate, diminish, and tear down the other person. Thus, if the joking around and fun are not being enjoyed by EVERYONE involved and starts to become frequently hurtful, vindictive, and nasty at the expense of someone else, this is not having fun. It is bullying. Bullying is not a one-time comment. It is not a one-time joke. Rather, when the joke becomes a repeated occurrence at the expense of someone's feelings or causes pain and the motive is to diminish a target's self-worth, it is bullying.

For example, when I was in the fourth grade, I was bullied by classmates because of my weight and good grades. What at first seemed like teasing later developed into bullying. I was an active, outgoing, and loud kid who excelled academically. However, being overweight, taller, and larger than a majority of my classmates and friends caused me to be self-conscious. I used to hate that my teacher used to line us up by rows in front of the class to test whether we knew our math skills. Since I excelled academically and was often the last one standing, verbal taunts such as "thunder thighs," "blubber butt," and "teacher's pet" from classmates who did not do as well would commonly occur. Of course, my classmates tried to downplay their bullying behavior by saying, "I was just joking," "We're only having fun," or "We're just playing." However, to me and to other kids like me, their comments were not funny but hurtful.

 TIP

How can you distinguish between friendly teasing and bullying? One of my teenage clients told me, "Teasing and joking make both parties smile. Bullying makes only one party smile. This person is not your friend. She's a bully; ditch the loser."

When joking around is obviously not being enjoyed by EVERYONE involved, the joking should stop. Everyone's feelings must be considered.

TOOLBOX TACTIC

It's not unusual to see elementary school children picking on or teasing one another. A common game is to tease a little girl who touched a boy and say she has cooties or vice versa. By the time these students are in middle school, they are no longer playing games such as these. Teasing and verbal abuse in middle school can include prank telephone calls at all hours of the day, yelling obscenities down the hallway, leaving incriminating notes lying around for others to find, and sending mean e-mails or instant messages. When investigating the difference between teasing and bullying, follow these steps.

- First, be observant. Look for signs of withdrawal and decreased social involvement.
- Second, watch the reaction of the child being teased to see if the impact is negative.
- Third, look at the teaser's motive and intention for the behavior. Follow up on your observations by speaking to each child.

Ask the following questions.

1. Is what is being said hurting someone's feelings?
2. Would you want someone to say that about you?
3. How did other people react to the comment made?
4. What was the intent behind the comment?
5. How did you feel when the person made the comment?
6. How did the child react to the comment?
7. Did EVERYONE laugh and smile?

Remember that the target's perceptions and experiences are what are important when differentiating between teasing and bullying, not just the reported intent of the offender.

The Myth Is Not The Reality

When you're being bullied, you don't tell anyone because you're used to it. You already know that no one ever tries to help when you ask even if it is a teacher or your parents. And because it's been happening for so long, you just keep on coping. When people say just ignore it, you know that they don't know what it's like because it doesn't help. It just makes things worse. Things need to be done, not said!

15-Year-Old Girl

In the past, misconceptions about the nature and consequences of bullying led adults to conclude that bullying was just part of the fabric of childhood. Children were often encouraged to solve the problem on their own, thereby increasing the stressors on an already stressful situation. Despite decades of bullying research that has proven many of these core beliefs to be inaccurate, these attitudes continue to persist among adults. Over the years, I have heard many myths about bullying. Here are some comments parents have told me.

Hah. I just keep telling my son that "they" are jealous and losers and will be working for him someday if he will just ignore them.

My days of being bullied, way back when, ended when I kicked the s*** out of the high school's top bully.... We are raising wimpy kids.... This is a mean world.... Adapt to it or get eaten up.

Unfortunately, bullying is part of growing up. Those people that feel insecure are generally the ones doing the bullying, but what is it that a school is supposed to do? You can't punish a kid for being mean to another. Everyone would be in detention if you did. Kids need to toughen up.

Because he lacks self-esteem, the other kids are picking up on that. He just needs to stand up for himself and the bullying should stop.

Standing up to people is a part of life, and for many people it begins with dealing with bullies. And sorry, but it's true...some people will only respond to a violent reaction. It is not easy. As a new parent, I am hoping that my son can avoid it. But as someone who was bullied, it is important that people are taught to stand up for themselves while they are young. Otherwise, life will be very difficult and painful, and their confidence will always be in question. Getting beat up isn't that bad. It's the mental drama that goes with it that can be devastating. If kids can learn that it's okay to lose just as long as you go down swinging, we'll have a much better world in years to come. It's quite simple. If someone bullies you, smash them so hard that they never do it again.

We had our own incident where a child that was 4 years older than my then 6 year old punched him in the stomach on a school bus while he was sitting down. When we called the school bus supervisor, he asked what he did to deserve it. My husband said, "Oh yeah, that's how that works. I feel like you deserve it right now. I'm going to come down there and kick your a** because I feel you deserve it.

Before dispelling the myths of bullying I want you to think about your core beliefs about bullying. What are your values regarding bullying? Use the activity below to examine your beliefs about bullying. Do your beliefs promote or prevent bullying?

POINT TO PONDER

What Are You Modeling to Your Children?

You are a role model for your children. They emulate what you do and what you say. How you conduct yourself and what values you live by not only define YOU and YOUR culture but also play a part in defining the people around you, particularly your kids. Think about the following statements. What are your values regarding bullying? Do your beliefs promote or prevent bullying?

1. Bullying is just part of growing up.
2. Kids will outgrow bullying.
3. Sometimes kids who are bullied are "asking for it."
4. The best way to handle bullies is to bully them back.
5. Bullying does not cause any serious harm.
6. Bullies are looking for attention. Ignore them and the bullying will stop.
7. All kids have the right to feel safe at school.
8. Sometimes a kid has to stand up for himself or herself and fight a bully.
9. Adults can be bullies, too.
10. Bullies are insecure and have low self-esteem.
11. Bullies have more power than their victims.
12. Targets should ignore bullying behaviors and learn to fight back.
13. If the target fights back, the bully will back down.
14. Targets of bullying need to follow the adage "sticks and stones will break your bones, but names can never hurt you."
15. Telling on a bully will only make the situation worse.
16. All bullies hit, push, or attack others.
17. Kids bully others because they have problems of their own.
18. Teachers often intervene to stop bullying.
19. Nothing can be done at schools to reduce bullying.
20. Parents are usually aware that their children are bullies.

Because effective intervention and prevention depend on debunking these long-held misconceptions, I want to clear up inaccuracies that perpetuate the cycle of violence. Listed below are the myths, realities, and solutions to bullying.

Myth #1: Bullying Is a Part of Growing Up

Reality. Bullying is not a normal part of growing up or a socially acceptable way to treat others. Not all kids bully others to get what they want. By accepting that bullying is OK, we give bullies the power they need to hurt and exert dominance over others. Kids are not born as bullies. Rather, bullying is a learned behavior. Kids learn how to bully by watching adults use their power for aggression.

Solution. You have the opportunity to set a good example by teaching your children how to solve problems by using their power in appropriate ways.

Myth #2: Bullying Often Resolves Itself When you Ignore It

Reality. Many times, ignoring a problem is a good way not to give attention to negative things. However with bullying, ignoring it is a reward. If we ignore it, we deliver the message that bullying is acceptable. Ignoring the bullying teaches the bully that he or she can continue to act as he or she always has without consequences. The level of bullying usually increases if the bullying is not addressed by adults.

Solution. Adults and other kids need to stand up for kids who are bullied, and to lend support to ensure they are protected and safe.

Myth #3: Children Need to Stand up for Themselves and Fight Back

Reality. It's safe to assume that children who are more confidently able to defend themselves are probably less likely to be a target of bullying. So telling already frightened and scared children to stand up to the bully by fighting back is placing them at risk for harm. In addition, fighting back gives kids the idea that violence is a legitimate way to solve problems. In fact, it only perpetuates the bully cycle. Although hitting back might bring a moment of satisfaction, it can potentially escalate the power imbalance or further escalate the problem. In light of reports of kids bringing weapons to school, fighting back could put both the bully and the bullied in danger. If the victim retaliates, it also makes it more difficult for the school to determine where the fault lies.

Solution. Teach kids to be assertive, not aggressive. Fighting back with verbal comebacks can be helpful if the target feels confident enough to tell the bully that he or she does not like being singled out or picked on. You can coach the target by showing him or her how to use a strong, firm voice (not yelling). Using statements like "I want you to leave me alone" or "I want you to stop doing this to me" might help the situation. Fight back by telling a trusted adult about what is happening so that the bully will be restrained and face consequences. Tell your children that it takes a lot of courage to come forward and reinforce that they are not weak or a tattletale for doing so.

TOOLBOX TACTIC

Tattling versus Telling

In helping your children distinguish between tattling and telling, teach the following:

- Tattling is about getting someone in trouble.
- Telling is about getting someone out of danger and/or preventing harm.

Use the following questions to discuss the difference between tattling and telling with your children:

- Is what you are about to tell me the truth, necessary, and kind?
- Are you trying to get someone in trouble or out of danger?
- What if you feel that telling someone will also put you in danger? What do you do? Is this the correct thing to do? Why or why not?

Myth #4: Bullying Builds Character and Will Make Children Tougher or Stronger

Reality. Research findings clearly show that being bullied increases the vulnerabilities of children. For example, we know that children who are passive and socially withdrawn are at a heightened risk of being bullied and that these children become even more withdrawn after incidents of harassment.[6]

Solution. Teach kids that character comes from being caring, compassionate, and considerate.

Myth #5: Nonphysical Bullying Does Not Cause Any Real Harm

Reality. Many adults tell children, "Sticks and stones can break your bones but words can never hurt you." Although physical bullying is easier to recognize, verbal and emotional bullying, both direct and indirect, does hurt children. Bullying is associated with a range of mental health problems. These include depression, anxiety, suicide, educational problems, antisocial problems, and relationship problems. Thus, a more realistic rhyme is "sticks and stones can break your bones but words can break your heart."

Solution. Teach kids that all forms of bullying are unacceptable and have consequences.

Myth #6: Children Will Outgrow Bullying

Reality. For some, bullying continues as they become older. Unless someone intervenes, the bullying will likely continue. In some cases, it can grow into violence and other serious problems. Studies have established a strong correlation between children who bully and have legal troubles as adults.

Solution. Teach kids prosocial behaviors that build up rather than destroy connections with others (covered in chapters 6, 7, and 8).

Myth #7 Bullies are Unpopular and Have Low Self-esteem

Reality. Research is finally catching up with what parents and teachers have known for years. Plenty of the most aggressive kids are confident and socially successful. Bullying and aggression can yield rich social rewards like attention, more friends, and power. That's one of the reasons it's so hard to get kids to stop being bullies. Gossip and exclusion bring kids together, even as these kids push others out.

Solution. Involve kids with high social status in antibullying programs at school.

Myth #8: Bullied Kids Need to Deal with Bullying on Their Own

Reality. Many adults encourage children to solve the problem on their own. This reinforces the belief that adults should stay out of it. Some kids have the confidence and skills to stop bullying when it happens, but many do not. Kids should not be expected to deal with bullying on their own since it is a form of victimization or peer abuse. Just as society does not expect victims of other types of abuse (e.g., child maltreatment or domestic abuse) to deal with it on their own, we should not expect children who are bullied to do the same.

Solution. Adults and peers play a critical role in helping to stop bullying and in supporting the targets of bullying.

POINT TO PONDER

Read over the myths and realities of bullying noted above. How many myths about bullying do you hold? How many beliefs aligned with the realities? What messages about bullying are you conveying to your children? Are they helping or hurting?

Is My Child In Danger of Becoming A Bully?

Research has shown a number of family, individual, peer, and school risk factors contribute to children's engagement in bullying. These risk factors for bullying behavior do not guarantee that a child will become a bully, but they do indicate an increased risk for bullying behavior.[8] These include:

BULLY RISK FACTORS	
Individual risk factors	• Impulsive, hotheaded, dominant personality • Lacking empathy • Difficulty conforming to rules and low frustration tolerance • Positive attitudes toward violence • Physically aggressive • Gradually decreasing interest in school (achievement) • Previous traumatic experiences of their own, including maltreatment or bullying
Family risk factors	• Lack of parental warmth and involvement • Overly permissive or excessively harsh discipline/physical punishment by parents • Lack of parental supervision • Parent(s) exhibit bullying behaviors or violence toward others, including toward both people and animals • Harsh, physical discipline at home, including physical abuse • Victimization by older siblings

Peer risk factors	• Friends/peers with positive attitudes toward violence • Exposure to models of bullying • Some aggressive children who take on high status roles may use bullying as a way to enhance their social power and protect their prestige with peers • Some children with low social status may use bullying as a way to deflect taunting and aggression that is directed toward them or to enhance their social position with higher-status peers.
School risk factors	• Lack of supervision during breaks (e.g., lunchrooms, playgrounds, hallways, locker rooms, and bathrooms) • Unsupervised interactions among different grade levels during breaks • Indifferent or accepting teacher attitudes toward bullying • Indifferent or accepting student attitudes toward bullying • Inconsistent enforcement of the rules • Weak policies against bullying and discrimination • Negative school climate

TOOLBOX TACTIC

Could You Be A Bully? Could Your Child Be A Bully?

Because children often model what they see, take the following quiz to see if you may display bullying behaviors. Then take the quiz as if you were your child. Next, give your child the same quiz to see if he or she may have engaged in bullying behaviors. Finally, compare the outcomes of the quizzes.[10]

For each question, circle whether the answer is "yes," "sometimes," or "no."

1. Do you enjoy teasing others?
   Yes   Sometimes   No

2. If you see that your teasing is upsetting someone, do you stop?
   Yes   Sometimes   No

3. Do you laugh if someone makes a mistake or hesitates?
   Yes   Sometimes   No

4. Do you think it's fun to embarrass someone?
   Yes   Sometimes   No

5. Do you pick on people who can't or are unwilling to fight back?
   Yes   Sometimes   No

6. When another person is harassing someone, do you go along?
   Yes   Sometimes   No

7. Do you feel you always have to come out on top?
   Yes   Sometimes   No

8. If someone makes you angry, do you have trouble getting over your anger?
   Yes   Sometimes   No

9. Do you blame others for the things that happen to you?
   Yes   Sometimes   No

10. If someone harasses you, do you feel the need to get revenge?
    Yes   Sometimes   No

Scoring: Give yourself 1 point for each "yes" you have circled, 2 points for each "sometimes," and 5 points for each "no."

- If your score is 25 or above: It is unlikely that you are someone who bullies.

- If your score is less than 25: It is likely that you have engaged in bullying behaviors. It might be a good idea to take a look at your behavior. Rather than harassing someone, ask yourself how you would feel if you were that person. How are you encouraging a culture of bullying at home? What behaviors do you need to change in yourself and in your family to prevent bullying from occurring in the first place?

What Are The Warning Signs that My Child Has Been Bullied?

Children who are targeted are often hesitant to tell an adult (e.g., parent, teacher, or administrator) about their experiences because of shame, fear of retaliation, and a sense that adults cannot help solve the problem. Because kids are so reluctant to admit that they are being bullied, you must familiarize yourself with the signs. Children who are being threatened or intimidated in this way may come home with torn or dirty clothing or with damaged property. They may seem anxious, sad, moody, teary, and/or depressed. They may complain of chronic pains such as headaches or stomachaches. They may have few friends (or spend little or no time with them), have changes in sleeping patterns (either too much or not enough sleep), or have frequent bad dreams. They may lose interest in schoolwork and may be reluctant or even afraid to go to school or other social activities.

If your children are being bullied, they may display one, all, or even none of these warning signs. So be alert for any changes in your children's behavior. Talk to them frequently about what is going on at school and in other activities. You may need to schedule a meeting with school staff to find out what has taken place.

Conclusion

As a parent, you must promote healthy relationships among young people. You, and other adults, are responsible for creating positive environments, promoting healthy relationships, and ending violence in the lives of youths. You are a role model and must lead by example. You must look for, listen for, and respond to bullying. Bullying is not about children of roughly the same strength or power arguing, quarreling, or getting into the odd fight about something. Rather, a child who is stronger, more aggressive, bolder, and more confident than the average child typically bullies others who are weaker, more timid, and tend not to retaliate or act in an assertive manner. Kids who get up the courage to complain about being bullied are saying they've tried and can't cope with the situation on their own. Treat their complaints as a call for help. Do not blame them. Do not dismiss them. Ensure that victimized children are protected and safe.

Chapter 3

Demystifying the Cycle of Bullying

This chapter provides an overview of the drama triangle: the bullying cycle, the reasons kids engage in bullying behaviors, and how brain development is involved.

Bullying and School Shootings

The combination of bullying, a penchant toward violence when one is angry, the availability of weapons, and the possibility of intoxication at school increases significantly the likelihood of retaliatory violence.

Michael Josephson,
Founder and President of the
Josephson Institute of Ethics

What do Columbine, West Paducah, Virginia Tech, and Chardon High School all have common? They have all been exposed to violent acts instigated by bullying. In extreme cases, targets of bullying may resort to violent retaliation. In 1999, Eric Harris and Dylan Klebold began the massacre in Columbine High School, killing 13 and injuring 24. Reports reveal that they were the targets of bullying who, in return, became bullies and began bullying others. In 2007 at Virginia Tech, Seung-Hui Cho went on a rampage, killing 32 people and taking his own life (*www.msnbc.msn.com*). According to MSNBC, Cho's former high school classmates reported his being mocked for his extreme shyness, quietness, and the strange way he talked. He would sometimes sign a question mark instead of his name. On Monday, February 28, 2012 in Ohio, 17-year-old T. J. Lane walked into Chardon High School and began a shooting rampage. He fired 10 shots at a group of students in the cafeteria, resulting in 3 dead and 2 wounded (*www.cbsnews.com*). Many students who witnessed the shootings describe the shooter as "an outcast who had been bullied." These tragic incidents appear to be the latest in a string of school shootings committed by bullied students. Although experts report that being bullied at school rarely leads to murder, they do agree that bullying is a common theme emerging in school shootings.

TIP

The U.S. Secret Service and the U.S. Department of Education studied 37 school shootings from 1974–2000. They found that almost three-quarters of the shooters had "experienced bullying and harassment that was long-standing and severe" and "approached torment."

www.secretservice.gov/ntac/ssi_guide.pdf

Josephson Institute of Ethics (*www.josephsoninstitute.org*) took a national sampling of 43,321 public and private high school students ages 15 to 18. The results indicated that 33% of students reported that violence is a big problem at their school, 24% reported they do not feel very safe at school, 52% of students have hit someone in anger, and more boys (37%) then girls (19%) stated it was OK to hit or threaten a person who makes them angry. In spite of all the attention that has been given to bullying lately, it appears that aggressive and intimidating behaviors continue to be prevalent. So why does this cycle of violence keep happening? To help answer this question, you need to understand the motives behind the behavior, how violence develops and is maintained, and how brain development is involved.

Why Do Children Bully?

Well, the only reason I bullied is because the same person I was doing it to did it to me like a week before. It wasn't the right thing to do, but at the time, it felt like I was getting revenge.

15-Year-Old Boy

Parents, teachers, and kids frequently ask me why children bully. Remember that not all children who bully come from chaotic environments or unstable homes. Many underlying factors can lead to their acting out or externalizing behavior. In the 1998 book *Choice Theory: A New Psychology of Personal Freedom*, renowned psychiatrist Dr. William Glasser states that all behavior serves a purpose that is motivated by what we want at the moment. Our chosen behavior can be justified as an attempt to meet one or more basic needs that are part of our genetic structure. The source of almost all human problems, such as violence and school failure, is feeling disconnected to others (e.g., peers, parents, teachers, etc.).

Additionally, Glasser asserts what happened to us in the past has everything to do with who we are today. Nevertheless, we can satisfy our basic needs only right now and can plan to continue satisfying them in the future. From a motivational perspective, this means the source of our problems lies in our previous experiences that threaten our feelings of competence, self-worth, self-determination, or relatedness to others. Consequently, our present behavior gives us a better sense of control over our life situations, including our relationship with others. Since kids continually try to find ways to fit in and belong, the key to understanding why they behave in a negative manner toward others is to recognize their intention or the purpose of the behavior.

POINT TO PONDER

According to Glasser, the source of all kids' problems can be explained by their unsatisfactory or nonexistent connections with other peers, parents, or adults. So how have you helped your children connect to people? Have your behaviors helped or hindered?

Seven caring habits foster relationships with others, while seven deadly habits break down relationships with others.

Seven Caring Habits	Seven Deadly Habits
1. Supporting	1. Criticizing
2. Encouraging	2. Blaming
3. Listening	3. Complaining
4. Accepting	4. Nagging
5. Trusting	5. Threatening
6. Respecting	6. Punishing
7. Negotiating differences	7. Bribing or rewarding to control

What habits do you identify with the most? With the least? What are some ways that you have used the seven caring habits to foster your connection with your children and with others? What are some ways that you have used the seven deadly habits to sever connections with your children and with others?

www.wglasser.com

Note that although kids choose their behaviors, they have direct control only over what they think and how they act. They can only indirectly control the way they feel (feelings) and their body's response to those feelings (physiological reactions) through their thoughts and behaviors. (I will discuss this point later on in the chapter under the section "the growing brain.") By understanding children's motivations you can help them make better choices (thinking) to behave in a positive way (behavior) that will help then meet their needs without hurting others and without getting in trouble. Seven motives or goals are behind bullying behaviors.

1: Power-Seeking/Control-Seeking Behavior

Kids who seek power ultimately want the upper hand. The goal of the behavior is to establish control, to be in charge, to run things, to have it their way, and to tell others what to do. Thus bullies usurp teachers', parents', or other adults' authority in or out of the classroom. They challenge others directly (let's fight, or argue) or indirectly (passive noncompliance) because they want to feel powerful and important. They want to achieve, win, or feel worthwhile. In pursuit of power, some kids choose to engage in bullying behaviors to gain a sense of power and control over their family, friends, or life situations.

 TIP

> While boys often display a strong need to dominate others and rely on bullying to enhance their physical dominance, girls have a strong need to socially dominate others, be the center of attention of a core group of peers, and rely on bullying to enhance their social status.

2: Love/Belonging

The most important need is to be loved and to belong. Connectedness with people you care about is a requisite for satisfying all of a person's needs. Some kids choose to bully because they feel disconnected from or unloved by their parents. They have a strong need to be a part of a group or to be accepted by their peers.

3: Fun

Kids' need for fun is found in their play. Thus they seek out activities that are pleasurable and enjoyable. Kids who bully seem to enjoy harassing others and get pleasure from seeing other people's pain. It feels good to make fun of others without regard for the feelings of others.

4: Freedom

Kids' desire for freedom is played out by the choices they make to fulfill this desire. Kids who bully may not believe they have the freedom to do things or engage in activities in their life. They may believe their choices are limited. By bullying others, they feel free to do whatever they choose to gain their independence, autonomy, or own space.

5: Revenge-Seeking Behavior/Survival

Kids who seek revenge are retaliating against real or perceived hurts or injustices. They believe they have been wronged in some way, have been treated unfairly, or have been bullied themselves. Consequently, they may be vindictive, lash out, sulk, or scowl. By intimidating others, they keep themselves safe. Sometimes kids want revenge on a school administrator, teacher, or another adult who may have hurt them. Since it is too risky to take their retribution out on the actual target, bullies take it out on someone safer—their peer. Revenge behavior may emanate from power-seeking behavior.

6: Feeling Inferior/ Inadequate

Kids bully others because they may feel inferior or inadequate in some area of their life. Their behavior is predicated on a belief system that they are unable to do things well. Procrastination, clowning around, noncompliance, feigned illness, ambivalence, and displays of inadequacy characterize their behavior.

7: Attention-Seeking Behavior

Some kids misbehave or bully to get attention. The message is "Look at me!" These kids require an audience. They never seem to get enough attention to satisfy them. Although this behavior is relatively benign, it can agitate teachers and other adults. This behavior can also trigger the fight or flight response. Keep reading to learn how chemical reactions in the brain can trigger the fight-or-flight response.

TOOLBOX TACTIC

Complete the activity with your children to examine how their needs are met. We are all born with the same basic needs. However, the things you may do to meet these needs may be different from what others choose to do. Think about your last conflict.

- What needs were you trying to meet?
- How were your needs met?
- If your need was not met, how could it be met?
- If your need was met in an inappropriate way, like hitting another child or talking back to the teacher, what are some ways you could meet your need in more appropriate ways?

Depending on your children's ages, you can have them draw a picture, write a story, or tell you how their needs were met and what happened once they were.

Unfortunately, kids will attempt to meet their needs in a way that makes sense to them at the time. Sometimes the choices and decisions they make are not healthy or safe. The answers to the questions in the previous box will help you to redirect your children. You will be able to help them find positive ways to meet and achieve their needs in a healthy manner. Understand that your children are not consciously plotting their misbehavior. Instead, it is based on their mistaken goal. You can show empathy and support when helping them develop and promote a respectful relationship with others.

TOOLBOX TACTIC

How are you getting your needs met?

The purpose of this activity is to examine what needs are being met when a child bullies others What is the child trying to get or avoid by misbehaving?

To help your children understand why kids engage in bullying or why your children bullies others, read together the seven reasons that children bully (listed earlier in this chapter).

After you read over the reasons do the following:

1. Have your children give a reason why they bullied.

2. Have your children write the need(s) that they identify with and list what need(s) they were trying to meet. For example,
   The needs I identify with are...for this reason...
3. Under each of your children's answers, have them list two positive things they can do to meet their needs in an acceptable way. For example, if your children want to belong to a group, they can join a group that interests them. Examples include key club, robotics club, skateboarding, etc.

The Theatrical Playground: The Place Where All Games Are Played

In 1968, psychotherapist Stephen Karpman created the drama triangle (*www.karpmandramatriangle.com*) to refer to the dysfunctional mind games people find themselves getting into with other people over and over again. The triangle represents the three states of mind or character roles that are dysfunctional responses to conflict. The triangle also shows how we use these roles to manage our anxiety when confronted with something new or emotionally uncomfortable. Most of us engage in these roles (patterns of communication) unconsciously based on our previous experiences. Our communication is based on our interpretation of what we have been told, what we have experienced in the past, and how we interpret current events.

Many children learn these roles from watching family dynamics and interacting with their parents. This means children are unconsciously very adept at taking a role that perpetuates the cycle and keeps them stuck in unhealthy behaviors. When children enter the triangle, they behave in a certain way to elicit familiar feelings such as feeling inadequate, useless, or unworthy. In other words, their behavior is driven by their internal negative critic. For example, if a critical parent has often said that the children are not good enough, the children will feel resentful and useless. Inwardly, the kids succumb to this persecutory voice, fearing it may be right. Because they need relief, they make excuses for their behavior by saying, "If it hadn't been for...I would be."

The goals of the drama are to avoid accountability, responsibility, growth, and change while blaming others for their misfortune. Therefore, each player in the triangle tries to get their emotional needs fulfilled. Simultaneously, none of the players acknowledge their own and others' contributions to the dysfunctional dynamic. They avoid the truth. They claim innocence. They reject any responsibility for the situation.

TIP

"The drama triangle does not refer to actual physical victimization such as witnessing or intervening in someone being physically assaulted or recanting an action or event that caused physical harm. The 'triangle' describes a state of mind or an attitude that plays out in a patterned role."

www.learningcommunityresource.com

It Takes Three to Play

The three roles that appear in people's relationship dynamics include the persecutor/bully, the rescuer/enabler, and the victim. Although not a part of Karpman's original drama triangle, a fourth role, bystander, is added. By understanding the roles designated in the drama, the way they interact, and the rules that trap us, we can learn to avoid becoming entangled in the drama. Figure 3.1 represents the theatrical playground, which is adapted from Karpman's drama triangle. The triangle can be played out between two or more players such as teacher-student, parent-child, child-child-child, teacher-parent-child, etc.

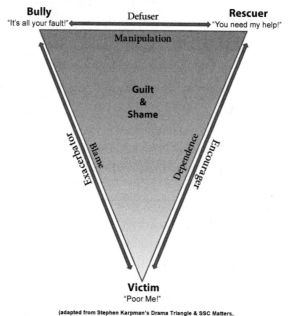

Figure 3.1: The Theatrical Playground

Bullies

Bullies operate from a position of power. They use fear and intimidation, either verbal or physical, as tools for keeping others down. For instance, they blame the victim and criticize the enabling behavior of rescuers. Bullies are highly judgmental of others, often pointing out the faults of others and become angry when others do not do what they say. Bullies use negative behaviors to cover up or deny their own weaknesses or take ownership of their problems. They are usually in complete denial about their blaming tactics. When these tactics are pointed out to them, bullies argue that the attack was warranted and necessary for self-protection. To them, to survive in this dangerous world means to strike first before someone strikes them. For example, the commando parent focuses on perfection and compliance rather than on being satisfied with growth and improvement. This parent is critical of the child by stating, "You must be perfect," "You always forget to bring home your papers for me to sign," or "You never put forth 100% effort into your studies."

TOOLBOX TACTIC

Ask yourself the questions below to check how often you play persecutor.
- Do I tell others what to do to solve their problems?
- Do I see others as powerless, incapable, and needing to be fixed?
- Do I criticize others?
- Do I speak and act in a rigid, dominating, or bossy manner?

Do you see your children playing this part? Ask your children the same questions. Do they identify with this role?

Rescuers

Rescuers see themselves as helpers and caretakers. They believe that their needs are unimportant and irrelevant. Thus, they need someone to rescue (victim) in order to feel vital, important, and loved. They need to be in control of others to avoid their own feelings and problems. Their self-esteem is derived from being seen as unselfish for someone else's own good. They have a strong sense of entitlement with the victim, claiming "You owe me because of all I've done for you." Unfortunately, rescuers help victims who have no idea of how to give back to the rescuers. Consequently, rescuers can become martyrs or even victims when they feel they have been taken advantage of by others. Rescuers often don't recognize themselves as ever being in a victim position since they are, after all, the ones with all of the answers. For example, the helicopter parent does everything for the child because the parent feels guilty over working long hours since the divorce. The parent, who is a rescuer, subconsciously keeps the child dependent by playing into the child's victimhood. The helicopter parent does everything for the child rather than allow the child to experience that he or she can do things independently.

TOOLBOX TACTIC

Ask yourself the questions below to check how often you play rescuer.
• Do I accept responsibility for fixing problems that are not mine?
• Do I believe I cannot say no to a request for help?
• Do I feel guilty when I say no to a request for help and end up helping nevertheless?
• Do I perceive others as incapable of making good decisions or of helping themselves?
• Do I perceive others as needing to be fixed or their lives needing to be fixed?

Do you see your children playing this part? Ask your children the same questions. Do they identify with this role?

POINT TO PONDER

You may think the rescuer position may be the best position to take. After all, it is a helping position. Wanting to be rescued isn't necessarily unhealthy. However, consider the following points.

1. It is healthy to want to help when one asks for help or needs it. Yet rescuers often meddle in other people's lives without the victim asking first or finding out whether and how the victim wants to be supported. What rescuers agree to do may not be what the victim really wants them to do. This means rescuers often feel resentful or unappreciated in some way, as though they have been victimized themselves.

2. Because rescuers need to be needed, need to be in control, and need to be right no matter the cost, they live their lives as if their own needs and wants are of little importance. Thus rescuers avoid dealing with any emotions or discomfort that might arise from addressing their own problems.

3. Because of the nature of the drama triangle, rescuers must have a victim—someone to take care of, someone to control, and someone, who by being needy, makes the rescuer feel good. In order to fill the need, they must have a victim whom they can "help." If there isn't one available, rescuers will attempt to create or find one.

4. By coming to the victim's rescue, rescuers indirectly communicate to the victim, "You are insufficient. You cannot take care of yourself. You are inept. Therefore, I should be in charge." This attempt to "fix" the victim's situation actually promotes a victim's dependence on the rescuers, which reinforces the victim's "one down" position.

Keep in mind the following. People who genuinely offer assistance to others do so free of expectations and free of fostering others' dependency upon them. Genuine helpers encourage self-responsibility. They demonstrate clear and drama-free communication and actions.

Victims

Victims feel helpless, hopeless, and incompetent. They believe they cannot take care of themselves. Victims see themselves as consistently unable to handle life. They often use guilt as a way to manipulate their rescuers into taking care of them. "If you don't do it, who will?" For example, a victim may say, "I can't do anything about my life because I am a loser. You won't understand what I had to do just to get to school today. This always happens to me when I try to get ahead in life."

TOOLBOX TACTIC

Ask yourself the questions below to check how often you play victim.
- Do I feel hopeless, powerless, or incapable of making decisions or making positive changes?
- Do I believe my life is just one problem after another?
- Do I manipulate others or use guilt to get help or get what I want?
- Do I blame others or circumstances for my difficulties?
- Do I focus on my problems?

Do you see your children playing this part? Ask your children the same questions. Do they identify with this role?

Bystanders

Three types of bystanders observe the drama and bullying: exacerbators, defusers, and encouragers.[1] Exacerbators, by their action or inaction, contribute to the creation, continuance, or aggravation of the harassment (bully) and victimization (victim) by stating, "You're right! She had no business talking to your boyfriend at the dance." Defusers attempt to neutralize the drama to reduce the conflict between the bully and rescuer by stating, "She didn't mean it that way when she said your shoes were so last year." Encouragers mediate the drama between the rescuer and victim by attempting to persuade the victim that the rescuer has the resources to help. For example, they may say, "You've faced more serious problems before, and Anna came to your rescue to help you to survive."

TOOLBOX TACTIC

Ask yourself the questions below to check how often you play bystander.
- Do I sit back and watch others be bullied?
- Do I believe that if I intervene, I will fall prey to being bullied?
- Do I encourage or support others to bully?
- Do I believe that if I intervene, I might make things worse?
- Do I believe the victim deserves it?
- Do I not know what to do?

Do you see your children playing this part? Ask your children the same questions. Do they identify with this role?

TIP

Remember that the triangle describes a person's state of mind or an attitude that plays out in a patterned role. Each person is playing out his or her dysfunctional pattern in an attempt to receive the kind of attention or control each unconsciously desires.
- Victims depend on a savior to take care of them.
- Rescuers yearn for a basket case to save.
- Bullies need a scapegoat to blame for living in a dangerous world.

As indicated in Figure 3.1, the roles of bully and rescuer are placed at the top of the inverted triangle. These roles assume a one-up position over others, meaning they relate as though they are better, stronger, or smarter than the victim. On the other hand, the victim is placed in the one-down position at the bottom of the triangle since the victim feels looked down upon or worth less than the others. The arrows on the triangle indicate the direction of the transactions. However, the drama in the triangle comes from the switching of roles. When one person changes roles or tactics, others in the triangle will then switch to match the change. This reinforces the never-ending drama of rescuing, persecution, and victimization.

TIP

Guilt and shame hook you into the drama. They are also powerful driving forces that perpetuate the triangle. Here are a few things you need to know about guilt.

1. Guilt is a signal that someone is attempting to pull you into the drama.
2. To stay out of the drama, you need to learn to give yourself permission to feel guilty without acting on that guilt. In other words, do not let the guilt push you into the rescuer position.
3. Learn to sit with the guilt and be uncomfortable. Feeling guilty is a learned response. It is not the same thing as losing your integrity.

Here's how the game is played. The bully, feeling inadequate in his or her abilities, becomes the victim of his or her own torment. The bully projects critical parental recordings toward the rescuer or victim. For example, the bully may think, "If all these other stupid people would do things my way, the world would be a much better place!" The victim, feeling resentful of the one-down position or lack of compliance from the rescuer, eventually retaliates against the rescuer and becomes the bully. The rescuer, feeling annoyed with a lack of response or any appreciation for his or her efforts, becomes a bully. The rescuer accuses the victim of failing to take responsibility for himself or herself. Thus the victim is back into the role of victim. By feeling guilty over not rescuing the victim, he or she returns to the role of rescuer.

CASE STUDY

Can you recognize the teacher-parent-child drama triangle?

Mrs. Smith: "Paul, since this is the third time you hit another student, you need to go to the principal's office, which means you can't go to the zoo next week."

Paul: "You didn't see, but he kicked and hit me first!"

Mrs. Smith: "Paul, it doesn't matter; you cannot hit another student. If I saw Tony hit you, he would go to the office too, but I didn't. Please get up and go to the office now."

Paul: "My mom says you are picking on me because you don't like me. I WILL go to the zoo next week."

Paul goes home and tells his mom.

Paul: "Momma. Mrs. Smith did it again. She yelled at me in front of everybody in the class and made me go to the principal's office. She says I can't go to the zoo next week. She always blames me for disrupting the class. I didn't do anything wrong, and it just isn't fair. She doesn't like me. She always picks on kids she doesn't like. She says we are too rowdy and disruptive. She doesn't have eyes in the back of her head. Everybody knows Mrs. Smith is a bad teacher. Because she can't control her class we have to pay for it by getting in trouble."

(Notice that Paul is placing the blame on someone else and talking for the class.)

Paul's mom: "Mrs. Smith, my son should not be punished for your inability to control your class. You always blame Paul for picking on other kids and disrupting the class. My son is not going to be punished when it is YOU that should be fired for not doing your job. You should be able to control your class. He is going on that field trip."

(Notice that Paul's mom uses the word "should.")

Mrs. Smith: "Your son is disruptive when he can't get his way. I understand that he has ADHD, but this is the third time he hit another student. What does it say if he goes to the zoo and isn't held accountable for the same standards as everyone else? It is not my problem that your son cannot control himself. Because he can't, he is not going to the zoo."

(Notice that at this point Mrs. Smith is defensive.)

Paul's mom: "I can see why my son says you are not a good teacher. You are blaming him and others for your incompetence. I am calling the school board—you can't keep my son off this trip. I pay your salary!"

Mrs. Smith: "Do what you think you need to do, but I'm not changing my mind."

Were you able to recognize the drama?

- Paul plays victim when he believes the teacher (bully) is picking on him.
- Paul brings in Mom to rescue him and solve the problem.
- Mom sees Paul as a victim who needs to be protected.
- Mom is unwilling to entertain the idea that Paul may shoulder some responsibility for his behavior (denial).
- Mom persecutes (bullies) the teacher (victim) by blaming the teacher for Paul's behavior.

- Because she believes she can't win with the teacher, Mom (victim) pulls in the school board for help.

As long as Mrs. Smith, Paul, and Mom are unwilling to talk to work things out, the problem will not be solved. The drama will continue, and trusting relationships will not develop.

No matter where we may start out on the triangle, no matter what role we have in the triangle, each role will eventually end up as a victim since each position is obtained as a result of feeling disregarded or disowned. The good news is that only one person needs to move out of the game and stop playing. When you are in the process of leaving the triangle, you are in the process of telling yourself the truth about your feelings, your motives, and the situation in general. You are willing to experience whatever feelings you are having. You are also willing to let others experience their feelings without you having to rescue them. Are you and your child ready to leave the game? In chapters 5, 6, and 7, I provide you with ways to get out of the game.

POINT TO PONDER

No matter how much a victim may want the bullying to stop, as long as he or she accepts the role, nothing will change. The bully maintains control. Rescuers feel obligated to intervene. Bystanders' stand by and watch.

Recall the old saying, "The definition of insanity is repeating the same behavior over and over again but expecting different results."

As long as the drama is maintained and the players do not rewrite their scripts, they will continue to switch and rotate between roles. This means the problems will not be solved.

Since children first learn their starting gate position in their family, what are some ways that you or your family dynamics reinforce their starting position? How can you help your children change their position?

TOOLBOX TACTIC

How We Play the Game. Can You Recognize the Drama?

Think back over a real-life experience involving you and another person where you suspect you have been a rescuer, a victim, or a bully, or all three. The purpose of this exercise is to become aware of the roles we play and how we relate through past patterns, fear, denial, conflict, etc. Using that situation, ask yourself the following questions.

Actions
- What am I not doing?
- What do I need to do?

Responsibility
- Who is taking responsibility for whom?
- Who am I taking responsibility for?
- Am I allowing the other person to take responsibility for himself or herself and for his or her actions?

Power
- Who has the power? How do I know?
- To what extent am I exercising my power appropriately?
- Have I agreed to more than I want to do?
- Am I doing more than half the work?
- Am I owning my power positively and appropriately?
- Am I using my power to take care of myself properly?

Boundaries
- Am I setting my own boundaries and taking responsibility for myself and my actions?
- What boundaries do I need to set up?

Authenticity
- To what extent am I being genuine and honest in my words and actions?
- To what extent am I asking/assisting others to be genuine and honest in their words and actions?

Feelings
- What am I feeling about this situation?
- How would I like to feel?

Respect
- To what extent am I showing appropriate respect for myself by my actions and words?

- To what extent am I showing appropriate respect for the other person in my actions and words?

Change

- What action do I need to take to make sure that I deal with this in the best possible way so that it has the best possible outcome?

Use the same exercise with your children to help raise awareness of how they play the game and feed into the drama.

Recognizing the Bullying Cycle

The phrase bullying cycle was developed by the pioneer of bullying research, Dan Olweus.[2] The bullying cycle is often used to help explain the unwritten code of silence that exists between the three players in a bullying situation, namely the bully, the target (the bullied), and the bystander. The code of silence, which operates on the premise of fear generated by the bully, is centered on the belief that if the bully's misbehavior is reported, things will only get much worse. Consequently, many kids are hesitant to break the silence and get help. Of course, this shared belief reinforces the bullying cycle since the bully is allowed to get away with being aggressive toward others. The bully continues the hurtful behavior without limits and consequences. For the most part, many kids long for the day when a teacher or another adult in the school could witness the bullying and take the burden off of them to tell.

 TIP

A 2011 study by the National Education Association (*www.nea.org*) found that 87% of school staff reported witnessing bullying. When surveyed about their response to bullying, 70% of the teachers surveyed believed that educators almost always intervened when they observed bullying. However, only 35% of 9th graders surveyed believed that teachers were interested in stopping bullying behaviors. In fact, 66% of victims felt that school staff did not respond well when they observed bullying.

There is an unspoken rule among children about telling adults—telling only makes you weaker, more vulnerable, and prone to being bullied even more. Some children are reluctant to tell because they do not want to worry their parents. Others remain silent in order to fit in and belong. They do not want to be seen as tattletales. Many are reluctant to report bullying because they feel ashamed at not being able to stand up for themselves. They fear that adults won't take them seriously. ("She just does it because she knows it bothers you.") Kids feel that adults won't help ("Just ignore her"), will blame them ("You should wear different clothes"), or will make matters worse by acting poorly.

Although estimates vary depending on how the data were collected, results from the 2009 *School Crime Supplement to the National Crime Victimization Survey* (*nces.ed.gov*) indicated the percentage of students breaking the code of silence decreases with increasing grade. In other words, elementary students are two times more likely than middle school and high school students to notify an adult that they have been bullied. Thus, as kids get older, they are less likely to report any type of bullying behavior. This stems from a need to be independent from parents and other adults and also to be able to solve their own problems.

Being bullied makes me feel really bad, and I often get depressed later at home. I would also plot revenge and privately express my "hatred" toward the bully, but I doubt I would really do anything about it.... I don't usually go to adults to "tattle" on people. Even though I know it's not tattling, it's real.

12-Year-Old Girl

POINT TO PONDER

Do You Share in the Blame?

- Do you encourage your children to stand up for themselves? If so, could their assertiveness be interpreted as bullying?
- Are you confrontational?
- Do you tell your children to hit back?
- Are you aggressive if another parent complains to you about bullying?
- Do you give your children space to talk about things that may be upsetting them?
- Are you critical of school staff in front of your children?
- Do you try to work on problems with the school?

What should we learn from this? Foremost, if your children take the courageous step of bringing their concerns about bullying to you, take your children seriously. Do not tell you children that bullying is an unpleasant fact of life and to accept it as a part of growing up. Very rarely will children make false allegations about bullying since there really is no positive to admitting this kind of abuse. Second, because bullying is a peer group issue, we need to change the group dynamics. One way is to encourage your children to be leaders in the school—to lead others in developing ways to campaign against bullying in order to break the code of silence. Lastly, to eliminate bullying behaviors, the roles that kids and adults play in actively or passively reinforcing bullying behavior must be addressed through school, family, and community efforts to change the norms and climate with respect to bullying. This means that all key stakeholders need to be actively involved in the process: teachers, administrators, parents, children, and community members. Chapter 8 provides you with ways you can help eliminate bullying behaviors.

CASE STUDY

Karen, who is in the 8th grade, is planning a slumber party to celebrate her birthday. Her parents have set a limit of eight girls, so Karen can't invite everyone she would like to invite. Two girls who are left out overhear the plans. They become angry, and plan their revenge for being excluded.

The girls make a "We Hate Karen" Web site. On the site, they note that anyone invited to the party should not go since Karen is fat, is ugly, and sleeps around. They tell everyone in school the site's address. The girls invite everyone to add new reasons why they hate Karen and to spread ugly rumors about her.

When Karen hears about the site, she gets a sick feeling in her stomach. Unable to ignore it, she checks the site often. Each day, she finds a new nasty comment or joke about her. She feels hurt and powerless to defend herself. She is too anxious to eat. She is too embarrassed to go to school, so she tells her parents she is sick in order to stay home and avoid everyone.

As Karen's parent, what advice would you give her? How would you handle the situation? What kind of support could you give her? Were there any signs that she has been bullied? Why do you think the girls harassed Karen? Do you think the girls were justified in their behavior?

Now read the case with your children. Ask them the following questions.

- If you were Karen's friend, what advice would you give her?
- How would you handle the situation?
- What kind of support could you give her?
- What warning signs did she show that she has been bullied?
- Why do you think the girls harassed Karen?
- Do you think the girls were justified in their behavior?

The Growing Brain

We have discussed many family, peer, school, environmental, and motivational factors associated with why some children bully others. However, those are not the only factors that explain the behavior of bullies. Biology can help explain what makes a kid want to bully another kid. All too often I hear, "You should know better than that." I agree. Many kids know right from wrong. In the heat of the moment, though, they may lack the ability to stop and think before they act. Why is this so? This is where neuroscience helps us understand how children's and adolescents' brains work.

TIP

For every $10,000 spent on decompression therapy, which is a promising treatment for youths with psychopathic tendencies, we save $70,000 that would have been spent to keep these individuals in jail. People with psychopathic tendencies exhibit poor behavioral control, impulsivity, and irresponsibility. They commit a wide variety of crimes and parole or probation violations. They hace a grandiose sense of worth and shallow affect. They are pathological liars, show a lack of remorse or guilt, are callous, and lack empathy, and fail to accept responsibility for own actions.

Scientific American Mind, October 2010

www.scientificamerican.com/mind

For some aspects of brain development, important abilities can be lost or diminished if they don't develop at the right time. Our childhood experiences affect how the brain develops. Our experiences, whether good or bad, cause changes in the brain. This is why we practice behaviors. The more we repeat things, the stronger the connections made in the brain. As the brain develops, it focuses on different functions:

1. **Physical life** functions (breathing, heart rate, blood pressure)
2. **Emotional** functions (happiness, anger, attachment)
3. **Thinking** functions (planning, impulse control)

As children age, we can see the physical changes. However, what we don't see are the emotional and logical changes that follow. Thus three interconnected brain structures—the amygdala, the hippocampus, and the prefrontal cortex—can shed light on how we think, feel, and react to events around us.[3,4]

POINT TO PONDER

Think back to when you were a tween or teen. Recall your behaviors.
- Did you engage in any risky behaviors?
- Did you do anything that got you into serious trouble?
- Would you deal with that same situation differently now as an adult?

How Emotions and Memory Are Closely Related

The dual activation of the amygdala and the hippocampus plus the dynamics between them may be what gives emotionally based memories their uniqueness. The amygdala, an almond-shaped brain structure, is involved in processing our emotions, storing emotional memories, and assigning emotional value to our experiences. For example, after a frightful experience (waiting to be rescued), a person can remember the logical reasons for the experience (did not evacuate but took shelter in my home). However, the person can also the "feel" the memory. The individual's body will have a physical reaction (increased heart rate, tension in the neck, headaches, and sweating).

So much of how we make sense of the world is gathered through our emotions. The amygdala houses our values and beliefs. It informs us of our gut decisions and reactions, of our relationships with people, and of our sense of belonging and purpose in life. Basically, all stimuli are filtered through our emotions. Every expression, posture, gesture, movement, touch, taste, sound, and behavior is processed through the amygdala. They each trigger different levels of emotional response, thus dictating behavior. The amygdala controls our reactions in social situations. It is also in charge of our fight-or-flight response. This is our body's primitive, automatic, inborn response that prepares our body to fight or flee from perceived attack, harm, or threat to our survival. This response also occurs in response to changes in the inner workings of our body's organs and glands.

TIP

The victim-rescuer-bully approach to speaking and thinking activates the amygdala to see the world and oneself in an ongoing fight-or-flight drama of right vs. wrong, good vs. bad, should vs. should not. The focus of victim-rescuer-bully thinking and speaking is to be right and dominate rather than to "be" and reach consensus or compromise.

In contrast, the hippocampus, which is a horseshoe-shaped, paired structure, is important in forming new memories. It connects emotions and senses, such as smell and sound, to memories. Subsequently, the hippocampus plays a vital role in long-term memory and spatial navigation. It's often described as our conscious recall of facts and events. To illustrate the synergistic nature of the amygdala and the hippocampus, consider the following case study.

CASE STUDY

Jamie lives in a tough neighborhood with her mom and two sisters. Her parents divorced due to her father's drug use, physical violence toward her mother, and verbal abuse toward her and her sisters. Jamie does not see or talk to her dad. Within the last year, several people in her neighborhood have been assaulted for various reasons. Because Jamie stayed after school for tutoring, she had to walk home alone since her mom was at work. As Jamie was walking home, she began to hear footsteps behind her. Afraid to turn around, she kept walking. However, the footsteps seemed to be getting closer. Jamie finally turned around only to find out that it was Melissa, a girl at school who constantly taunts Jamie about her grades (calls her a loser), about living in a poorer neighborhood (calls Jamie trailer trash), and about not being pretty (calls her zit face).

Because Jamie began to feel hurt and threatened, her emotional response (amygdala) stimulated the hypothalamus to initiate a sequence of nerve cell firings and release of stress hormones like adrenaline and cortisol. These caused Jamie's breathing and heart rate to increase, pupils to dilate, pulse to quicken, sight to sharpen, awareness to intensify, perception of pain to diminish, and blood to be directed into her muscles and limbs in preparation for Jamie to either confront or flee from the threat—Melissa.

Memories stored in Jamie's hippocampus now told the amygdala how she should respond. Remember that Jamie comes from a home where she has been verbally abused by her father and where her father was physically abusive to her mother. Stored memories in the hippocampus recall those aggressive events where her father would destroy furniture, punch and kick her mother, and make derogatory comments toward Jamie—causing Jamie to retreat and hide under the bed to keep herself safe. Therefore, the message sent to Jamie's amygdala when Melissa appeared was to escape from feeling ridiculed, unloved, discarded, unworthy, and not safe. Since two out of three needs of the amygdala were violated (e.g., need to be safe, wanted, and successful), the fight-or-flight system bypassed Jamie's rational mind and moved her into attack mode. Instead of confronting Melissa (fight), Jamie started running (flight) to keep herself safe.

Have you been in a similar situation to Jamie? What did your hippocampus tell your amygdala to do? Did you decide to fight or to flee? What do you do in situations where you are stressed?

Now imagine Jamie is your child. Do you think Jamie did the right thing by running away? Do you think she should have stood up to Melissa?

TIP

Are Your Children Overly Emotional?

Because the amygdala seizes control of all behaviors when the stimuli are perceived to be emotional, some children are born hypersensitive. Children who are hypersensitive experience sensory overstimulation to light touches, loud noises, bright lights, and rough textures as distressing.

They may show stress when routines change. These kids are very shy and clingy in new situations, have a limited ability to self-soothe, and express excessive fears and worries. They may be slow to engage in new experiences, are aggressive when provoked, and exhibit compulsiveness and perfectionism.

Minnesota Association for Children's Mental Health

(*www.MACMH.org*)

The prefrontal cortex, the last area to develop, is the part of the brain that controls our logical reasoning. It handles our decision making, problem solving, and high-level reasoning. The prefrontal cortex controls impulse control. It allows for learned behaviors versus just emotional responses. Consequently, the prefrontal cortex intercedes against the amygdala's innate and impulsive responses. During adolescence, the prefrontal cortex is the part of the brain that develops the most. New connections are made among centers of higher abstract thinking. Neurotransmitters are altered in number and type. However, these changes—particularly in higher judgment, wisdom, and forethought—are not in place until the early 20s.

Do you ever wonder why your tween or teen can be a model citizen one moment and reckless the next? This happens because the adolescent's prefrontal cortex is not fully developed.[5] Dr. Stephen W. Phillippi, from Louisiana State University Health Sciences Center School of Public Health, simplifies the point. He states, "adolescence is like giving a teenager a car with (1) a new body with a lot of horsepower (physical); (2) a sensitive gas pedal that can go from 0–60 mph in a few seconds (emotional); and (3) a brake system that won't work completely for several years (thinking)."[6] In other words, Andy now has the physical capacity to engage in activities that give him an instant rush or high (pleasure-seeking emotions) like rock climbing, bungee jumping, drinking, or driving fast. He participates in these behaviors in order to save face and not look like a coward in front of his peers. Consequently, his focus is on what he will get now (acceptance from peers and the thrill from the activity) and less on what might happen in the future (broken bones, accidents, or death). Since his prefrontal cortex is not yet fully developed, he lacks the ability to control his impulsive and risky behaviors.

Over the years, I've heard common phrases such as "You're being so immature," "Stop being so immature," or "Grow up" to describe the outcome of many adolescent's behaviors. I've made the same comments when talking about my son's behaviors. Based on neuroscience, parents are partially correct in these assertions. We know that children's brains are not always capable of making the right choices because the synapses (connections) are not yet formed. Thus the children's behaviors can result from an immature brain. Research indicates that engagement in risky behaviors peaks in mid-adolescence. As we get older, we spend more time thinking before acting, are more resistant to peer pressure, are more willing to delay gratification, are less impulsive, and less likely to engage in sensation-seeking behavior.[1]

POINT TO PONDER

During adolescence, teens are susceptible to peer pressure (e.g., looking for affiliation, social approval, and risk). They become highly concerned about what others think of them. One reason for their susceptibility to peer pressure is explained by an area of the brain called the dorsal medial prefrontal cortex.[3] This region activates when adolescents think of themselves and others. It is one of the last areas to develop before adulthood.

Functional MRI scans reveal more activity in this region during adolescence than in adulthood. This explains why during adolescence, teens begin to separate from the focus of what you, the parent, thinks.

Think back to when you were a child—when most of your world revolved around home and family. When did that start to shift to your peers? When did you stop telling your parents everything you did with your peers? How did your peers influence your decisions?

TOOLBOX TACTIC

Bullying and Television Shows

Your children are probably aware what bullying is, but are they able to understand why it happens? Television shows are filled with incidents of bullying and messages about bullies, targets, and bystanders.

Watch a television show with your children to see if they can recognize the games people play that keep the characters stuck in the bully drama. Can your children pick out different examples of bullying? Can they tell you how and why the roles of bully, victim, and rescuer are reinforced? Some TV shows that show bullying are *Gossip Girl*, *Glee*, *South Park*, *The Simpsons*, *Revenge*, *The OC*, and *The Office*.

Ask your children?

- Who is the bully, victim, and rescuer? Why?
- What is the underlying message that keeps each character role playing the game?
- Can your children identify with any of the characters? How do they see themselves in each role?
- How do your kids think they can get out of the game?

TIP

Since bullying behavior is primarily learned, it can also be unlearned. In other words, conditions can be changed so that bullying is not learned in the first place.

Conclusion

For most of us, our behavior serves a purpose. It is our best attempt to meet one or more psychological needs. At times, we use these behaviors in unhealthy ways to meet our needs. Kids are no different from adults. Although bullies use unhealthy behaviors to meet their needs, the good news is that children are still learning how to meet their needs in appropriate ways. As I noted earlier, it may be difficult for some kids to resist giving in to their impulsive behavior because their synapses (connections) are not yet formed. However, as parents we play a critical role in how our children's brains grow and develop. What we teach, what children watch us doing, and the experiences we give them all contribute to the physical structure of the developing brain—whether good or bad. By repeating or practicing behaviors, the connections in the brain become stronger. Part of our job as parents is to help guide and teach our children healthy ways to achieve their needs and goals without infringing on the rights of others to meet theirs. We are responsible for ensuring that the connections made during childhood are built on positive, healthy interactions that foster strong, trusting relationships.

Chapter 4

Gathering the Players On and Off the Playground

This chapter describes the three main roles that kids play in bullying situations. It also includes the subgroups within each role and the consequences of bullying. A model is presented that shifts the role of bystanders to become defenders, not offenders.

The Bullying Trifecta

There is no respect for others without humility in one's self.
Henri-Frederic Amiel (1821–1881)
Philosopher, Poet, Critic

TIP

It is not always easy to identify those who bully and those who are bullied. These are not personality types. No one is born a bully or a target of bullying. This is about behavior and interrelational conflict. Some children both bully and are bullied by others.

Millions of people all over the world have now seen the 40-second video of Australian 16-year old Casey Heynes (*www.youtube.com/watch?v=isfn4OxCPQs*). He was being taunted and punched repeatedly. Then he fought back with one dramatic move. He picked up Ritchard Gale, the smaller 12 year old who was attacking him, and slammed Ritchard to the ground (*www.caseyheynes.com*). The incident was recorded on a cell phone camera by a group of boys egging Ritchard on. The situation seemed to be set up to humiliate Casey by creating an online video of him being taunted. The video went viral all over the world as the scenario turned on its head into a "kid snaps on bully" story. In an interview with Australia's "A Current Affair," Casey, dubbed "The Punisher," stated, "I wasn't really thinking, I was just like, 'Yeah, finally it's over.'" He said of the experience, "I was scared" (*nydailynews.com*).

Casey's story illustrates the three characters involved in bullying. The bully was Ritchard. Casey was the bullied. The people watching were the bystanders. Ritchard repeatedly harassed and tormented Casey to the point that Casey felt lonely and worthless. Casey even considered suicide. The bystanders joined in, watched, and cheered Ritchard on. The school suspended both Ritchard and Casey for four days for fighting. The bystanders received no punishment. Do you agree that Casey should have been suspended? Did you know that 3 out of 10 children in grades 6 through 12 are involved in bullying—as bullies, as victims, or as both—each year (*www.cdc.gov; nces.ed.gov*). Although children within each of these groups share many similarities, each group can be further divided into subgroups of students with different personalities, motivations, and behaviors.

POINT TO PONDER

How do you know if you are or have ever been a bully? Ask yourself these questions.
- Does it make you feel better to hurt other people or take their things?
- Are you bigger and stronger than other people your age? Do you sometimes use your size and strength to get your way?
- Have you been bullied by someone in the past and feel like you have to make up for it by doing the same thing to others?
- Do you avoid thinking about how other people might feel if you say or do hurtful things to them?
- If you have bullied other people, think about why. Think about how or what you were feeling at the time. Think about how you felt afterwards.

Bully Characteristics

As you read in chapter 2, not all bullies are the same. They come in all shapes and sizes, ages, genders, backgrounds, and intellectual abilities. Some children who bully learned their aggressive behaviors from their family or school environment. Some bully because of peer pressure. Some bully because their parents reinforce grandiosity. Some bully as a result of being the target of another bully. Despite these differences, children who bully share one thing in common. They thrive on power and feed on fear. Bullies use their poisonous words, gestures, fists, or social exclusion like an arrow to puncture and penetrate their target's soul and psychosocial well-being. Listed below are characteristics that distinguish the five types of bullies.

POINT TO PONDER

> Kids who bully others feel contempt for their target. Contempt has three characteristics:
> 1. A sense of entitlement
> 2. Intolerance toward differences
> 3. A liberty to exclude
> Have you noticed your children showing contempt for another?
>
> Barbara Coloroso

Type A: Aggressive Bullies

Aggressive bullies are the most common. They are characterized by physical strength, fearlessness, belligerence, coerciveness, confidence, positive attitudes toward violence, relative popularity with their peers, and mercilessness toward their targets. They seek excitement through their aggressive behavior, take pride in exerting control over less powerful peers whom they victimize, and are often rewarded for their behavior through fear, attention, and possessions. They can be psychologically defensive, react against rules and authority, become easily frustrated, and refuse to accept responsibility for their actions. Aggressive bullies are often bullied by family members. They usually come from a family culture of violence where there is little closeness and unity. Instead, the family focuses more on power over one another. Consequently, family members often lack empathy or compassion for their target.

My ex–best friend always used to threaten me just because I didn't give her what she wanted and sometimes sent hurtful e-mails to me. She sent e-mails that were mean when she was mad at me and she didn't get her way. And she'd threaten me because I lost her socks. I always tried to make her happy so she wouldn't do anything bad to me, but it didn't help at all.

11-Year-Old Girl

Type B: Passive Bullies

Passive bullies, who are also calles anxious bullies, rarely provoke others or take the initiative in a bullying incident. They tend to be insecure. Thus, they associate with and lend support to the aggressive bully. For instance, an aggressive bully initiates a bully situation. The passive bully supports the aggressive bully's behavior or begins to participate in the interaction. Passive bullies may feel peer pressure to bully, especially in school settings, in order to obtain control in a complex social environment. These children are also seen as the "wannabes" because they want the power that aggressive bullies exert over others.

Type C: Bully-Victims

Bully-victims represent a small percentage of bullies who have been bullied themselves and then go on to bully other kids. Many times, kids find that when they are lacking something essential in one environment, they will overcompensate in another. For instance, children may be targets at home and bullies at school. They possess some of the same characteristics as provocative victims (described in a later section). Bully-victims often struggle to control their emotions. For example, bully-victims may unintentionally prompt others to bully them again by reacting very emotionally to initial teasing, threats, or physical aggression. Bully-victims may have similar problems controlling feelings of anger and frustration, predisposing them to retaliatory aggression. Bully-victims often feel less safe and more disconnected to their school environments than children who have not been the targets of bullying. Bully-victims may have been targets all through childhood. When emerging into adolescence or adulthood, they may decide it is time to take control—control over others.

> *I recently picked on an old friend of mine. For what I will not reveal because it was unusually cruel. However, she had done something to me that was equally as wrong, if not worse. I was disappointed in her. For that I decided not to be her friend any longer and spread her deepest secrets to everyone, which made her look like a complete fool. I felt somewhat guilty because I had known her for years. At the same time, it was a payback. I think she learned from it some, when it comes to attempting to mess around with me.*
>
> 17-Year-Old Girl

Type D: Entitled Bullies

The phrase "entitled bully" is a relatively new category used to refer to kids who have no noticeable social or mental problems but appear to bully others for pure enjoyment or sport. Entitled bullies are usually popular, have high social status, and are socially skillful. Thus, they harass others because they believe they are superior to anyone who is different from them. They are concerned with their own wants and pleasures, not the needs and rights of others. Basically, entitled bullies believe everyone should cave in to their wishes. Contrary to the popular belief that bullies lack social skills, research has shown that bullies are actually quite adept at reading social cues and perspective taking.[1,2,3] However, rather than using these skills toward prosocial behaviors, i.e., to empathize with others, they instead use these skills to identify and prey on peer's vulnerabilities.

Although entitled bullies have high self-esteem, their sense of humility is low to almost nonexistent. *Dictionary.com* defines humility as modesty, lacking pretense, and not believing that you are superior to others. Bruna Martinuzzi, author of *The Leader as a Mensch: Become the Kind of Person Others Want to Follow*, wrote, "Humility is all about maintaining our pride about who we are, about our achievements, about our worth— but without arrogance."

Many of these children come from well-respected families and are seen as "the good kids in school." They usually do not get into trouble, have a good relationship with teachers, are academically high achievers, and are involved in school-related activities. Sometimes parents unknowingly reinforce these children's grandiosity by indulging their every wish to the point of worshipping their existence. For example, almost on a daily basis, I receive numerous Facebook postings where many of my friends post pictures of their children's awards, accolades, and milestones. Although it is wonderful that their children are excelling, they fail to consider parents who have children who may work just as hard but do not achieve the same success. Have you noticed the same thing?

Type E: Cyberbullies

Children who cyberbully use social media to harass or intimidate others online. Unfortunately, there is no "one size fits all" for children who cyberbully. Therefore, the following chart breaks down the types of cyberbullies, their definition, and the reason for the harassment. This chart could be helpful if and when a cyberbullying incident occurs, so you can record and report it to the school or authorities if needed.

Cyberbullying Type	Definition of Type	Explanation of Type
Vengeful angel	Youths who bully online do not see themselves as bullies. They see themselves as righting a wrong and protecting their friends.	These cyberbullies have been bullied or have a friend who is experiencing bullying and is looking to get even.
Power hungry	Youths who bully online to exert their authority; control others by using fear tactics similar to traditional bullies; frequently the target of off line bullying.	Typically, these are shy or more reserved youths who can hide behind the computer to feel empowerment.
Revenge of the nerds or retaliators	Youths who bully online to exert power and control; use technology to frighten or embarrass targets. They are empowered by anonymity to settle the score or get back at the people who are or who have harassed them.	Although typically quiet in person, they may appear tough online. May be considered "a nerd" by fellow students; do not receive much respect. They use social media platforms to retaliate since they possess the technical knowledge and skill without their identity being discovered.
Mean girls	Youths who bully online because they are bored or looking for entertainment. Traditionally ego based, they bully online to promote their own social status.	Typically done in a group setting. They are looking for entertainment or to fit in with a particular group. Boys can also fall into this category, but less commonly.
Inadvertent	Youths who bully online without realizing that it is bullying. They typically do not mean to cyberbully anyone.	Typically role playing or responding to others. Those who do not understand their online actions. Meant in fun but misunderstood as serious. Once they have an understanding of their actions, they generally feel remorse.

POINT TO PONDER

Since parents are often role models for their kids' behaviors, can you identify with any of the above motives behind cyberharassment? Have you engaged in cyberharassment for any of the reasons stated above? If so, what did you do? What happened? What did it feel like to be the sender or the receiver of the message? Was it your intent to harass or embarrass?

TOOLBOX TACTIC

Sharing a Story, Building Trust

In August 2010 during the Bullying Prevention Summit, the U.S. Secretary of Education, Arne Duncan, a father of two children, stated, "A powerful testament to the fact that bullying is not part of the natural order of things is that most people can remember, even decades later, the feeling of being bullied or bullying another individual. Or they may feel haunted by the memory of standing by while a friend or classmate was bullied" (*www.ed.gov*).

Think back to when you were a kid. Can you remember times...

- When you were repeatedly teased, humiliated, or shut out of a group?
- When you were forced to do something you didn't want to do by someone you considered more powerful than you?
- When you intentionally hurt someone who was timid or shy or when you witnessed this happening to someone else?
- How did you feel?
- What did you do?
- Did you tell someone?
- How did you get support?

Fast forward to now. How have your past experiences affected you now as an adult? Share your bullying experiences with your children. By hearing your stories, they may be more willing to open up to you about their experiences with bullying.

This exercise is an excellent way to strengthen your relationship and build trust and rapport with your children. Plus it sends a message to them that you will listen and will be there in their time of need.

1. Discuss what they think of their stories amd how the stories made them feel.
2. Using your stories, brainstorm suggestions for things your children can do to stop or prevent bullying.
3. It may be helpful to write down your children's responses so you can weigh the pros and cons of implementing prevention and intervention strategies.
4. Invite your children to tell, write, or draw stories about their bullying experiences. Young kids benefit from drawing pictures or using puppets to tell their stories. These may be the preferred options for kids who are uncomfortable sharing their experiences aloud.
5. Discuss your children's stories together.
6. Remind your children that bullying is unacceptable behavior and that they have the right to attend school or other activities free from harassment.
7. It is never the children's fault if they are targeted.

The Impact of Bullying on the Bully

Targets of bullying are not the only ones who are adversely affected. Those who bully are more likely to engage in vandalism, shoplift, be truant, drop out of school, and use drugs and alcohol. Some acts of bullying can result in suspension or expulsion from school and the loss of valuable learning time. A bully who learns to use aggression toward others may find the negative behavior a hard habit to break. Even though people who bully cause a great deal of pain to others, bullies need help too. Without intervention, children who continue to bully others may embark on a downward spiraling course for the rest of their lives because of their inability to deal with conflict and violence. If they do not learn how to change their behaviors, they usually end up in trouble with the law. By age 24, 60% of children who were childhood bullies have at least one criminal conviction and 40% have committed three or more crimes.[4] As adults, they have higher substance abuse rates, have poorer social skills, have greater mental health problems, and exhibit increased aggressive-impulsive behaviors. With continual use of control and power exerted in their interpersonal relationships, they experience increased social isolation, difficulty creating close friendships, and low life satisfaction. Children who were childhood bullies are more likely to permit their own children to bully others, thus raising a new generation of bullies.

POINT TO PONDER

The most difficult thing for some parents to accept is that their children may actually be bullies.
- Are your children aggressive around other children or even adults, exhibiting physical or verbal hostility?
- Are they ill tempered or anti-social, showing no sympathy for targets of bullying?
- Do they have a hard time following rules or been involved with acts of vandalism or theft?

If so, it is important that you talk to your children and follow up with school staff.

TOOLBOX TACTIC

Point out to your children that you have been referring to victims of bullying as "targets," not "victims." Ask them why you might have made this distinction. (The term "target" is used because the word "victim" implies powerlessness and passivity. In contrast, the term "target" does not imply anything about that person's ability to respond. Individuals who are targeted by bullies can, with support, take action.) Do they agree with this distinction? Why or why not?

Target Characteristics

A target is a child who suffers from destructive acts, either emotionally or physically. Targets of bullying tend to be perceived as being different, exceptional, or marginalized from their fellow students. They may behave in a manner that may elicit negative peer reactions. There are two types of targets: passive/submissive and provocative.

Type A: Passive or Submissive Target

Passive or submissive targets are generally characterized as quiet, anxious, insecure, unassertive, and socially isolated. Passive victims represent roughly 80% to 85% of all victims.[4] Because they have difficulty making and keeping friends, they lack a network of friends who can be supportive and help deflect a bully's attack, which makes them easy targets. They are seen as physically and emotionally weaker, lacking self-confidence, overly sensitive, more withdrawn, and overly dependent on adults. Studies show that passive targets have a higher prevalence of overprotective parents or school personnel. Thus these targets often fail to develop the skills to cope with the bullying. When faced with opposition, they may withdraw, run away, break down, or cry.

I still cry when I think of what she said. After a while, you start believing all of the things people tell you that aren't true. When I look in the mirror, I wonder if I'm fat (I'm not) after what my ex-friend said.

14-Year-Old Girl

Type B: Provocative Targets

Provocative targets typically possess behaviors that are often seen as inviting peer bullying and harassment. They represent a small portion of targets, comprising just 5% of those children who are bullied.[5] In many cases, children with behavioral difficulties may trigger peer victimization and social exclusion because they do not know how to conform to traditional ways of relating to others. These targets usually lack good social or emotional regulation skills (i.e., children with autism or Asperger's). For example, children diagnosed with attention-deficit hyperactivity disorder (ADHD) may aggravate peers by engaging in obnoxious, irritating, or other annoying behaviors due to their high energy, impulsivity, and incessant talking. In return, they are bullied by their peers, which triggers provocative targets to use verbal taunts rather than physical force to "egg on" the situation.

Because provocative targets tend to be quick tempered and try to fight back if they feel they have been insulted or attacked, they in turn bully other children. Provocative targets try to salvage their pride and defend their honor. Thus these targets can become a bully-victim. However, the significant difference between a provocative target and a bully is that the provocative target loses in the end. Rather than back down, they are prone to lose the fight.

CASE STUDY

A 7th-grade girl named Carol (not her real name) has had the same best friend, Ann (not her real name), for the last six months in school. They have sleepovers every weekend, talk or text on the phone every night, and know everything about one another. Keep in mind that the shared information includes every boy each one has liked since kindergarten, what teachers they do and do not like, what if anything they have ever done physically with a boy, and what other students they do and do not like.

Now imagine one day Carol goes to school and her so-called best friend is not talking to her. Carol has no idea why. Not only that, but Ann is telling everyone all the secrets that she was supposed to keep for the rest of her life. There is no way that Carol will be able to concentrate on anything academically. All day, she is worrying about what will happen next and when she will be able to get an answer about why Ann is mad at her.

If the bullying is bad enough, Carol might pretend to be sick and go to the nurse's office so she can go home and escape all the secrets and talking behind her back.

Now imagine that Carol is your child. How would you handle the situation? What kind of support could you give her? Were there any signs that she has been bullied? Would you contact Ann's parents? The school? Why do you think Ann treated your daughter that way?

In some cases, girls have friends like the one noted above and keep going back to them, thinking she can change them for the better. However, the victim will once again be treated badly and miss more school, thus missing more work and getting poor grades.

POINT TO PONDER

According to legend, an old Cherokee told his grandson the following. "My son, there is a battle between two wolves inside us all. One is Evil. It is anger, jealousy, greed, resentment, inferiority, lies, and ego. The other is Good. It is joy, peace, love, hope, humility, kindness, empathy, and truth." The boy thought about it, and asked, "Grandfather, which wolf wins?" The old man quietly replied, "The one you feed." What are you feeding your children?

The Impact of Bullying on the Victim

But I know because I have myself been bullied. It lowers my self-esteem. It makes me feel really crappy. It makes me walk around the rest of the day feeling worthless, like no one cares. It makes me very, very depressed.

13-Year-Old Girl

Constant ridicule and torment can have lasting effects on children's sense of who they are in the world and how they think about themselves as they develop. Children who are frequently targeted ask themselves "Why me?" They feel embarrassment, guilt, and shame when they can't stand up to the bully and deal with what is happening to them by themselves. Most spend their energy at school being afraid and worrying about when, where, and how they will be bullied again. Because they are often reluctant to tell you or another trusting adult about the harassment, they may simply suffer in silence. In other words, targets experience immediate and long-term effects. These effects fall into 5 categories.

- *Psychological:* lower self-worth, lower self-esteem, lower self-confidence, higher rates of depression, increased anxiety, feelings of loneliness, confusion, anger, frustration, sadness, self-blame, feelings of insecurity and helplessness, and psychological trauma
- *Academic:* lower grades, loss of interest in school, low school commitment, disliking school, absenteeism, decreased ability to concentrate resulting from psychological symptoms, and dropping out of school
- *Social:* poor social skills, decreased or lost friendships, increased social anxiety, withdrawn or isolated, having disrupted relationships with parents or guardians, drinking alcohol, smoking, associating with friends who engage in risky behavior, becoming more violent or aggressive, and acting out—either externally through fights, school delinquency, and sometimes criminal behavior, or internally through self-harm and suicide
- *Physical:* more headaches, stomachaches, loss of appetite, sore throat, mouth sores, and sleep problems
- *Long term:* greater and prolonged violence and later criminal behavior; for example, being a target of bullying during adolescence is linked to higher levels of depression and anxiety in early adulthood

TOOLBOX TACTIC

Bottled Emotions

Remember that the physical symptoms noted above do not always stem from a biological cause. In my experience working with families, parents often become frustrated with their child because, according to the doctor, there is no medical reason for the child's ailments. Yet the child continues to complain about the symptoms. When this happens, I usually talk to parents about how the mind and body are interconnected. I state, "Perhaps these symptoms are occurring because your child is holding all of his or her anger and frustration inside. By keeping the bullying to himself or herself, the symptoms discover physical ways to be revealed. For example, our emotions are like a soda bottle. If you shake it, it will expand and become bloated with increased carbonation. Once you take the top off, the pressure is released, soda sprays everywhere, the bottle begins to deflate, and then it returns back to normal."

You can use the same analogy with your child to help him or her understand what happens by bottling up their emotions because he or she is afraid to tell someone about the bullying.

TIP

Sometimes it may take a long time for your child to recover fully from bullying, particularly if the bullying happened over a long period of time. Therefore, the quicker the problem is recognized and dealt with, the quicker your child can start to put it behind him or her and get on with life.

Bullying and Self-Harm

Being bullied makes me feel bad and rather depressed. It makes me feel like I don't want to be a part of this world anymore.

14-Year-Old Girl

Recently, the overabundance of news stories about the targets of bullying committing suicide has caused great concern. It highlights the potential destructive consequences that result from being bullied. Here are a few of these tragic cases. In Chadbourn, North Carolina, 10-year-old Jasmine McClain hanged herself after repeatedly being bullied at school. Her mother, Samantha West, found her in her bedroom. "I just lost it because she took her last breath in my arms," West said when interviewed. "She was a loving child. I just don't understand" (November 16, 2011, *www.wral.com/news*). In Joshua, Texas, 13-year-old Jon Carmichael committed suicide following being bullied (March 31, 2010, *www.cbsnews.com*). In Massachusetts, another student, 15-year-old Phoebe Prince, hanged herself at her family's home after she was mercilessly harassed for months (*www.puresight.com*). Carl Joseph Walker-Hoover, an 11-year-old football player and Boy Scout, hanged himself after school bullies repeatedly teased and taunted him by calling him gay. Sadly, these children felt that taking their own lives was the only way they could escape the pain and achieve peace.

According to the American Association of Suicidology (*www.suicidology.org*), suicide is the third leading cause of death for young people. By internalizing their pain, young people who are bullied contend with emotional issues such as depression and anxiety. This is called an internalized response. Unfortunately, in the face of persistent bullying, they are significantly more likely than others to have suicidal thoughts. A recent study reported in the *Journal of the American Academy of Child and Adolescent Psychiatry* indicated that children who were bullied over a long period were six times more likely than their peers who weren't bullied to have suicidal thoughts and were more likely to consider suicide by the time they are 11 years old.[6] For more information on bullying and suicide, read the book *Bullycide in America* (compiled by Brenda High, published by JBS Publishing Inc. in 2007). It chronicles stories by mothers of children who have committed suicide as a result of being bullied.

CASE STUDY

The Tragic Case of Hope Witsell

Hope Witsell was a 13 year old who grew up in Sundance, Florida. One day, she decided to send a "sext"—a nude photo of herself—to a boy she liked. Another girl borrowed the boy's phone, found the image, and forwarded it to other students. The image began to spread like a virus to other kids in Hope's school as well as other schools. Since the photo went viral, Hope was taunted and harassed with insults such as "whore" and "slut" by her peers at Beth Shields Middle School.

Hope wrote in her journal, "Tons of people talk about me behind my back and I hate it because they call me a whore! And I can't be a whore, I'm too inexperienced. So secretly TONS of people hate me."

School authorities found out about the nude photo toward the end of the school year. They suspended Hope for the first week of eighth grade, which started in August. When she returned to school, a counselor observed cuts on Hope's legs and had her sign a no-harm contract. Hope agreed to tell an adult if she felt inclined to hurt herself. The next day, Hope hanged herself in her bedroom.

On September 12, 2009, Hope wrote in her journal, "I'm done for sure now. I can feel it in my stomach. I'm going to try and strangle myself. I hope it works."

As you read Hope's story, what are you feeling? Thinking? Now imagine this girl is your child. How would you handle the situation? What kind of support could you give her? Were there any signs that she had been bullied?

Puresight

http://www.puresight.com/Real-Life-Stories/real-life-stories.html

TIP

Bullying does not cause suicide. Rather, children involved in bullying, in any role, especially bully-victims and chronic victims, are at increased risk for suicide ideation and suicidal/self-injurious behavior in preadolescence.

The following story illuminates the devastating internalizing effects of bullying.

I was pushed into walls, called names, and sexually assaulted. Three years of pure hell at high school, I now can't trust anyone. I'm very shy and depressed, I have low self-esteem; I have no friends as I don't know how to communicate with people. In high school I did not have many friends; I would get picked on by people I did not even know; I would miss a lot of school because I would pretend to be sick or I would go home crying. This then caused problems with my grades. I missed out on a lot of learning, due to low self-esteem. I thought about suicide to end it all. I started starving myself, and I never stopped. I became very thin. I still have problems with not eating, and I have very low blood pressure. My stomach has shrunk so I can try and eat but it makes me sick—all of this is due to the stress of being bullied.

                                                                    18-Year-Old Girl

The girl's story noted above reports the lasting physical, emotional and psychological traumatic effects that bullying has on a child's well-being. Some kids are able to rise above the bullying and not suffer any long-term effects because they are resilient. Nevertheless, not all kids are equipped to handle such abuse. Children who are bullied have feelings of shame, guilt, and embarrassment, which are normal reactions when they are harassed and tormented repeatedly and over a long period of time. These feelings can last long after the bullying has stopped. Over the years, I've noticed many parents forget that even though the actions of the bully have stopped, their children have not totally recovered from the emotional damage they suffered as a result of being bullied. Without being able to resolve some of these emotional issues, kids are at risk of becoming a bully or of projecting lingering feelings of rejection and worthlessness onto themselves.

I have been bullied since I was in middle school. I have cut myself and have been in psychiatric hospitals for what they did to me. They crushed my self-esteem for a long time. These people were relentless. They made my friend commit suicide after bashing him twice without punishment. And still it continues.

                                                                    17-Year-Old Girl

TOOLBOX TACTIC

A teacher in Newfoundland was teaching her class about bullying. To help them understand the devastating effects bullying has on its target, she conducted the following exercise. She had the children take out a piece of paper and told them to crumple it up, stomp on it, and really mess it up but do not rip it. Then she had them unfold the paper, smooth it out, and look at how scarred and dirty it was. She then told them to tell it they're sorry. Even though they said they were sorry and tried to fix the paper, she pointed out all the scars they left behind and that those scars will never go away no matter how hard they tried to fix the paper. This is what happens when a child bully's another child. The bully may say he or she is sorry, but the scars are there forever. By the looks on the students' faces, she figured they got the message.

Conduct the same exercise with your children. In addition to gauging their facial expression, ask them what they think the moral of the story is about. Have they fallen prey to a bully? Do they have any warning signs of being bullied?

Corinne Costantino, Boston Early Childhood Parenting Examiner

http://www.examiner.com/article/bullying-and-suicide-it-never-ends

Bystander Characteristics

Bystanders play an important role in understanding bullying and victimization. Because children gather in schools, neighborhoods, and playgrounds, they have probably been involved in bullying as a bystander in some role—joining in, cheering, passively watching, and, on occasion, intervening. A recent study found that peers were present in 85% of bullying episodes but intervened in only 10%.[7] This means if there are 100 episodes of bullying, a bystander will intervene only in 10. Generally, nearly one-half (48%) of all bystanders use appropriate behavior (e.g., tell another student, tell the bully to stop, help the student, or tell an adult) when they see or hear about someone being bullied. A small percentage (10%) of students use only inappropriate behavior (e.g., joined in, made a joke, found a way to retaliate, or did nothing).[8] However, most bystanders (41%) use a combination of appropriate and inappropriate behavior.[8] There are three bystander roles.

Role 1: Active Bystanders

Active bystanders assist and support the bully by actively joining in the bullying. They position themselves nearer the bully and face and/or circle the target. The active assistants are the bully's sidekicks who reinforce and encourage the bullying by offering positive feedback through laughs or encouraging gestures (e.g., "Yeah keep doing that!" "You got' em!") or by focusing on the target (e.g., "You have no chance here!"). By just being present, active bystanders may give the bully more confidence. They encourage the taunts so the bully can keep bullying. They also enhance the power differential. ("Don't you think this kid is bully worthy?").

Bystanders who laugh when they see someone being bullied are making the situation worse because their actions encourage the bully.

12-Year-Old Girl

Role 2: Passive Bystanders

Passive bystanders simply stand aside, circle around, and watch the bullying in silence. They usually position themselves anywhere in view. Many passive bystanders either escape to avoid the event or gossip to others who were not there about it and then spread the information. Passive avoiders facilitate victimization by denying personal responsibility and may use scapegoating to shed responsibility for not becoming actively involved. It is difficult for children to step up and try to help a child who is being bullied. One study found that while two-thirds of students say they should do something to stop a bully, only 25% actually do.[9]

Role 3: Defender Bystanders

Defenders usually position themselves nearer the target and/or between the target and bully. They may risk their own safety to intervene for their close friends or other peers who are being bullied. They usually mobilize personal or social resources to help reduce or even stop bullying. For example, they may defend victims, take sides with victims, inform and seek help from adults, comfort victims, or try to make bullies stop. Defenders support the target. Their characteristics include friendship, use of a productive style of coping, self-esteem, altruistic actions and feelings, the ability to avoid retaliation when angered, and high emotional support from friends. What does this mean? We need to increase the opportunities for children to acquire these characteristics in order to empower bystanders to become involved and become defenders, not offenders.

TIP

Peers who used a productive style of coping at school were more inclined to support the target and less inclined to support the bully. This suggests that teaching peers to cope effectively when a bullying situation occurs may help combat bullying on the peer level.

The Consequences of Bullying on Bystanders

In addition to the devastating effects that bullying creates for the bully and target, according to the U.S. Department of Education (*www.ed.gov*), bystanders may experience the following.

Be afraid to associate with the target for fear of either lowering their own status or of retribution from the bully and becoming targets themselves. One girl commented, "I was bullied by this girl a year older than me because I told her to stop bullying my friend. So she stopped harassing her and turned to me."

Fear reporting bullying incidents because they do not want to be called a snitch, a tattler, or an informer. A 15-year-old girl commented, "Once I got into a huge fight because these girls were bullying one of my friends. I tried to tell them to stop, but they turned on me instead. They insulted me very badly, and I insulted them all the same. They printed out what I said but not what they said and showed the principal. I got in a lot of trouble but talked my way out of it by telling the TRUTH (something THEY didn't do) and got let off with a warning."

Experience feelings of guilt and helplessness for not standing up to the bully on behalf of their classmate or friend. A 12-year-boy commented, "They made threats to beat my friend up; what else could I do?"

Be drawn into bullying behavior by group pressure.

Feel unsafe, unable to take action, or feel a loss of control.

Assume the adults at their school are uncaring or cannot do anything to stop the bullying.

Begin to think bullying is acceptable school behavior. One 10-year-old boy commented, "Kids get bullied every day; that's just the way it is. I just sit and watch as one boy picks on another boy. I know I should do something to help, but then I decide, 'Really, it's none of my business.'"

It is clear that bystanders display distinct patterns of behavior during a bullying incident. These responses represent students' attitudes toward the problem of bullying (e.g., positive, neutral-indifferent, negative) as well as the actions they are likely to take during an actual incident. Despite their fears, however, bystanders must learn that their supportive involvement is critical. Studies show that when a bystander intervenes, 57% of the time bullying usually stops within 10 seconds.[10] More often than not, bystanders give positive attention to the bully more than to the target, which reinforces the bully's dominance over the target and the bully's position within the peer group. Bullies like an audience. Although many factors influence bystanders' decisions to intervene in a bullying episode, they will more than likely get involved if they perceive the peer pressure to do so.

CASE STUDY

Playground Scenario

The third graders are outside at recess. A group of three boys is off playing by themselves. Another boy, Andy, approaches them and asks if he can play with them. One of the three boys says that they have formed a club, and since Andy is not a member, he cannot play. Andy asks about the club. The boy says that Andy cannot join. Andy keeps persisting, saying he wants to play and asking how he can get into the club. Finally, the same boy says that if Andy smears dirt on his own face, they will let him in the club. Andy points out that none of the other boys have dirt on their faces. The boy replies that it does not matter. If Andy wants to be in the club, that is what he needs to do.

Questions to discuss:

- What are some thoughts and feelings that you had while reading this scenario?
- At which point in the scenario do you think bullying has occurred?
- How should a teaching assistant (or other adult outside at recess) respond to this situation?
- Who are the bullies in this scenario? The bystanders? The target?
- What could have been done to prevent this situation?
- If you were Andy's parent and he told you what happened, what would you have advised him to do? Would you encourage him join the club to fit in?
- The boy says it is the "cool" club and that Andy is not cool enough to be in the club. How would you respond to his comment? How do you think your child would respond?

TOOLBOX TACTIC

Bullying and the Movies

Your children are probably aware what bullying is, but are they able to spot it when it happens and the reasons why it happened? As you saw in chapter 2, sometimes kids mistake a joke or funny comment as playing or joking when, in fact, it is bullying. This is because many believe everyone is just having fun. The child on the receiving end of the joke, though, may not think it's funny. You also read in chapter 3 the reasons why kids engage in bullying behaviors. Watch a movie with your children that has bullying in it. Then start a conversation with your children to see what they know about bullying, help them clarify what bullying is, and find out if they have been involved in bullying.

Here are some examples of movies you could use that show bullying, conflict, and joking: *Harriet the Spy*; *Diary of a Wimpy Kid*; *Bridge to Terabithia*; *Stand By Me*; *Mean Girls*; *Heathers*; *Clueless*; *Karate Kid*; *Happy Feet*; *Powder*, *Bring It On*; and *Never Been Kissed*.

During and/or after the movie, use the following questions to test your children's knowledge.

- What do you think the difference is between being a bully and just joking or fooling around?
- Why was the person being teased?
- Is it OK to tease other people?
- When is it acceptable to tease others?
- How does it feel to be teased and bullied?
- What type of bullying did you see?
- What type of bullying was involved?
- What type of bullying is most hidden from other peers?
- How often do they think peers intervene when they see bullying?
- How did the bully acquire power?
- What was the bully's motivation for being cruel?
- How can a target take back power?
- How would you feel if any of the types of bullying happened to you or to a friend?
- What could you do if you were being bullied?
- What could you do if you saw someone being bullied?
- Have you ever bullied?
- Why were you bullied?
- How did you feel at the time?
- How do you feel now, knowing you bullied someone?
- Have you been bullied by a friend, teacher, or sibling? If so, how did you feel?

From Bystander to Upstander

Although most attempts to reduce youth violence have focused on the bully or the relationship between bullies and targets, such interventions do not go far enough in creating safe schools and communities. It is critical to consider the role of bystanders, whose influence in perpetuating or escalating violence has often been overlooked. We must empower bystanders to become actively involved in a bullying incident. One way we can accomplish this task is to create a shift in the school's climate by giving the bully and active bystanders much less power, by giving the target and defenders more safety and support, and by inspiring involvement from passive bystanders. The goal is to shift the bystanders' attitudes along this continuum, away from accepting bullying behavior and toward support for targets and their defenders. The school climate is positively impacted when students stop seeing bullying as funny, entertaining, and a way of life at school.

Conclusion

Since the development of self-esteem in youths depends largely on the positive acceptance of their peers, being rejected or excluded can result in long-term negative outcomes. Persistent feelings of shame and guilt can develop in the minds of all parties involved. Given these facts, it is clear that the bully, the one bullied, and the bystander are at risk for developmental problems that could persist into adulthood if left unattended. Therefore, if we, as parents, fail to intervene in bullying situations, these issues can become a significant hurdle in a child's development.

Chapter 5

Decoding the iGeneration of Bullying: Cyberbullying

This chapter provides answers to some frequently asked questions about cyberbullying. What is cyberbullying? Does it differ from face-to-face bullying? How are kids cyberbullied? How common is it? Why do kids use social media to cyberbully? What are the effects? What are the warning signs? How do I respond? When should I get the school and authorities involved?

> *With communication like texting and instant messaging, they can be meaner. There's lots of bullying going on. There has always been bullying, but it's taken a new form. Online bullying can be anonymous, so there's an ability to be mean and not have repercussions.*
>
> 17-Year-Old Girl

POINT TO PONDER

If I were to ask you how much time per day kids spend with various media—cell phones, computers, tablets, televisions, video games, etc.—what would you say? Do you think it is more time than they spend at school on any given day? Now that you have a number in mind, read on to see if you were right or even close.

In 2011, the Kaiser Family Foundation found that youths of ages 8–18 years devote an average of 7 hours and 38 minutes (up from 6 hours and 21 minutes) to using social media in a typical day (more than 53 hours a week). Since this generation spends much of that time media multitasking (using more than one medium at a time), they manage to jam about 10 hours and 45 minutes worth of media content into those $7^1/_2$ hours.[1]

Are you surprised by this amount? How close were you? How much time do you think your kids are spending with social media each day? Do you know what they are doing online?

Introduction to Cyberbullying

As you read in chapter 1, kids today do not know a world without technology. They are hardwired into digital media. In other words, kids continually leave one form of media and go to another form to complete everyday tasks. They use technology for work, for play, and to form relationships with people they have never met. They cannot imagine life without cell phones. About 95% of all youths ages 12–17 are now online, and 80% of those online use social media sites.[2] Smartphones, laptops, and tablets are common devices that youths use to access the Internet. Nielsen noted that about 40% of social media users access websites from their smartphones.[3] This means where kids go, their devices go with them—to school, to the movies, to the shower, and to bed. They never seem to be disconnected from social media. Social media refers to online platforms for interactions and relationships. It has created a whole new world of social communications. Young people use text messaging, instant messaging (IM), chat rooms, Facebook, other social networking sites (SNS), Twitter, Skype, and Instagram to stay in touch with friends and to make new ones Young people also use social media to share their creations, do their schoolwork, play online games, shop, and more. Because technology is a way of life for many kids, and they can access social media and digital communication technologies 24/7, not surprisingly they have turned to technology to antagonize, harass, and exploit others. Consequently, a new variation of bullying called cyberbullying has transitioned it from the physical (i.e., face-to-face bullying or F2F) to the virtual world (i.e., bullying in cyberspace).

 TIP

According to the American Osteopathic Association, 52% of parents are worried their child will be bullied via social networking sites.

TOOLBOX TACTIC

Using Social Media and Leaving a Digital Footprint

When youths go online, they leave a "digital footprint." This phrase describes the trail, traces, or "footprints" that people leave online through forum registration, chats, e-mails, attachments, uploading videos or digital images, and any other form of transmission of information completed online. All of these examples leave traces of personal information that are available to others online. Much of our digital footprint is left through the use of social media.

Find out how your children are using social media platforms and discover their digital footprint by asking the following:

- How much time do you spend online?
- How often and when do you access the Internet? Other social media?
- Where do you access the Internet? At home? At friends' houses? At school? Elsewhere?
- How do you access the Internet? Via cell phone? Via computer? Via tablet?
- What do you do while online? What are your favorite places?
- Do you have a webpage/Facebook account? Who are your friends?
- What screen name or user name do you use?
- Have you posted personal information online? Pictures? Where? How do you protect the information?
- Have you seen inappropriate content online? What did you see? Where did you see it? What did you do when you saw it?
- Do you know how to be safe online? How?

Use these questions to start a dialogue with your children about online safety. The goal is to make sure you understand how they use social media so you can respond appropriately.

TIP

Over 1.5 million children reported being cyberbullied on or off school grounds.

Results from the 2009 School Crime Supplement to the
National Crime Victimization Survey

What Is Cyberbullying?

Cyberbullying is a form of intentional psychological cruelty where an individual or group uses electronic devices, the Internet, mobile phones, or other social media platforms to intimidate, threaten, or humiliate another individual or group of individuals repeatedly.[3] Common technologies used by digital aggressors include instant messaging, e-mail, text messaging, social networking sites, Instagrams, chat rooms, blogs, websites, online gaming, vlogs, and Geotagging. Cyberbullying is similar to other forms of bullying but differs in that it takes place in the hidden online world of youths. In the past, bullies needed a physical location to harass the victim. However, because children who cyberbully typically harass their targets away from the watchful eyes of adults, social media is the perfect tool for reaching their target anonymously—anytime, anyplace, 24/7, often without consequence. Consequently, unlike face-to-face bullying, home is no longer a place of safety and refuge for many kids.

A Form of Psychological Control

Children who cyberbully can humiliate their target by reaching a potentially huge online audience with the stroke of a few keys, while simultaneously gaining instant gratification when the target responds due to the immediate confirmation that a message was received. The reasons kids are so cruel online are quite complex. The reasons are not limited to the traditional power-seeking relationship in the schoolyard. Because of the very nature of this faceless behavior, cyberbullies have either perceived or actual power over their target. This power is not physical. Rather, it is a form of psychological control. Consider the following actual scenarios involving cyberbullying.

> When 15-year-old Lauren went to hear a band play in the spring, the drummer autographed her stomach. It was meant as a joke among friends, a parody of rock stars and their groupies. However, the musician's jealous girlfriend did not see the humor. "I'm gonna shoot you and bury you alive," the girlfriend threatened Lauren in her online journal, which was read by many of Lauren's friends.

> Jesse, a round, socially awkward seventh grader was humiliated online by classmates for two years after another boy created a website mocking him and inviting comments from others.

High school sophomore Lauren was the subject of nasty postings on a website message board started by a former friend at her school. The thread, which was called "Lauren is a fat cow MOO BITCH," made fun of her weight ("People don't like you because you are a suicidal cow who can't stop eating") and her bout with multiple sclerosis ("I guess I'll have to wait until you kill yourself, which I hope is not long from now, or I'll have to wait until your disease [M.S.] kills you"). The site urged Lauren's boyfriend to break up with her. The postings on the message board were not only vicious attacks on Lauren. The aggression escalated into Lauren's offline world. Lauren's car was egged, "MOO BITCH" was scrawled in shaving cream on the sidewalk in front of her house, and a bottle filled with acid was thrown at her front door.

Ryan, a handsome and popular tenth grader, was shocked and angered to discover his name was included on a website that named the school's "top five biggest homosexuals" and the "top 20 gayest guys and gayest girls."

Fifteen-year-old Jodi was horrified to discover an entire website had been created to insult and threaten her. The site contained abuse concerning her weight and even had a date for her "death." Jodi found out about the website when a classmate tried to take a photograph of her with a digital camera and said it was for the web.

These are just a few examples of how youths have used cyberspace and social media to unleash a dark, cruel world of spite and vengeance. Regrettably, children who cyberbully are malicious aggressors who seek pleasure through sending angry, vulgar, argumentative, cruel, offensive, and insulting messages. They make threats and false promises for the purpose of their own enjoyment and at the expense of their targets' self-worth.

 TOOLBOX TACTIC

Download a news story about a child who has been cyberbullied and use the story as a conversation starter with your children. For example, "I found this story about cyberbullying. Has anything like this ever happened to you? Do you know someone who has been cyberbullied?" Ask them to come up with a definition for cyberbullying. The purpose of discussing the story is for you to learn what your children know and to find out the latest social media trends.

TIP

Because most teens believe bullying and cyberbullying happen only in elementary or middle school, they use the terms "drama" or "digital drama" to represent the interpersonal conflicts that occur in high school.

Urbandictionary.com defines drama as a way of relating to the world in which a person consistently overreacts to or greatly exaggerates the importance of benign events. People who engage in drama will usually attempt to drag other people into their dramatic state as a way of gaining attention or making their own lives more exciting.

CASE STUDY—PART 1

The Incident: A Parent's Experience with Cyberbullying

When Tara's daughter Sasha was in 10th grade, Sasha became the target of both face-to-face bullying and cyberbullying by a small group of female classmates. Sasha had recently become friends with Lisa. However, they had disagreements over whether Sasha was willing to drive Lisa somewhere and whether Lisa was willing to return a sweater she had borrowed from Sasha. At school one day, Lisa and two friends confronted Sasha in a hallway and began berating her. Sasha ran off in tears. Lisa and her friends followed Sasha and continued verbally attacking her until a teacher intervened. Sasha was upset but seemed willing to put the incident behind her and to accept that she was no longer part of Lisa's clique.

The next day, one of Sasha's friends told her that a Facebook page had been created attacking her. She showed me the page, supposedly for a user named Pissog Slrig, which is "Gossip Girls" spelled backward. (At the time, the Gossip Girl books about a group of scheming high school classmates were popular). Pissog Slrig posted a message on her Facebook wall (message board) page that "Sasha is about to feel the H-E-A-T!...guess she knows now that she shouldn't have been a bitch...but Sasha, don't bother running or hiding, because wherever you go, Lisa and co will find you... Sasha, you're about to wish you never did anything to anyone." Pissog Slrig then sent Facebook friend requests to at least 14 other classmates, inviting them to link to the page and read the threats. Pissog Slrig posted additional threats over the next two days.

After the Facebook threats, Sasha was verbally abused by Lisa, Lisa's older brother (who followed Sasha into a classroom and told her that she "couldn't run and couldn't hide"), and other members of Lisa's clique. Sasha was fearful, hurt, frustrated, and embarrassed. Thus, she came to me and her father for help. If you were Sasha's parent what would you do?

- What is your first reaction to this case?
- How would you support Sasha?
- How would you handle the situation?
- Would you contact Lisa's parent's? The school? The authorities?
- What method(s) of cyberbullying were used in this case?
- Why do you think Lisa and the others cyberbullied Sasha?

A Breakdown of Relationships

I believe a troubling aspect of cyberbullying is centered on the breakdown of human relationships. Social media creates a world away from physically interacting with and relating to others. Although the digital world is creating new opportunities for your kids to grapple with social norms, explore interests, develop technical skills, and experiment with new forms of self-expression, it removes them from the real, face-to-face, social world of connecting with others at school, work, social events, and college and job interviews. In others words, social media technologies cannot accurately replicate human interaction. For example, I can post a comment on my friend's Facebook page. The context of my comment can be easily misinterpreted or lost on the intended audience. This misinterpretation of meaning can lead to complications within my relationships. Consequently, social media can inadvertently undermine the quality of human interactions.

 POINT TO PONDER

Research shows that youths are increasingly connecting to the Internet wirelessly (81%). A large proportion (65%) use social networking sites for friendship, socialization, and relationships.[5] However, some sources on these sites may provide inaccurate, incomplete, or inappropriate information that kids may use to imitate in their own on- and offline relationships. Thus if kids are using social media platforms to connect and maintain relationships, are you sure they know what a healthy relationship is supposed to look and feel like?

Communicating Online vs. Face to Face

Most youths prefer socializing online than in real life because online is more comfortable, more fun, and less risky (*www.jwt.com*). Nobody judges them online. Nobody can know their real intentions. They can gain validating feedback from others without feeling rejected or ridiculed. Since they are interacting online, if they do not like what they are reading, they can delete the message or the person (i.e., unfriend someone). Consequently, kids do not have to know how to deal with others face to face. What will they do or say, though, if they do not like what someone says in a face-to-face interaction? A person cannot be deleted or defriended by a stroke of a button.

Furthermore, kids do not have the time and/or are not interested in holding extended face-to-face conversations since they crave constant and immediate feedback when talking with someone. Remember, our kids are the iGeneration or iY Generation (see chapter 1). Their world has been defined by technology—iPod, iBook, iPhone, iChat, iMovie, iPad, and iTunes. For many of them, life is pretty much about "I." They are defined by their technology and media use, their love of electronic communication, and their need to multitask. Although they are adept at multitasking, they may find it harder to have old-fashioned, face-to-face conversations since they spend so much time in front of a screen. Instead of having a single face-to-face or phone conversation that may cover a multitude of topics over several minutes, kids would rather communicate in spurts of shorter but more frequent bursts of information through texts, instant messaging, blogging, and so on.

TIP

The level of distance granted by technology creates a superficial understanding of what being social means. Children will likely learn and grow from real-world social interactions differently than from online social situations.

Because social media takes kids away from the real world, they do not have the opportunity to engage in social situations. Although youths can introduce themselves online and hold a conversation online proficiently, many do not know how to introduce themselves properly to others, how to start or maintain a conversation, how to make eye contact, how to talk loud enough, or how to stand up straight. They do not really know how to act around people in real-world interactions. Consider the following quotes from two teens.

15-year-old Shelly indicated that social networking sites keep individuals away from the real world. She stated, "You can connect with people using Twitter or YouTube, but in the end, you don't know them unless you talk to them in real life."

15-year-old Alise agrees. "Although we believe that we are connecting when we text, write, or webcam our friends and family, we are not connecting," she said. "True communication is when you can physically see, hear, and talk to another person."

Some may argue that Skype, Facetime, Skypito, and Google Chat provide face-to-face interaction and that kids are communicating in a "real" way with friends and family members across the country, or even around the world, without being in the same physical space. Kids agree. Nearly 2 in 5 online teens (37%) say they have video chatted with someone using applications such as Skype, iChat, or Googletalk.[6] In meetings held with students, I asked them why they agreed. Below are some of their comments.

Skype allows me to see my dad since he lives in another state and I don't get to visit him often. This way he can keep up with me and I don't miss him as often.

I use videochat because I can talk to my grandparents who I don't get see because they live out of state. This way I can get to know them and who they are. If I didn't Skype them, then I probably won't talk to them as much even if they lived close to me.

It is easier to say "Skype me" then going over to my friend's house. I don't drive, so my parents have to bring and pick me up. Instead of hearing them gripe and complain because they are busy, I Skype my friend so we can see each other more often.

As the students noted above, social media platforms are a fantastic way to keep in touch with loved ones. However, I believe they should be used in conjunction with face-to-face interactions and not be used as the sole or main method of connecting with others. After all, we still live in a real world and need to interact with real people. Do you agree or disagree?

TOOLBOX TACTIC

Healthy Relationships

Work with your children in developing good relationships in order to ensure that your children clearly understand what a healthy relationship is supposed to look and feel like online and offline.

- Create healthy relationships with your children by making sure you spend quantity and quality time with them to build relationships of mutual respect and trust. In order to build trust, this must be done.
- Be a good role model. Surround your children with people who demonstrate qualities of a being a good friend. These qualities include trust, honesty, being supportive, being a good listener, sticking with you during both the good and the bad times, accepting people for who they are, and being someone you can have fun with.
- Create a puppet show or use paper, pencils, crayons, or paints so your children can draw pictures to show you what they know about friendships. Topics should include:
  1. Have them come up with a definition of what makes a friend.
  2. Give you examples of what a good friend looks like and what a bad friend looks like.
  3. Give you examples of how they know the other person is being a good friend. What are things that a good friend would do or not do? What would a good friend say or not say?
  4. Give you examples that show how they know if their online and offline friends are happy, sad, mad, etc.
  5. Teach them how to introduce themselves to others. For example, "Hi, how are you?" "My name is Kim. What is your name?" or "What do you like to do for fun?"
  6. Teach them to make eye contact when talking. For example, ask them what color your eyes are. What color are the puppets eyes?

What if you don't have any puppets? Pull out some paper lunch bags. Get out the crayons, yarn, and whatever else you can find around the house. Create your own puppets! Even using simple socks will work. Kids love this activity as it not only challenges their creativity but also provides great quality time as a family.

Differences Between F2F and Cyberbullying

Like traditional bullying, cyberbullying can lead to significant emotional harm of young people. However, bullying in the digital world is a distinct form of bullying in several ways. The following table compares face-to-face bullying and cyberbullying. I will explain these differences later in the chapter.

F2F Bullying	Cyberbullying
Direct	Anonymous
On school campus	Anywhere
Lot of energy and courage	Not so much
Mostly verbal and physical	Multimedia
Poor relationships with teachers	Good relationship with teachers
Fears retribution	Fears loss of technology
Requires strength	Requires skills & knowledge

 TIP

According to new research published in the Archives of Pediatric & Adolescent Medicine in July 2012, one-fourth of teens admitted to having sent a sext. Sexting is the practice of electronically sending sexually explicit messages or images from one person to another. Boys are more than twice as likely to ask for a sext than girls. Girls were nine times more bothered by someone asking them for a sext than boys. In light of these findings, I encourage you to monitor your kids' cell phone very closely. Cell phone monitoring can be done either physically or with the help of a software service like Mobile-Spy or WebWatcher Mobile.

Different Ways Kids Cyberbully

Cyberbullying can be carried out through both direct and indirect means. Direct attacks are when a cyberbully directly sends a message to the target. Indirect attacks, also known as cyberbullying by proxy, are when a cyberbully gets someone else to help harass the target with or without the accomplice's consent. In other words, the cyberbully gets someone else to do their dirty work. Cyberbullying by proxy is considerably the more dangerous type of cyberbullying because the aggressor can deny that he or she has taken any part in the harassment. Therefore, many cyberbullies by proxy go unpunished.

TIP

Only 7% of U.S. parents are worried about cyberbullying even though over 43% (4 out of 10) of middle and high school teens aged 13 to 17 report that they have experienced some sort of cyberbullying in the past year.[2]

CASE STUDY

A group of 6 fifth-grade girls (from the same class) had a slumber party at one of the girl's houses. They listened to music and downloaded songs, played games, called friends on their cell phones, and sent e-mails back and forth to other acquaintances from their class and from the other classes at school. Throughout the evening, you poked your head into your daughter's bedroom to ask if the kids needed anything. Otherwise, your daughter's door was closed all evening while the kids took part in their activities.

At some point, one of the girls suggested that they choose a boy from their class and make a list of the "Ten Things They Hate" about him. A couple of the girls seemed a bit hesitant. However, the stronger personalities prevailed. The next hour was spent with this group sharing their hate list with the other girls in the class during e-mail chats. A variety of lists were circulated. By the time they were done, probably 20 girls in the fifth grade had seen at least one version of the list.

One of the girls in another class printed out a version of the e-mail that had some very hurtful language (He's fat, he's ugly, he has pimples, etc.) and brought it into school on Monday. She passed it around to several of her friends. When the classroom teacher saw these girls

giggling, she came over and asked to see the piece of paper. After reading what was on the page, the teacher contacted you, the parent, regarding the mean, hateful words.
- What is your first reaction to this case?
- How will you handle the situation with the teacher?
- How will you handle the situation with your child?
- What will you say to her?
- What consequence will she have?
- What method(s) of cyberbullying were used in this case?
- What technology was used to cyberbully?

Your child could be a target of cyberbullying in 8 ways. At times, cyberbullies may combine several tactics in order to intimidate or harass their targets. No matter what form is being used, its effects have serious social, emotional, and health effects long after the harassment has stopped.

Type 1: Flaming

Flaming is an intense argument or online fight that contains forms of hostility, aggression, intimidation, insults, sarcasm, and the use of unfriendly tones and uninhibited language. These messages can be very personal, intense, and evoke a strong emotional reaction. These messages usually contain capital letters, images, and symbols to add emotion to the person's argument. Although flaming usually lasts for a short period of time, if your child continues to respond to the messages in anger and haste, it can become an ongoing issue.

In a chat room for girls who enjoy surfing, Megan disagreed with a comment made by another member regarding overweight people being allowed to surf. Another chat room member responded by insulting Megan's physical appearance. When Megan tried to defend her position, the insults got worse.

Type 2: Harassment

Harassment involves aggressors tormenting their target by repeatedly sending hateful, offensive, rude, and insulting messages at an individual or group. Aggressors can send hundreds of insulting e-mails or text messages at odd times throughout the day and night. Unfortunately, the target of the message, your child, then has to sift through every message.

Amanda reported to the principal that Cara was bullying another student. When Amanda got home, she had 35 angry messages in her e-mail box. The anonymous cruel messages kept coming—some from complete strangers.

POINT TO PONDER

Think about it. How would you feel if someone sent you a message that said, "You are a whore and a slut"? If it happened only once, you would more than likely ignore it. However, what would you do if you received the same message, on the hour, every hour, for a day, two days, or every day of the week?

Type 3: Cyberstalking

Cyberstalking is similar to harassment. However, cyberstalking is highly intimidating. It includes threats and intrudes on a person's privacy. Cyberstalking involves following targets through cyberspace, moving with them to different sites, and/or posting where they post. It is facilitated via computers, global positioning systems (GPS), cell phones, cameras, and more. Cyberstalkers may monitor their target's online activities via spyware, which tracks the location of the target using GPS technology, and/or intercept phone calls or messages using software. They can also watch and monitor the target through hidden cameras. The goal of a cyberstalker is to incorporate persistent behaviors that instill apprehension and fear. In the mind of the target, there is a fear that the virtual stalking may escalate to stalking in the physical world. Consequently, the target must deal with not only the emotional anguish but also the potential for physical danger.

When Annie broke up with Sam, he sent her many angry, threatening, pleading messages. He followed her where she went online and tracked her every move through her cell phone. In his messages, he stated that he would never leave her alone; that she would never leave him, and if she tried to leave him, he would make her life a living hell.

TIP

Only a certain amount of cyberstalking cases involve strangers. More often, targets are cyberstalked by people they know such as a bully at school, a friend, or a neighbor. Cyberstalking commonly begins after a relationship ends. The person who was dumped becomes jealous and enraged. He or she begins to stalk the ex online through text messaging or social networking sites.

Type 4: Denigration

Denigration refers to putting someone down, dissing someone online, and sending or posting cruel gossip or rumors about a person to damage his or her reputation or friendships.

Some boys created a "We Hate Joe" website where they posted jokes, cartoons, gossip, and rumors, all dissing Joe.

Type 5: Happy Slapping

Happy slapping is a relatively new type of cyberbullying. This occurs when an unsuspecting victim is physically attacked, in person, as an accomplice films or take pictures of the incident. The image or video is then posted online or distributed electronically. Often the attackers will say it was only a prank or joke, hence the term "happy slapping." Happy slapping is becoming more common since most cell phones now include cameras.

Type 6: Impersonation/Masquerading

Impersonation or masquerading refers to pretending to be someone else online. The aggressor sends or posts material online to make someone look bad, to get the person in trouble, to place the person in danger, or to damage the person's reputation or friendships. Impersonators usually steal someone's password by watching the person type it in, which is called "shoulder surfing." Then the cyberstalkers create fake e-mail addresses, websites, or instant messaging names. They also steal e-mail addresses or mobile phone numbers to bully others. The online aggressors' real identities remain hidden. All too often, friends share their passwords with each other. However, after they are no longer friends or get into a fight, the ex-friend—the impersonator—uses the target's password and screen name either to harass someone else or to sign up for inappropriate chat rooms or websites.

> *Laura watched closely as Emma logged into her account and then captured her password. Later, Laura logged on to Emma's account and sent a hurtful message to Emma's boyfriend, Adam. Since the message was sent from Emma's account, he thought it was from her. Angered by the message, he broke up with Emma.*

 TIP

> One out three teens report sharing one of their passwords with a friend, boyfriend, or girlfriend. Four out of ten middle school students have had their password(s) stolen and changed by a bully, who then locked them out of their own account or sent communications posing as them.
> Pew Research Center's Internet and American Life Project

Type 7: Outing and Trickery

Outing is sharing someone's secret or embarrassing information online through personal communications such as text messages, pictures, e-mails, or instant messaging. Even reading out loud the saved messages on a person's mobile phone is a form of outing. Trickery is deceiving someone into revealing secrets or embarrassing information, which is then shared online. Cyberbullies often enlist their friends, also known as proxies, to assist them in their dirty work and to "join in on the fun" to further the humiliation and emotional damage caused to the target. Furthermore, many cyberbullies print out instant messaging conversations, often containing personal or sexual information, and show them around to other people. If the message is supposed to remain private, it can cause real psychological harm to all person's involved.

> *Katie sent a message to Jessica, pretending to be her friend and asked many questions. Jessica responded, sharing really personal information. Katie forwarded the message to several of her friends with her own comment, "Jessica is a loser."*

Mandy, an obese high school student, was changing in the locker room after gym class. Lisa took a picture of her with her cell phone camera. Within seconds, the picture was flying around the cell phones at school.

Type 8: Exclusion and Ostracism

Exclusion and ostracism refer to when an individual is intentionally singled out and excluded from a group by removing or blocking someone from buddy lists, chat rooms, Internet groups, or gaming websites. For example, kids who do not have a cell phone are often excluded from the group of kids who do—77% of those ages 12–17 have a cell phone.[5] Because communicating online has become a normal part of kids' daily lives, being socially cut off can be devastating for many of them.

11-year-old Amber recalled in a newspaper interview how every girl in a class but one was invited to a recent sleepover. The girls at the party went on the Internet that night and taunted the one who had been left out.

TIP

Griefer

A griefer refers to someone, usually in an online game, who intentionally and repeatedly attempts to degrade another person's experience or torments that person. Griefing usually takes place in massive multiplayer online role-playing games (MMORPG) like Battlefield, Halo 4, and Counterstrike.

Tactics used by a griefer:

1. Player vs. player abuse: Singling out the same person and killing him/her over and over when he/she is defenseless until the person logs off.
2. Kill stealing: Repeatedly trying to steal another person's kills so that his/her time is wasted.
3. Gang banging or dog piling: Recruiting others (usually their online friends) into joining them in targeting the victim.
4. Making "clever" comments: Spamming a person with vulgar, hateful, or offensive messages. The comments stay within the rules while violating the spirit of the rules.
5. Flame baiting: See #4 above. This is done in order to provoke the victim into responding out of anger in a manner that violates the rules, causing the victim to be punished or banned by the forum administrator. This is also known as trolling.

6. Blocking: Getting in another's way so he/she cannot move or get out of a particular area.
7. Training: Triggering many monsters, almost always impossible to fight and survive, with the intention either to run someone out of an area or to kill him/her indirectly if the server is not player vs. player enabled.
8. Stalking: After driving the target off the forum, following him/her to other forums to continue the attacks.
9. Drive-by: Signing up under a different name in order to take a cheap shot at the target. Griefers also frequently use other tactics, including using a fake IP address, in order to avoid punishment.

These tactics are typically bannable on the first offense. However, many griefers rarely get punished for their actions.

www.urbandictionary.com

Separating the Facts from the Hype

Recently, cyberbullying has received more media attention. It seems like the issue is everywhere. It is on the television news, in the newspaper (in paper and electronic form), on the radio, on the Internet, YouTube, and in blogs to name a few. It has been a growing issue because kids have incorporated technology in all facets of life. Currently, 1 in 5 children ages 12-18 are using social media platforms to antagonize, intimidate, and exploit others. Text messaging is the most common method of harassment (*nces.ed.gov*). In fact, 1 in 10 children have been a cyberbully and also been cyberbullied.[7,8] Girls, who are more likely to spread rumors, are twice as likely to cyberbully as boys, who are more likely to post hurtful pictures or videos.[2] Cyberbullying crosses all races and geographic boundaries. It does not discriminate, because the majority of kids have access to some social media platform.[2,5]

 TIP

Cyberbullies spend more time online (38.4 hours) compared with other teens who have not bullied others online (26.8 hours). Cyberbullies are more likely to have engaged in sexting (31% vs. 19% for teens overall).[6]

Not surprisingly, there is often a crossover between being cyberbullied and being bullied face to face. Targets of cyberbullying were more likely to get into a physical fight (15.6%) at school and to be the target of a crime (12.8%) than students who were not cyberbullied (5.1% and 3.3%, respectively).[2,7] This fact indicates that although cyberbullying takes place off school grounds, the school environment is being affected by it. School personnel are forced to deal with the consequences. Unfortunately, less than 8% of public schools are aware of the extent of cyberbullying among students (*nces.ed.gov*). In addition, kids who have cyberbullied or who have been cyberbullied perceive a negative climate in their school. This means they do not enjoy going to school, do not feel safe at school, do not feel teachers at their school really try to help them succeed, and do not feel that teachers at their school care about them. In contrast, those who have not experienced cyberbullying do not perceive a negative climate in their school as often. So this issue leads to school safety concerns. Subsequently, kids who report being a target of cyberbullying are eight times more likely to carry a weapon to school.[2,7]

TIP

According to the Pew Internet Research Center, 88% of social media-using teens have witnessed other people be mean or cruel on social network sites.

How Do Kids Respond to Cyberbullying?

When kids act meanly or cruelly on social network sites, most kids report that they just ignore what is going on (35%), defend the victim who is being harassed (25%), or tell the person to stop being mean or cruel (20%).[2] Despite the good news that most kids report seeing bystanders responding positively by standing up for or defending the person under attack, kids are also likely to witness others joining in the harassment. One in five (21%) social media–using teens who have witnessed online cruelty say they have joined in. Two-thirds (67%) of them witnessed others joining in the harassment they have seen.[2]

Get Advice

About one-third of teens who witness online cruelty seek advice, while nearly two-thirds of teens who have been cyberbullied have sought advice about what they have witnessed or experienced online.[2] Of the teens who have witnessed online cruelty and then sought advice about how to handle it, more than half sought help from a friend or peer. Another third sought advice from parents. A much smaller numbers of teens said they look to a sibling, cousin, or teacher for advice. Additionally, the source of the advice varied depending on the sex and age of the victim. For example, boys are less likely than girls to seek advice from any source. Younger kids, ages 12–13, are more likely to seek advice primarily from their parents. Older kids, ages 15–17, are more likely to report and discuss these concerns with friends.

Don't Tell

Most older teens do not tell their parents about cyberbullying. They do not believe that adults can help them fix the problem, they think they can solve the problem on their own. They also fear that their technology privileges will be taken away. As one 16-year-old girl told me, "If you take my cell phone away, it is like death. It's like I am invisible to the rest of the world because I can't connect with my friends." In some cases, disclosure only made the situation worse. "I think most kids are reluctant to tell someone because they think it makes them look like a little kid who is 'tattling,'" commented one parent.

TOOLBOX TACTIC

Youths use their own methods to counter cyberbullying. Some ask the cyberbully to stop. Some block communication. Some do nothing about it. Some go offline. Do your children know how to protect themselves from being bullied online? To find out, let them show you how.

Children love to teach adults about technology. They love the idea that they get to teach you something. So allow them to show you step by step how they can block or ban an e-mail, text message, website, YouTube video, and friend request on Facebook (or other social networking sites). Let them show you how they can disable the GPS location permissions on their devices.

The Attraction to Cyberbullying Using Social Media

I think most people who bully online just do it to act tough. Since they're not saying it to someone's face, it makes them seem more of a wimp.

15-Year-Old Girl

Kids use social media to be mean and vindictive for several reasons. First of all, the reasons discussed in Chapter 2 about why kids bully others face to face apply to why kids bully in cyberspace. Kids behave in ways that will often meet a need that is devoid in their life, such as wanting to be loved and feel connected to others. They may want to achieve a sense of competence and personal power. They may want to act with a degree of freedom and autonomy. Bullies often want to experience joy and fun. However, kids who cyberbully have additional motives for using social media to harass others. Social media platforms create an environment where anonymity is paramount (you don't know me). Identity, norms, and ethics are challenged (you can't see me). Power and authority are equalized. Additionally, they believe this is a type of entertainment (it's just a game).

Reason1: You Don't Know Me

Anonymity. The ability to remain anonymous on various social networking platforms is becoming the leading reason that many cyberbullies choose to exploit. Under the veil of anonymity, kids' inhibitions disappear (called the disinhibition effect). They can tease and humiliate their target without their identity ever being known. This means cyberbullies can hide their identity behind their laptops, cell phones, and screen names or aliases by using anonymous e-mail addresses or fake screen names. Clearly, targets often do not know who the cyberbully is or why he or she is harassing them. Anonymity is a powerful force that allows cyberbullies to do or say whatever is on their mind. It helps loosen them up. Cyberbullies are thus free to express themselves more openly. In cyberspace, kids share more personal aspects about themselves and reveal more secrets, emotions, fears, and wishes than they would normally do in the real world. On the other hand, anonymity may free them to be ruder, harsher in their criticisms, instill anger, or even threaten individuals. Sadly, social media has become a refuge for bullies. The mask of anonymity is commonplace. It is virtually impossible for targets to confront their digital aggressors face to face.

It seems that whenever anonymity is allowed, intelligence takes a nosedive. Sure, people are more likely to give their true opinions if anonymity is allowed, but the bad tends to outweigh the good. I'm fine with people having different opinions and speaking what they feel, as long as they are held accountable for what they say and they are respectful. Too many people just want to "vent," and that just ends up spreading negativity.

17-Year-Old Boy

TIP

Although using the Internet may feel safe, anonymous, and impermanent, the opposite is actually true. What teens don't often realize is that what gets posted on the Internet stays on the Internet. You are never really anonymous online.

Experimentation with multiple identities. Youths use social media to experiment with their identities due to the anonymous nature of cyberspace. Virtual identity play can aid the identity formation process by providing new tools and diverse spaces for self-expression, self-reflection, and feedback from others. Social media platforms provide the perfect forum for kids to create and experience different online personas (known as avatars) and to hang out with their friends. However, it is also a place where cyberbullies can use online personas as weapons to degrade and ridicule other kids (whether they know them offline or not).

In real life, 16-year-old Megan is a model child and student. She makes good grades, rarely gets in trouble, and is polite to others. She is on the academic team, is captain of the cheerleading team, and volunteers for several civic organizations. On the other hand, Megan's virtual life is remarkably different. Online, she uses profanity in her language, is cruel to others, is very opinionated, and dresses very provocatively for someone her age. Even her avatar does not resemble what she looks like in real life. Remember that, online, adolescents can be whomever they want to be. The faceless cyberspace provides them with opportunities to separate their virtual identity from their real identity. Cyberspace allows them to experiment with their identity without disappointing parents, family members, teachers, and friends. It allows youths to escape from the realities of life. Given that the usual constraints of real-life roles are nonexistent online, their identities can grow and change as they grow and change. Sometimes this happens for the better. All too often, though, some adolescents engage in high levels of identity reform (or transformations) as part of playful experiences or fantasy, seamlessly transitioning between honesty and deception.

TIP

Teens who use social networking sites are twice as likely as nonusers to say they have misrepresented their age online in order to gain access to websites and online services (49% vs. 26%).[2] A *Consumer Report* study suggested that 7.5 million American children under the age of 13 were Facebook users and that approximately 5 million were age 10 and under.[9]

Sense of entitlement. These hidden bullies are known as the popular-aggressive children who cyberbully others because they believe they are superior, prettier, and smarter than others. They believe they have the right to harass or demean others, especially if the person is different. Hidden bullies enjoy high status and esteem from their peers and, surprisingly, their teachers. They are socially skilled and competent, are good students, make good grades, have good relationships with adults, and are involved in extracurricular activities. Although entitlement cyberbullies have high self-esteem and self-worth, their sense of humility is almost nonexistent. Sometimes parents unknowingly reinforce these children's superior, highly confident attitude by showering them with attention and high expectations and by constantly praising them that they can do and achieve anything.

Empowerment. When kids either cannot find the courage to confront someone they are in conflict with or their social status makes them feel disempowered, cyberbullying can seem like a safe way to retaliate. Whereas F2F bullies have the courage to harass their target in person verbally or physically, cyberbullies, who are less inhibited online, do not have to exert a lot of effort and muster up much courage to confront or harass their target online. It can help them achieve the power and control they seek without retaliation. Sometimes because of the anonymous nature of online environments, cyberbullies brag about their online cruelty. The power they feel when bullying someone online is not enough to feed their need to be seen as powerful and intimidating.

TOOLBOX TACTIC

Since youths' online self-expressions tend to reflect aspects of their offline selves, explore different social networking sites and blogs on the Internet. Read some of the posts with your children. Use the following questions to discuss the information with them and to discover their thoughts about how they and others explore their identities online.

- What do you think the person is trying to say?
- Do you think the person's response makes sense?
- Do you think the person would say the same thing in real life?
- Why do you think people feel freer to say things online?
- Do you think people are anonymous online?
- Have you written anything online that was untrue?
- Do you have an online avatar?
- What type of feedback have you received from people online? How does this differ from the feedback you have received in the real world? How is it similar?

Remind them who they are online also represents who they are offline. So if your children would not use lewd or foul language in the real world, they should not use it in the virtual world. Their identity should be one and the same.

Reason 2: You Can't See Me

Illusion of invisibility. Cyberspace creates an illusion that kids are invisible because it is faceless. The power to have their identity concealed overlaps with anonymity, because anonymity is the concealment of an identity. The opportunity to be physically invisible amplifies being anonymous. The freedom to express one's belief or emotions without censorship is enticing. In light of the cloak of anonymity and invisibility, it is easy to see why many kids believe if you can't see me, you do not know who I am, and for that reason, there is no way I will get punished. Given that the Internet is faceless, cyberbullies do not see the hurt and pain they have inflicted on the person on the other side of the screen. For example, when cyberbullies act out certain hostile feelings, they do not have to own or to take responsibility for their behaviors. They do not have to worry about what they say, what they do, or how they sound. The illusion of invisibility makes it easier for them to rationalize their irresponsible or harmful action due to the lack of potential for detection and punishment.

> *Being bullied over the Internet is worse. It's torment and hurts. They say "sticks and stones may break my bones, but words will never hurt me." That quote is a lie, and I don't believe in it. Sticks and stones may cause nasty cuts and scars, but those cuts and scars will heal. Insulting words hurt and sometimes take forever to heal.*
>
> 14-Year-Old Girl

TOOLBOX TACTIC

Should freedom of speech protect anonymous harassment, people who speak with no accountability because they can hide behind false names and identities? Do your children think speech should be protected? Do this activity to find out.

Each of the scenarios listed below contains a form of expression by one person about another and is presented electronically in some form for many people to see. The question arises, "Is this an acceptable form of free speech or is it cyberbullying?"

1. Amy finds that photos of her, which were taken by her ex-boyfriend, have been uploaded to his Facebook page. Then they were copied and reproduced in many more places, including photo-sharing sites. Her ex-boyfriend says that he is not responsible for what was done with the photos after he uploaded them.

2. Baily creates a website that is intended to mock another student in her class that will likely lead to the student being harassed at school. The site was not created at school and is not hosted on school computers (though it can be accessed from them).

3. Chet discovers that other students in his class have created an online forum in which students are invited to vote on whether or not he should be beaten up.

After reading the scenarios, discuss them using the following questions.

• Was the subject of the scenario kept anonymous? If so, does this make the action more acceptable? Why or why not?

- Did the creator of the expression reveal his or her identity? If so, would this make the action more acceptable in this scenario? Why or why not?
- Was anyone's reputation negatively affected by this action? Explain.
- Do you believe the intent of the action was to hurt someone else or just express an opinion? Explain.

Now rate the scenario on a 1 to 5 scale with 1 being totally acceptable and 5 being totally unacceptable. Be sure to explain your rating as your response will more than likely differ from your children's responses.

After reviewing and rating the scenarios, discuss both your and your children's ratings using the following questions.

- Describe your rating of the scenario and the reasons why you rated it as you did.
- Compare and contrast the seriousness of the actions in the scenario. Were they public for anyone to see? Were they private so only the target saw the message? Would the action be more acceptable if the target's privacy was maintained?
- Describe what you would do if you were the person targeted in this scenario.
- Describe what you would do if you discovered this activity and knew the people involved.

Remember the two points of the discussion. First, you want to find out about your children's thoughts. So it is important that you do not challenge or blame their way of thinking but, instead, listen and learn. Second, use the discussion time as a teachable moment—to teach your children about your family's morals and ethics about how a person should be treated. Teach them about the limits of free speech.

The illusion of invisibility encourages kids to go to places and do things that they would not otherwise think about doing in the real world. They can browse and visit many different sites without anyone even knowing who they are—so they think. Unfortunately, many kids believe that what they do or say online is private. Many young kids believe if the message or picture is deleted, then it is gone forever. For example, Katie was sending harassing and degrading text messages to a girl in her class. She deleted the messages to get rid of the evidence. However, Katie was shocked to find out that the girl's parent was able to trace the messages back to Katie's cell phone.

TOOLBOX TACTIC

Remember—tell your kids they are really never invisible online. Teach them to think before they post. Once they put it out there in cyberspace, it is for the whole world to see. Once it is out there, they can never get it back.

To help your children think before they post visit *http://www.netsmartz.org*. The NetSmartz videos are age appropriate to help children learn the importance of being safer online and offline.

- For children ages 5–10, use the "Bad Netiquette Stinks" video.
- For tweens ages 8–12, use the "Post to be Private" video.
- For teens ages 11–17, use the "Cyberbullying: You Can't Take It Back" video.

Different online social norms. Social media creates a world in which there is a different set of rules, norms, and/or values from the real world. The virtual environment is devoid of standard rules of conduct that many parents teach their children. Many kids believe "everybody does it," "life online is just a game," or "it's not me—it's my online persona." Once again, being anonymous leads to inhibited behaviors. In return, these behaviors reduce the influence of real-world social norms and constraints. Consequently, deregulated behaviors are unleashed.

The rules that many parents teach their kids, such as "be kind to others" or "if you don't have anything nice to say, then do not say it at all," seem not to apply to online environments. Fourteen-year-old Julie commented, "I have a free speech right to post whatever I want, regardless of the harm I cause. I have the right to use any language I want to because there is no adult hovering over me, monitoring my behavior." Many kids believe if you have mean things to say, then say it online. Unfortunately, these harmful online social norms support cyberbullying. In light of this finding, many kids no longer listen to the old parental saying, "Do as I say and not as I do." They see this as hypocrisy. Daniel commented, "I hate when my parents tell me 'Because I said so.' If they don't want me to do something, then they shouldn't do it either."

TIP

Although parental awareness of their teens' online activities has risen significantly, 41% of teens said their parents had no clue about what they were doing online. Interestingly, 48% of parents admitted they do not always know what their kids do online.

Norton Online Living Report

Reduced social cues. The faceless social media platforms create a world where kids do not see nonverbal social cues such as body language, voice tone, and facial expression (excluding video chats). They do not see a child crying, hurt, stressed, or scared. They do not see the pain they have caused to another human being. All they see is a computer or phone with a screen that contains words or pictures. Unfortunately, the lack of tangible feedback from the person on the other side of the screen interferes with cyberbullies recognizing that they actually caused harm to another person (empathic response). Clearly, this reduction in social and emotional cues impedes cyberbullies' ability to empathize or be remorseful for the harm they have caused. Likewise, because cyberbullies cannot see the damage caused to another person, they can easily rationalize their irresponsible or destructive behaviors. Consequently, in their minds, they did not really hurt anyone.

Underdeveloped empathy skills. Empathy is one of the foundational moral emotions. It is a skill that requires understanding how another person feels as well as understanding that what happened to someone else could happen to you. It takes years to develop. Empathy deepens and expands as one gets older. It is a feeling that compels people to act compassionately. Generally, preadolescents have a difficult time empathizing since their brains are not fully developed. At this age, there is a lot of focus on self (see chapter 3). It is like the kid who shouts out, "Hey mom, look at that fat lady." If kids already have difficulty empathizing with others in the physical world, how do adults expect them to be able to learn and express empathy toward another person in the virtual world? The faceless Internet does not provide a medium in which they can read someone's nonverbal body language or see their facial expressions. If kids cannot see the damage or the pain they caused, then they cannot learn how to be compassionate and caring human beings.

I am not blaming social media platforms for kids' lack of empathy or saying that it is the only cause. Rather, kids choose to sit in front of their computer screens or cell phones rather than going out and seeing their family and friends face to face, where they can learn and practice social skills. It is a matter of how they use the Internet and also the purpose and function of the Internet. More troubling, the Internet does not provide kids with opportunities for them to learn and practice being tolerant toward others. More and more studies have shown that those who engage in cyberbullying have been found to lack empathy for others. Certainly, the faceless social media platforms create a barrier where the other person's reactions or nonverbal cues are absent. In this environment, kids let go of any inhibitions. Because kids have grown up with technology, they do not differentiate between the online and offline environment. If their virtual persona engages in mean and hurtful behaviors, these behaviors can transfer to their real-life persona, where their sense of warmth and open-mindedness can be stifled.

"On the Internet, nobody knows you're a dog" (*cartoonbank.com*) is a phrase popularized by Peter Steiner's famous cartoon—which first appeared in *The New Yorker* in July 1993—that describes the anonymity of the Internet. This cartoon featured an illustration of a dog seated at a computer telling his canine friend that "On the Internet, nobody knows you're a dog." The cartoon summarizes the world we live in today. Under the cloak of anonymity, kids are free to be whomever they want to be, behave in any manner they choose, and say whatever they want to say on the Internet—all without consequence. Additionally, the cartoon illustrates how younger children look up to older siblings, to someone in a mentoring role, and to you the parents, for guidance and direction in cyberspace.

For example, if younger siblings view their older siblings writing degrading, harassing, or provocative language, the younger siblings may learn that this type of behavior is acceptable in online environments. If your children see you write or post inappropriate information or pictures that can be used as a weapon to damage another's self-esteem, your children may believe that it must be OK for them to do it too. Your actions thus reinforce the online social norm that anyone can write anything and say anything without consequence.

POINT TO PONDER

The parent-child relationship is crucial to developing empathetic teens. One of the most powerful ways to teach children empathy is to be empathetic yourself in your parenting. Frequent parental punishment and restricting kids' privileges most or all of the time has been implicated in increasing the odds of an adolescent being an online bully. How do you define your relationship with your children? Do you model empathetic behaviors? What type of behaviors do you want your children to model?

Mass audience. Cyberbullies can achieve their goal of humiliating their target by reaching a potentially huge online audience with the stroke of a few keys. Because of the sheer speed of digital communication, the damage can spread much faster than traditional F2F bullying. Ironically, cyberharassment can be far more public than F2F bullying. The audience is limited only by the aggressor's imagination. Social networking sites, blogs, wikis, online journals, and websites can achieve the same effect of the bathroom walls of generations past but with an unlimited number of recipients. What helps drive the cyberbully is the perception that everybody knows about the online cruelty.

Reason 3: It's Just a Game

Entertainment. For many kids, they believe their behaviors or actions exhibited in cyberspace are not real. It is only a game they play to pass the time. Thus the ego-based cyberbully harasses his or her target because he or she is bored or looking for entertainment. The drama that surrounds adolescent relationships is perceived as fun for teens unless, of course, you are the target. If the goal is to have fun and be entertained, a cyberbully's aggression grows when fed by group admiration, by cliques, or by the silence of others who stand by and let the bullying happen. On the flip side, the bullying quickly dies if a cyberbully does not get the entertainment value he or she is seeking.

It's one thing when you get made fun of at school, but to be bullied in your own home via your computer is a disgusting thing for someone to do. I think anyone who gets kicks out of it is disgusting. It makes me feel badly about myself. It makes me wonder how people can be so rude and disrespectful of others and makes me lose faith in the human race. It decreases my self-esteem. I often wonder what I did to make someone treat me that way.

16-Year-Old Girl

Lack of impulse control. Many kids tend not to think before they act. They have a hard time hitting the pause button. They often race right from thinking something is a good idea to jumping into behaviors without any in-between steps and without considering the consequences. The Internet allows them to turn thoughts into actions at lightning speed. Impulsive kids are more likely to say or do something online that they will later regret. All too often, I have heard adults say, "They should know better." As a parent myself, I have said the same thing. I have told my teenage children, "I taught you better than that. You know right from wrong." I forget that many kids lack impulse control due to immature internal behavior control (see chapter 3). This means that kids react quickly without restraint and without thinking about the consequences of their actions. Because they have an underdeveloped prefrontal cortex (the part of the brain that controls their reasoning and ethical decision making), cybercommunication interferes with their ability to connect their actions with harmful consequences.

TIP

> According to the AP-MTV survey, only about half (51%) of young people say they have thought about the idea that things they post online could come back to hurt them later. In other words, about half of the young people do not think before they post!

Ineffective problem-solving and decision-making skills. Many kids lack the ability to problem solve effectively. This is related to impulsivity. Problem solving forms part of our thinking, whereas decision making is the outcome of our thought processes. In cyberspace, an adolescent's ability to make effective decisions is diminished because of the impulsive nature of the adolescent mind as noted above. Many youths make poor decisions based upon instinct or the first thought that enters their heads. For example, many adolescents act before they think. They respond inappropriately to messages in anger and haste. Often, they write information online before they have an opportunity to weigh the pros and cons of the outcome. Unfortunately after posting a response, they cannot get it back. Once the information is in cyberspace, there is no way of getting it back.

POINT TO PONDER

How do we, as adults, expect adolescents to make effective decisions and solve their problems if they have not developed the capacity to do so or have never learned how to make effective decisions? The majority of the cybercommunication feedback they receive is based upon ineffective, unhealthy, and inappropriate types of information.

As a parent, remember that boys take longer than girls to mature, Most teenage brains will not fully develop until the age of 25. So if you find yourself in a situation where you have to deal with the consequences of your children's impulsive, unhealthy decisions, do as they should do. Stop and think. Ask yourself if your children have the brain power and skills to avoid making poor decisions.

TOOLBOX TACTIC

Help your children refrain from engaging in cyberbullying by fostering empathy and understanding. Use the following example to open up a dialogue with your children to help them understand that someone is on the other side of the screen. Remind them words do hurt. For openers, you can state, "I came across this message and was shocked by what I read. I was wondering if you have seen anything like this before."

> Divagirl10: Hey, loser, watch your back.
> Tam479: What r u talking about?
> Divagirl10: Why don't you kill yourself while u r ahead?
> Tam479: Why can't you just leave me alone?
> Divagirl10: Ugly girls like u need to be put in their place.

You can ask your children the following questions to discuss the message.

- Why do you think Divagirl10 sent the message?
- What would you say to Divagirl10 if you knew who she was in real life?
- How do you think Tam479 felt when she read the message?
- How could you support Tam479?
- Have you witnessed cyberbullying? How did you respond?
- Have you ever sent a mean message because you were upset?
- Do you think you were justified in sending the hurtful message?
- What could you do differently instead?
- Would you tell Divagirl10's and Tam479's parents that they have been involved in cyberbullying?
- Who would you talk to if cyberbullying happened to you?

The Consequences of Cyberbullying

Even though it may not take place in person and it might not cause physical injuries, the emotional and psychological effects of cyberbullying are just as destructive. The majority of youths who have been cyberbullied suffer the same negative effects as those who are involved in traditional F2F bullying (noted in chapter 4). These effects include issues surrounding their physical health, academics, behaviors, and emotions.

The sheer amount of time young people spend using media makes it plain that the potential of media to impact virtually every aspect of young people's lives cannot be ignored.

Kaiser Family Foundation

The Internet is not a place to harass others or hurt them. The Internet is supposed to be a place that is safe and fun for people, not a place to be criticized or harassed. I used to be bullied at school frequently. I was sometimes hurt so badly that I had to fake being sick at school just so I could go home. One girl actually told me she would come and murder my parents and kill me personally. She made me cry so hard that I threw up. So I know firsthand what it's like to be bullied beyond your imagination.

12-Year-Old Girl

I was harassed and threaten online because I was gay. I started skipping school because I didn't want to face people at school. I used to make As and Bs, but my grades dropped to Cs and Ds because I never did my homework or I was not in the class to get the assignments. I just didn't care anymore.

15-Year-Old Boy

Yeah! I wrote and posted some pretty nasty stuff about my ex-girlfriend. Although she deserved it, I was the one who suffered for it. We were at school and got into a huge fight. To get back at her, I posted the pictures when I was at school. So I got suspended. To let off steam, I got a buddy of mine to buy me a six-pack to drink my troubles away.

17-Year-Old Boy

I know because I have myself been bullied. It lowers my self-esteem. It makes me feel really crappy. It makes me walk around the rest of the day feeling worthless, like no one cares. It makes me very, very depressed.

12-Year-Old Girl

TIP

> Children who demonstrate greater resiliency and less distress in response to cyberbullying have parents who use a parenting style that involves active and positive engagement—providing warm emotional support along with clear limits. Resilient children also demonstrate higher levels of individual self-control, including the ability to avoid responding impulsively.

Cyberbullying and Suicide

Meet 15-year-old Amanda Todd from British Columbia, Canada. She posted a cry-for-help video on YouTube. She used note cards to detail the torment she endured from classmates and strangers in the wake of a revealing (topless) video chat photo released to her Facebook friends and others by an extorting stranger. She got depressed and anxious. She experimented with drugs and alcohol. She cut herself and made at least two previous attempts at suicide. People commented on her Facebook page that she should try harder to kill herself: "I hope she dies this time and isn't so stupid." Unfortunately, on October 10, 2012, she succeeded (*nydailynews.com*).

Cyberbullicide is defined as suicide indirectly or directly influenced by experiences with online aggression. Similar to traditional bullying, there is a link between cyberbullying and suicide ideation for aggressors and targets. Several high-profile cases have involved teenagers taking their own lives in part because of being harassed and mistreated online. This reveals the harmful effects cyberbullying can have on a child (e.g., Ryan Haligan, Phoebe Prince, Megan Meyers, and Tyler DiClemente to name a few). Some kids become so depressed that they believe they have no other choices and no other way out than to die. In their minds, they just want the pain to stop and the only way to achieve peace and stop the pain is through death. This faulty way of thinking is unfortunate. Nevertheless, to adolescents who are hurt, tired, and hopeless, their way of thinking becomes clouded and their judgment compromised by visions of quietness and serenity.

TIP

Being cyberbullied does not cause kids to commit suicide. It is unlikely that experience with cyberbullying by itself leads to youth suicide. Rather, cyberbullying tends to aggravate or worsen the instability and hopelessness in the minds of adolescents already struggling with stressful life circumstances.

Cyberbullying Research Center

Has My Child Been Cyberbullied?

The biggest red flag that your children might be a target of cyberbullying is a withdrawal from technology. On the next page are some early-warning signs. If you notice any of these signs, do not ignore them. Targets of cyberbullying need to feel that you are taking the problem seriously and that you are going to do everything that you can do to help.

WARNING SIGNS	
• Spend long hours on the computer • Close windows on their computer when you enter room • Are secretive about Internet activities • Behavioral changes • You may find unexplained long distance telephone call charges • Won't say who they are talking to • You may find unexplained pictures on their computer • Trouble sleeping • Stomachaches and headaches • Lack of appetite, throwing up • Fear of leaving the house • Crying for no apparent reason • Stories that don't seem to make sense	• Lack of interest in social events that include other students • Often complain of illness before school or community events • Frequent visits to the school nurse or office complaining of feeling sick—want to go home • Lowered self-esteem • A marked change in attitude, dress, or habits • Unexplained broken personal possessions, loss of money, loss of personal items • Being aggressive at home • Missing or incomplete schoolwork, decreased success in class

How Should I Respond if My Child Is Being Cyberbullied?

You have gained a better understanding of cyberbullying and the technologies used. You are now able to recognize the warning signs. By using the case study given at the beginning of this chapter, I will outline specific actions that you and your children can take to stop the cyberbullying, as well as what not to do once you discover your children have being cyberbullied. Because cyberbullying can range from making rude comments, to spreading rumors, to making threats, how you and your children respond may vary depending on the nature and severity of the message. Regardless of the message, early intervention is essential as it may prevent the online harassment from escalating.

Seven Steps to Cyberbullying Intervention

Teach your children to respond in several ways. Do not respond to the bullying messages. Don't retaliate. If the messages continue, take a break and then reply strongly. Tell the sender to stop. Block or filter all further messages. If necessary, change your e-mail address, account, user name, or phone number. In the case of young children, teach them to turn off the monitor but leave the computer on so they can seek your or another adult's help.

Step 1: Preserve the Evidence

Don't delete. Do not delete any message or picture. This first step is crucial for making a case of cyberbullying and identifying the aggressor. You should document the activity by keeping a record of any online activity (text messages, Web pages, chat sessions, blogs, etc.), including relevant dates and times. In addition to saving an electronic version, you should print out a copy for your records. This can be done by e-mailing the text message or picture to your e-mail address.

Take a screen shot. A screen shot is an image captured by the computer to record the items visible on the monitor. This will copy the image on your computer monitor so you can paste it into a Microsoft Word document.

Filter the message. If the messages come through e-mail, you can set the filter to direct all messages from the cyberbully to go directly into a specific folder you have created. This way the evidence is saved without having your children see the message in their general inbox.

 TOOLBOX TACTIC

PC/Windows Directions for Taking and Saving a Screen Shot

1. Have the content you wish to "photograph" clearly displayed on your monitor.
2. Press the "PrtScn" button on your keyboard. It is typically located in the top right corner of your keyboard.
3. Open a new document in Microsoft Word (or an equivalent).
4. Right click your mouse and select "paste" from the menu that pops up.
5. A copy of the screen should appear in the document.
6. Type any other relevant information, such as online nicknames, e-mail addresses, date, time, and anything else which you might need later to document the incident.
7. Save the document onto your computer's hard drive in a location you will remember.

Apple Directions for Taking and Saving a Screen Shot

1. Have the content you wish to "photograph" clearly displayed on your monitor.
2. Press "Apple (Command) Key + Shift +3." This captures the entire desktop to a file on the desktop as "picture #."

3. You can also be more selective with what content you "photograph" by pressing "Apple (Command) Key +Shift +4." This allows you to use your mouse to select a specific part of your desktop for capture. When your pointer turns into a cross, hold down the mouse button. Drag to select the part of the screen you want to capture.

4. When you release the mouse button, a snapshot will be captured of that part of the screen. Press "Esc" to release the screen capture feature and switch back to the normal cursor arrow.

Step 2: Avoid Engaging in the Situation

Do not respond in anger. Teach your children to avoid escalating the situation. Explain to them that responding with hostility or taking vengeance will not help solve the problem. Rather, it will likely provoke a cyberbully and escalate the situation. If they engage in flaming, pinpointing who first instigated the cruel messages could be difficult.

Ignore or block the cyberbully. If the offense is minor and has occurred only once, ignoring the cyberbully may be the best option. Often, cyberbullies thrive on the reaction of their targets. If the cyberbullying is coming through e-mail or a cell phone, you can block future contact from the cyberbully by using the block feature for instant messaging or text messaging. Of course, the cyberbully may assume a different identity and continue the cyberbullying. However, blocks may provide enough time for you to investigate the situation.

To enable the block feature, go to "options" or "preferences," click "block," and then input the cyberbully's screen name or e-mail address. You can also use blocking software like SafeEyes or CyberSitter to stop the messages from coming through.

A word of caution: blocking may not be easy for children to do because social media is a major part of their lives. Their curiosity to know what is being said or done may override their hurt feelings. For example, one teen girl commented:

> I started obsessing a lot on the computer. I started going on a lot more. Like just checking out sites, making sure that nobody's talking about me. Checking my Facebook page or site to make sure... I just over-obsessed about it. I'd go on every day for like 2 hours, 3 hours sometimes, just making sure that no one's talking about me, there's no websites about me.

TOOLBOX TACTIC

Privacy Controls

Facebook allows you to control:

- Who can see your profile
- Who can post to your wall
- Who can contact you on Facebook
- Who can see your contact information and e-mail address
- Who can see your search results on Facebook and in search engines
- Who can interact with you on Facebook

On your Facebook home page, click "account" in the upper right corner of the screen and then "privacy settings."

If someone is harassing you on Facebook, use the "report/block" button found at the bottom of the screen.

- To report a person for cyberbullying or abuse, you must first remove them from your friends list.
- Users are not notified when they are blocked.
- All reports are kept confidential.

Delete all old accounts and create new ones. If your children are receiving unwanted e-mail messages, change their e-mail address. If the harrassment is through their cell phone, change their number. If it is occurring by instant messaging or chat, change their username and password. If the cyberbully does not gain access to the new information, the problem may stop. On the other hand, if the cyberbully continues to send or post messages to the new account, you may have a stronger case for legal action. Furthermore, make sure your children keep their password private. They should treat their password like their toothbrush. Do not let anyone else use it (but you, of course).

TOOLBOX TACTIC

Use Multiple Passwords

You and your children should never use the same password for every system or program you log on to. You should use multiple passwords to help prevent them from being discovered. Use these tactics when choosing a password.

- Do not use passwords that are based on personal information that can be easily accessed or guessed.
- Do not use words that can be found in any dictionary of any language.
- Develop a mnemonic for remembering complex passwords.
- Use both lowercase and capital letters.
- Use a combination of letters, numbers, and special characters.
- Use different phrases as your password.
- Use different passwords for different accounts.

Step 3: Tell the Cyberbully to Stop

In some minor cases (cases not involving threats to harm), it may be appropriate for your children to respond to the cyberbully in an attempt to get the harassing messages to stop. If you choose this option, the first step is to make sure your children do not respond when they are emotionally upset. They should count to 5 or 10 so they do not respond in anger or haste. Even better, they should wait a day or two before communicating with the cyberbully. This will provide them with a cooling off period where they can write down how they feel or what they might want to say to the cyberbully. However, they should not send it to anyone. They should walk away and read it later. Also during this cooling off period, together you and your children can write a strong message that demands the harassing communication to stop or harmful material to be taken down. The message should include a statement that suggests if the material is not removed or taken down, further steps will be taken to resolve the problem. The warning message should be a simple, nonemotional reply indicating that you will either go to their parents or the police if the cyberbullying continues. The message should be firm enough to get your point across but gentle enough not to enrage or anger the aggressor even further.

TOOLBOX TACTIC

The following is an example of what your children can write to the cyberbully.

Dear KTZJ0004:

I would appreciate it if you would stop sending me harassing messages, take down the pictures you posted of me on Facebook, and delete the voting website you created about me. These messages are unnecessary and are a violation of the "terms of use." Since you have violated the terms of use, you are subject to adverse action. If the material is not removed or taken down, my parents and I will take the necessary steps to resolve the problem by either contacting your parents or the authorities.

Thank you for your attention in this matter,

Judy Doe and John and Jane Doe (Your child's name and your name)

Step 4: Investigate the Sender

Try to identify the individual doing the cyberbullying. Even if the cyberbully is anonymous (using a fake name or someone else's identity), there may be a way to track them through your school's Internet system or Internet or mobile service provider. Most of the time, children are not very clever in concealing their identity online. They usually make mistakes and leave clues that can identify who they are. More than likely, the cyberbully is someone your children go to school with. Other kids usually know the individual doing the harassing. If this is the case, the school can use its Internet system to try to identify who the cyberbully is by examining the Internet use records and talking to potential bystanders. If the cyberbullying occurs off campus, you can contact school officials (the principal, counselor, teacher) to see if they would be willing to talk to other students who might know the identity of the cyberbully. Some states have laws that mandate schools investigate off-campus hate speech. If the cyberbullying is criminal, such as making threats or posting nude photos, contact the police or an attorney. Leave the investigating to them.

Step 5: Get the Information Removed

You can take several avenues to stop the communication or to get the harassing material removed.

Contact the cyberbully's parents. The cyberbully's parents may be unaware that their child has engaged in this type of activity. They may be very concerned to learn that their child has been cyberbullying others. Thus they may act quickly to put a stop to the online harassment. On the other hand, the parents could be very defensive and react poorly. So proceed cautiously.

If you decide to contact a cyberbully's parents, communicate with them in writing—not face to face. To show proof their child has engaged in cyberbullying, send them a certified letter informing them that if their child does not refrain from sending or posting harmful messages, you will contact law enforcement. You should also include a copy of all of the material you have collected (e.g., copies of e-mails, text messages, websites, pictures, etc.) and the repeated attempts to tell their child to stop the cyberbullying. It is important to let them know that after notifying them of the situation, and if they fail to take corrective action, they can be held liable for their child's behavior if you choose to sue them. Of course, this should always be your last resort.

Contact the ISP or MSP. If the cyberbullying continues, you can contact the Internet service provider (ISP) and/or mobile service provider (MSP) to file a complaint to get the material taken down. Sending or posting inappropriate language may violate the terms and conditions of using these services. Therefore, violators are subject to adverse action. The ISP or MSP should respond to your complaint in a reasonable amount of time. In your complaint, include the link where they can access the harmful material posted on the Internet as well as copies of all harmful messages. Keep a copy of all communications.

TOOLBOX TACTIC

Depending on the technology used, follow these directions to file a complaint.

1. If the cyberbully's comments are on a website or if a fake profile has been set up about your children on a social network site, go to the site's home page. The following instructions specifically describe what to do if the cyberbully is harassing your child via Facebook.
   - Go to Facebook's home page (*facebook.com*). File a complaint by clicking on the "contact us" or "help" link.

- Click "report abuse or policy violations." There are four different categories you can click on, depending on the type of speech. There is also a tool for reporting without a Facebook account.
- Once you click on the appropriate link, the site will show you how and where to report the abuse.

2. If the cyberbully is using e-mail, contact his or her ISP. You can determine the ISP from the e-mail address. Go to the ISP's website, and follow the complaint procedures. For example, AOL has a "notify AOL" link found at the bottom of the website.

3. If the cyberbully is using his or her own website domain name, you can find the owner of the site and the company that hosts the site by going to any of the following:
   - *http://www.yougetsignal.com*
   - *http://www.whois.net*
   - *http://www.greatstatistics.com*

4. If the cyberbully's comments are coming through text messages on the cell phone, trace the number and contact the MSP.

Contact an attorney. Some forms of cyberbullying can constitute crimes, torts, or statutory violations depending on the content of the messages. In cases of serious cyberbullying, civil law permits a victim to sue the cyberbully and the cyberbully's parents in order to recover damages for defamation, public disclosure of private facts, invasion of privacy, assault, or intentional infliction of emotional distress. An attorney may also be necessary to get a court order for the cyberbullying to stop. Because cyberbullying is committed by a minor, some states have parental liability laws that hold parents financially responsible. Parents can also be sued for negligent supervision.

Step 6: Work with the School

School administrators have an obligation to intervene if cyberbullying occurs through the school district's Internet system or if a cyberbully uses a cell phone on school grounds or on a school-sponsored event to cyberbully. If this is the case, note the time the message was sent or posted to demonstrate that the actions occurred while your children were at school or attending a school event. If the identity of the cyberbully is known and found to be another student, the school may help you mediate and resolve the situation informally by communicating with the cyberbully's parents and facilitating counseling for all parties involved without involving law enforcement or lawyers.

If the cyberbullying is off-campus speech, there is a strong likelihood that cyberbullying may be supplemented by face-to-face bullying at school. Depending on the offending text or posted material, the school, which may have separate policies for dealing with cyberbullying activities that involve students off campus, may be able to impose formal consequences. For example, in Kentucky, Rowan County Senior High School officials suspended 16 students for sexting after nude pictures were found on their cell phones.[1]

School personnel are encouraged to respond to your inquiry by:

- Listening and not arguing with you
- Stating the school's position and goal of creating a safe and caring environment
- Validating your concern why this may be a problem
- Problem solving how all parties can work together to fix the issue
- Informing you of the school's response and how it is monitoring the situation
- Avoid arguing and trying to change your perspective
- Setting clear expectations and consequences for cyberbullying

CASE STUDY—PART 2

The Resolution: A Parent's Experience with Cyberbullying

Tara's parental response included one of initial success followed by frustration and then failure. The success occurred with the Facebook page itself. Tara and her husband e-mailed Facebook and demanded that they remove the page. Facebook did remove it within 24 hours. Tara stated, "We think that they acted so quickly not because of the content of the page but because it was a clearly fictitious name and therefore violated Facebook's terms of service, which require all profiles to be in the real name of the page owner."

The parents' experience with the school administration was far from satisfactory. Believing that Lisa had posted the Facebook page, they asked the principal to discipline Lisa for it. The principal called in Lisa, who denied posting the page. Lisa then bragged on her own Facebook profile about how she had defied the principal. When the parents advised the principal of this, she suspended Lisa for disrespecting her (the principal). The principal also suspended Lisa's brother for verbally threatening Sasha. So Lisa and her friends described themselves to their classmates as victims of an "oppressive school administration." This led to further ostracizing of Sasha. Ultimately, Tara and her husband decided to transfer Sasha to another high school. Her first few months there were unhappy. Ultimately, Sasha made friends at the new school and graduated at the top of her class.

To help bring closure to the situation, Tara and her husband decided to try to find out who had posted the Pissog Slrig page. Tara's husband contacted Facebook and was told that they could not release that information without a subpoena. Tara and her husband are both attorneys, so they prepared a document request in state court, obtained a subpoena, contacted a process server in California, and served the request to Facebook. Facebook complied with the subpoena, providing documents that showed that Pissog Slrig was not Lisa but was Janine, a wannabe follower of Lisa. Unfortunately, the school did not have the authority to discipline the two girls for their cyberbullying because it happened off campus. The parents then filed a civil suit against Lisa's parents. Although the pleadings sought damages for Sasha's emotional distress, Sasha's parents decided early on that they did not want to make Sasha relive the incident in depositions or court testimony. Therefore, the family agreed that they would be satisfied with an apology and reimbursement of the several hundred dollars spent in court costs and fees to learn Pissog Slrig's identity. Janine's parents initially seemed willing to negotiate a resolution, but then stopped returning their calls and e-mails. Sasha's parents decided that it was not worth pursuing Janine's family any longer.

- What is your first reaction to the resolution of the case?
- Can you identify any steps of cyberbullying intervention?
- Do you think Tara was justified in filing charges? How would you feel about filing charges?
- Do you think the consequences that Lisa faced were appropriate?
- Do you think it was fair that the school did not hold the girls accountable for their cyberbullying behaviors?
- Would you transfer your child to another school?
- Would you give up pursuing the matter because the bully's parents were uncooperative?

TIP

If you discover that your children are sexting, view it as an opportunity to engage them in a discussion of what constitutes a healthy relationship and how they can stay safe both physically and emotionally.

Step 7: Work with the Authorities

If you are uncertain if cyberbullying violates your jurisdiction's criminal laws, contact your local law enforcement. They can advise you of your rights. You should contact your local law enforcement immediately if cyberbullying involves direct threats of violence, extortion, obscene or harassing phone calls or text messages, stalking, hate crimes, sexual exploitation, or child pornography.

In 2012, at least 13 states introduced or are considering bills or resolutions aimed at sexting—the practice of sending sexually explicit, nude, or seminude photos of children by cell phone. Three states—Hawaii, Pennsylvania, and South Dakota—enacted legislation in 2012. Since 2009, when the National Conference of State Legislatures (*www.ncsl.org*) began tracking sexting legislation, at least 20 states and Guam have enacted bills to address youth sexting. Visit *www.cyberbullying.us* or *bullypolice.org* to check the laws against cyberbullying in your state.

If your children are being cyberbullied, let them know that they should come to you first. Then assess the level of severity and type of bully. If the cyberbullying is severe—threatening physical harm to your child, family, or friends—contact the local police department, especially if the cyberbully is anonymous. If you or your children know the cyberbully, contact the school administration and have them approach the bully's parents. Engaging with the cyberbully directly can escalate the situation. So make sure your children do not respond to or delete messages from a cyberbully. This evidence can be kept as a record of the malicious behavior while disengaging helps prevent additional negative material from surfacing. Cyberbullying is easier to prevent than to fix. So change your children's account information and have them turn off the computer. By walking away, they become less accessible to bullying and harassment and are also affected less by the situation.

Conclusion

As youths spend an increasing amount of time online, they are more likely to participate in destructive or potentially dangerous acts. Aided by tools of new media and digital communication technologies, youth cultures are developing alternative notions and practices of citizenship. Some kids cyberbully because they think they are supervisors over others. Some do it for entertainment. Some cyberbully to seek revenge or right a wrong. Some do it to boost their confidence and image in order to advance or reinstate their social standing in their physical world. Given that the virtual worlds have become an extension of children's real worlds, social media platforms can inadvertently undermine the quality of human interactions. The platforms allow destructive emotional impulses freer rein under specific circumstances.

Although social media holds tremendous promise for creating a more peaceful and respectful world, this world cannot be created through laws or through technology protection measures. We, as parents, must take an active role in identifying cyberbullying behaviors. We must work with our children by teaching them the values, skills, and motivation to make safe and responsible choices in both their online and offline worlds.

Part III

Responding to Bullying

Chapter 6

Helping Your Children Cope with Being Bullied

This chapter focuses on the do's and don'ts of responding, ways to help your child cope, and when to get the school and authorities involved.

My Child Fell Prey to a Bully: How Do I Respond?

My 10-year-old son recently fell victim to bullying. The signs were not as explicit and obvious as they might appear. By the time my husband and I knew that something wasn't right, we felt the damage had already been done.

A Frustrated Mom

Any child can be a target of bullying. However, children who are passive or shy are at a greater risk for becoming targets of bullying. Children who bully often choose shy children to harass simply because they believe the victim will never tell and they know they can get away with it. Thus being alert and observant is critical since victims are often reluctant to report bullying. Many of them do not report it to you or to any adult because they are embarrassed or humiliated by the bullying. Victims assume that adults will accuse them of tattling, will judge them, will tell them to deal with it themselves, or will fail to protect them. By the time they may report the bullying to an adult, they have likely exhausted their strategies for responding to the bullying.

If your children tell you that they are being bullied, be understanding and supportive. Victims often need a lot of courage to admit to being bullied. The last thing you want is for your children to shut down, remain quiet, or refuse to speak to you about what is going on in their lives. As a result, your role as the parent will be to help your children build resilience and gain the necessary skills to act on their own behalf. In addition, when something goes wrong at school, your children need to know where they can turn for guidance and support and what action to expect. You can help your children understand the importance of reporting harassment. You can guide them through the complaint and investigation process. This chapter will give you the do's and don'ts of dealing with bullies. It also contains a step-by-step process for supporting and teaching antibullying skills that will help restore your children's confidence and build resilience.

TIP

The goal of intervening on behalf of the child who is a target of bullying is to

- Support the child in a way that allows him or her to regain self-control, avoid embarrassment or humiliation, and feel safe from retaliation
- Work to strengthen the social standing of the child and to develop a buddy system to ensure the child is not alone at school
- Support the child's development of social skills, confidence, assertiveness, and ability to respond to bullying

CASE STUDY—PART 1

Beth and the Rumor Weed

You, the mom, just received a phone call from your friend Susie. Susie's daughter, Elise, and your daughter, Beth, have been best friends since 2nd grade. The girls are now in 7th grade. Susie called to let you know that Elise came home from school the other day and stated Beth has been teased, taunted, and a victim of vicious rumors being spread by a group of girls in their classes. These rumors are now on the Internet. The group of girls created a website called Busty Beth's Sex Forum. From what Elise reported, this has been going on for several months. Shocked and in disbelief, you become angry and upset because Beth hasn't told you anything, even though you've asked her every day about what is going on at school. You've noticed that she has been moody lately, but you thought it was just regular teenage hormones. Beth will be home in a couple of hours from school. What will you do? How will you respond?

The Three D's Response Model

Pretend that you have just learned that your children have fallen prey to a bully like in the case study. Instinctively, you would want to confront your children and say, "Why didn't you tell me?" When this thought enters your mind, "STOP and THINK" before you do. Think about the reasons why children keep information to themselves. They may prefer to handle things on their own. They might think you will get upset. They might think you won't believe them; they might just find it embarrassing to have a parent involved. Using the case scenario above and using the three D's response model (discover the story, discern your options, and develop a plan of action), you will learn what not to do followed by how to respond to the news that your children have fallen prey to bullying.

Phase 1: Discover the Story

Girls would tease me in the halls. They call me four-eyes, tell me I'm not important. At one point, I was telling myself I just wanted to die.

Jamie, a 6th-Grader

Remember that children will talk about the harassment to you when they know you will listen and help. As you talk with your children, the conversation will help you determine your level of involvement and plan of action. Consider the following questions as you listen to your children's stories about harassment.

1. Do my children need my help or protection?
2. How can I help my children stay safe?
3. What information do I need?
4. Where can I go for help?

TOOLBOX TACTIC

When helping your children (or any person) manage a crisis situation, you must remember to implement the three S's of crisis management:
1. Safety and security—Let the children know they are safe from harm and will be protected.

2. Stability—Keep their environment stable by maintaining their current routines, such as waking up for school at the same time, participating in scheduled extracurricular activities, eating dinner at the same time, having the same bedtime, etc. Given that a crisis usually dictates some change, a stable environment can be comforting to scared and frightened children.

3. Support—Be supportive by validating their fears and thoughts regarding the crisis situation. Reassure them that you love and care for them and that eventually the crisis will subside. You will always be there for your children.

Don't Wait to Respond

Talk with your children immediately to explore what is going on in their offline and online lives. If you wait, they may perceive your hesitation to mean that you do not believe them, that the bullying doesn't warrant your attention, or worse, that you don't care. The longer you wait, the worse it usually gets. It can be a mistake to come straight out and ask, "Are you being bullied?" Your children may become defensive and deny everything. So here are some direct and some subtle questions that can get the discussion going.

- I'm worried about you. Are there any kids at school who may be picking on you or bullying you?
- Are there any kids at school who tease you in a mean way?
- Are there any kids at school who leave you out or exclude you on purpose?
- Do you have any special friends at school this year? Who are they? Who do you hang out with?
- Who do you sit with at lunch and on the bus?
- Are there any kids at school who you really don't like? Why don't you like them? Do they ever pick on you or leave you out of things?

Do Initiate and Assess Immediate Safety

Once you know bullying has occurred, begin the conversation by stating, "Someone is bullying you and this concerns me. Bullying behavior is unacceptable and should not be tolerated. You are important, and you have a right to feel safe. So we need to do something about this." It is also critical that you gauge your children's immediate safety by looking out for the warning signs. These include overreacting to minor frustration, fearing new social situations, experimenting with drugs or alcohol, having difficulty sleeping or eating, extreme isolation and withdrawal, chewing fingernails, inability to make friends, disinterest in school activities, lethargy, stomach complaints, or open anger, hostility, or rage. (See chapter 2 for additional warning signs.)

Don't Be the Volcano

It can be upsetting when your children are being bullied. Your first reaction might be to say, "I am going straight to the school or police" or "I am going to contact the girl's parents." All of these people should become involved in resolving the bullying situation. However, don't freak out and overreact. Don't immediately leap to the phone and call the principal or teacher. It doesn't help to berate the people who can be your ally. Also, if your children are being cyberbullied, like in the case study, you may be inclined to immediately take their cell phone away or revoke Internet privileges. However, technology is not causing the problem. The way the technology is being used is causing the problem. If you take away cell phone or Internet privileges, your children will see this only as being punished for something that they did not do. They will become reluctant to talk with you. Plus, this will only lead to your children feeling more socially isolated, because of the importance of technology to adolescent peer interactions. The reality is that removing all forms of technology from the house will not completely protect your children from seeing additional harassing messages. Eventually, your children will return to using these technologies either at home, at a friend's house, at school, or at the library.

Do Be in Control of Your Emotions

Your parental protective instincts stir strong emotions. First and foremost, tend to your hurt and lonely children. When talking with your children, stay calm and show concern. It is appropriate to show emotion, but be careful not to become overly emotional. If you overrespond, your children may shut down and not talk about the bullying anymore in order to protect you. They may worry that you will charge in angrily to the school and make things worse. So remain calm. That way you can support your children and later plan a course of action with them. Remember, it's your children's problem, so help them solve it first. Help them choose a path that they feel comfortable pursuing.

Don't Be the Brick Wall

Don't say, " You should have..." or "I would have..." Be careful not to jump to conclusions by not listening and trying to solve the problems before gathering all of the information. Your children may perceive your response to mean that you blame them for not putting a stop to the harassment.

Do Be a Good Listener

Before taking any action, listen to their story and gather the facts. Focus all of your attention on them. Give your children plenty of time to express themselves and tell you how they feel. Thank them for sharing this information. By actively listening and not interrupting, you can use the time to gain a sense of their concerns and allow the development of trust.

Don't Be the Cynic

Don't say, "You're overreacting." Your children may perceive your response to mean that their pain doesn't warrant your attention.

Do Be Supportive

Let them know you are there for them and support them. State, "Now that I am aware of the bullying, I will be here to support you and I do not blame you or feel disappointed in you. It takes courage to talk about what is going on and admit you need help dealing with the bullying. I am here to help you generate some solutions. You are not alone." Let your children know that you are determined to persist until their concerns are adequately addressed. This willingness to keep at it lets them know that their concerns are valid, their safety is paramount, and that they are worthy of your time and effort. Tell them you love them often.

Don't Be the Steamroller

Don't say, "They're only words, do not listen to them." Your children may perceive your response to mean that you are blindly insensitive to their hurt.

Do Be Empathic

Empathize with your children by telling them that bullying is wrong and how painful the past few months must have been for them. For example, "I am here to support you through this painful and stressful time in your life. You are not alone." Also, it is important that they know you believe them. It's not their fault. You are glad they told a friend. Make it clear that they should never be ashamed to ask for help. When you show that you believe what your children have told you, when you take their concerns seriously, and when you are willing to persistently stand up for them, your children's self-worth can begin to grow again.

Don't Be the Martyr

Don't say, "That's nothing. When I was a kid..." They may perceive your response to mean that they are unimportant. Even if you think you've been there, done that, and heard it all, it can still be surprising how harsh kids today can be.

Do Be the Validator

Let your children know that you understand what they are going through. Acknowledge their hurt. Tell them, "It bothers me that you have been bullied, and I'm sorry that you had to deal with the hurt by yourself. We will get through this together." Let them know it is normal to feel hurt, fear, embarrassment, shame, and anger. Other responses include:

- I am sorry this happened to you.
- I am glad you told me.
- Sounds like you have been putting up with this for a while.
- I imagine this might be difficult in several ways.

Don't Be the Critic

Don't say, "What did you do to make them so mad at you?" "Why don't you just log off?" or "I told you so." Although made unintentionally, these comments can be perceived as blaming your children for being harassed and criticizing them for how they handled the situation. Be careful not to fall into the pitfall of asking "why" questions. These sorts of questions generally elicit rationalizations and defensive posture. Also, if you disagree with how your children handled the bullying situation, do not criticize them. Rather, discuss alternatives. It is often very difficult for children to know how best to respond.

Do Be Curious and Investigative

Change "why" questions into "what: or "how" questions. For example, instead of asking your children, "Why didn't you just turn the computer off?" you can ask them, "What prevented you from logging off or deleting the site?" or "What keeps you from logging off?" By asking your children the questions listed below, you will learn how they have been harmed by the bullying. Ask the following:

1. What did you think when you realized what had happened?
2. What impact has this incident had on you and on others?
3. What has been the hardest thing for you?

Additionally, find out what other parents or children know about the bully, but do not mention the bullying. Ask these parents or children if they have witnessed your children being bullied or if they think your children are being bullied. Sometimes those who are not emotionally involved may see things differently and may help you see things more clearly.

TIP

While investigating the bullying, be careful not to bash the bully or school in a way that may tarnish your own integrity (i.e., gossiping). Rather, make sure to enlist the help of everyone and anyone that is in a position to address the situation and help bring the bullying to a stop.

Don't Be the Interrogator

Don't say, "I want to know everything" or begin the conversation by asking too many questions. Avoid "why" and "you" statements. This can cause your children to become defensive and shut down the line of communication. Refrain from asking too many questions before they have an opportunity to tell you their stories.

Do Be the Clarifier

Thank your children for sharing their story with you. Restate the facts in order to gather further information about the bullying. Find out what tactics are being used and where and when it is happening. Try and draw them out by saying, "Tell me some more about it..." As they tell you how they feel, be sure to repeat back their thoughts and feelings using phrases like, "I know you're feeling worried" or "I can see that you are distressed over the situation." When they feel understood by you, they will be more receptive to your help and any advice on coping that you may offer.

Do Be the Journalist

Be clear on the facts. It is important to document the bullying by keeping a journal of all bullying incidents and to take pictures of any injuries. This is so you are able to tell the school or authorities exactly what happened. Record as much detail as possible since memory tends to be short and details can get easily and understandably distorted by emotion. Then again, it is time to take action as soon as you know that bullying has occurred. Don't wait for your children to fill up a page in the reporting journal.

TOOLBOX TACTIC

Follow these directions to document the bullying incident(s) and file an accurate complaint. You and your children should write down:

- What happened
- Where and when it occurred
- The names of the people involved
- If anyone else witnessed the incident
- What tactics were used
- How your children reacted
- How the bully and bystanders responded

Don't Be the Bully

Don't say, "Stick up for yourself" or "If you get a black eye the other guy better have two black eyes." Telling already frightened and scared children to stand up to the bully by fighting back is placing them at risk for more harm.

Do Be the Teacher

Teach your kids safety strategies by showing them nondefensive reactions to defusing the situation (e.g., avoiding). Coach them on the three D's of when and how to involve adults to help. I will cover specific strategies later in the chapter.

Don't Be the Rescuer

Don't say, "Leave it to me, I'll take care of it." It can be very embarrassing for your children if they have Mom sort out their problems.

They may perceive your response to mean that you believe they are weak, incapable of dealing with the situation, and incapable of being a part of the solution. Likewise, if your children have a learning disability, they may have enough to deal and cope with without the whole school knowing that there is yet another thing they are unable to deal with on their own. Also, threatening the bully yourself, while occasionally successful, is probably not a good idea. The bully may just decide to pick on another child for a while.

Do Be the Collaborator

Collaborate with your children to deal with the situation and generate solutions to the problem. Boost their sense of empowerment and control by involving them in the process and working as a team. Reassure them that the situation can be handled discreetly and safely. By asking them the questions listed below, your kids can explain what they have already tried to fix the problem, and what they need to help make things right. Ask the following.

1. Who else have you spoken to?
2. How you have dealt with this so far?
3. Do you feel safe?
4. What have you tried before to help make it stop?
5. What worked and what didn't?
6. What do you think needs to happen to make things right?
7. How do you think I can be helpful? What would you like me to do?
8. What steps can be taken to make you feel safe?
9. How can we make sure this doesn't happen again?
10. What can we do to help you?
11. Will this make things better?
12. What do you think we can do to avoid this from happening again?

CASE STUDY—PART 2

Information Gathered

You spoke to Beth when she came home. She said she thought things were going well at her new school since all the popular girls were being so nice to her. Then she found out that one of them had posted mean rumors about her on a website. When she asked the girls why they were being so mean, they just laughed in her face and called her more names. Beth cried herself to sleep at night and started going to the nurse's office, complaining of a stomachache to avoid the girls during study hall.

Phase 2: Discern Your Options

Our goal must be to raise children who can handle the bumps and bruises the world has in store. We need to prepare them to cope with difficult challenges and bounce back. We must help them find happiness even when things aren't going their way. We want them to develop deep, strong roots now so that their wings will carry them successfully and independently into the future.

Dr. Kenneth Ginsburg,
Author and Professor of Pediatrics at
the University of Pennsylvania School of Medicine

Now that you have discovered your kids' stories, the next step is to discern how to help your children cope. Many children who are targets of bullying need to learn to trust again, to win back their strength as individuals, and to improve their self-esteem. They need to understand what happened to them and learn why it occurred. They also need the right tools to prevent bullying from ever happening again. Because there are no good or bad people, just desirable and undesirable behavior, you can teach your children the tools and skills needed to deal with dominant behavior and help them become resilient to bullying. As you use and teach these skills, keep in mind that each child's journey along the road to resilience will be different. What works for one child may not work for another child.

 TIP

Research indicates that individuals who daily have 3 times as many positive emotions as negative emotions (3-to-1 ratio) are more likely to be resilient and have a successful reintegration.

Donald Meichenbaum, Ph.D.
Research Director, The Melissa Institute

What Is Resilience?

Resilience is the process of adapting well and the capacity to bounce back from adversity, trauma, tragedy, threats, or other significant sources of stress.[1] Resilience describes one's ability to recover from or adjust easily to all the changes and misfortune an individual experiences day by day. We are not born with resilience.[2] Resilience is not a trait that individuals either have or do not have. Rather, it involves behaviors, thoughts, and accompanying feelings that can be nurtured, developed, and learned.

 TOOLBOX TACTIC

Explore Resilience

Teach your children about resilience and what it means to be resilient. Resilience is the ability to handle stress and respond positively to difficult events. Children can build their own resilience, much like building muscles, by practicing special bounce back strategies.

Use a ball to demonstrate. Explain that even though a ball falls and hits the hard floor, it manages to rebound and bounce back so you can catch it. Now bridge how the ball can represent your children's lives. Ask them the following.

- How are you like the ball?
- Have you been able to overcome obstacles before? If so, how?
- Think back to a time when you faced up to your fears. How did you get through it? What did you do? What did you say to yourself? How did you feel when you overcame the obstacle?
- What kinds of situations have been most stressful for you?
- How have those situations typically affected you?
- To whom have you reached out for support to work through your stressful experience?
- What have you learned about yourself and your interactions with others during difficult times?
- Has it been helpful for you to assist someone else going through a similar experience?
- What has helped make you feel more hopeful about the future?

POINT TO PONDER

What Characterizes Resilient Children?

1. Sociability (form healthy relationships)
2. Optimism (positive view of self and future)
3. Flexibility (change is part of life)
4. Self-confidence (move toward goals, base decisions on confidence in one's abilities)
5. Competence (be good at something and take pride in it)
6. Achievement orientation
7. Community engagement
8. Access to positive adult models
9. Insightfulness (understand people and situations, be able to see other sides)
10. Perseverance (don't give up)
11. Perspective (view crises as challenges to be faced, not insurmountable obstacles)
12. Self-control (manage strong feelings and impulses; internalization of locus of control)

What characteristics do you think exemplify your children the most? The least? How have you helped foster these resilient traits in your children?

www.melissainstitute.org

Because we are role models for our children, by viewing challenges as opportunities for growth, we display a resilient mindset. We are the models who demonstrate healthy coping strategies. We are the ones who, through our examples, make it safe for our children to admit their vulnerabilities and personal limitations. What we do to model healthy resilience strategies for our children is more important than anything we say about them.

TOOLBOX TACTIC

Six Steps to Teaching Life Skills

Do you know how to work effectively with your children and prepare them to use the antibullying strategies needed to deal with being bullied? Over the years, I've come to realize that not all parents know how to teach their children various information. You may know what type of information you need to cover, but how you reinforce the information is a different story. Therefore, listed below is a six-step model you can use that will help you teach, show, practice, and reinforce your children's repertoire of life skills.[3]

1. Instruction (teach)—Present an overview of the social, emotional, or thinking skill. Talk about the benefits of the skill in enhancing relationships as well as the risks for not learning the skill. For example, when teaching the social skill of being assertive, ask your children, "What does being assertive mean to you? How is being assertive different than being aggressive?" Then talk about the differences between assertiveness and aggression.

2. Modeling (show)—Model what being assertive looks like to your children. This will help your children visualize the process. The model can be live (you) or a media simulation (a movie).

3. Discussion (process)—Invite discussion of the skill that was just modeled. Did any of the situations observed remind you of a time that you used the skill? Were there any barriers to success?

4. Role-play (practice)—Allow your children to attempt the desired behavior in a safe environment. Assign the roles, and set the stage to practice. For example, have your child be the bully and you be your child, the target. Have a friend or siblings be the bystanders. Set the stage for the role playing. Ask, for example, "Where will you be talking? What will be the time of day? What will you be doing?" Coach and prompt role player(s) when needed.

5. Feedback (reinforce skill)—Mix general praise with corrective or constructive feedback. How well were the behavioral steps followed? What did your children like? Dislike?

6. Own work (apply skill)—Practice this "homework" in and out of school and the home. Your children need to be able to transfer their newly developed skills to real-life situations. Application also strengthens these skills.

All of these components are used to reinforce desired behavior. For example, social skills are generally acquired through learning (e.g., observation, modeling, rehearsing, and feedback) and are maximized through social reinforcement (e.g., receiving positive responses from one's environment). Deficits or excesses in social performance can be remediated through direct instruction and modeling. Behavioral rehearsal and coaching reinforce learning. Hence, your children need these skills to combat dysfunctional behaviors and enhance their resilience during stressful events.[3]

A Road Map to Building Resilience

Children need to develop their social and emotional resilience by developing their social survival skills so they can create true friendships, build a supportive network, and block bullying. The following is a roadmap to resilience. It details a variety of antibullying skills and strategies that you and your children can use to bolster resilience and deal with the effects of bullying. The goal is to help your children move from viewing themselves as victims, to survivors, and even to the point of becoming thrivers (i.e., helping others and transforming their pain into something good).

In all of the strategies listed below, help your children practice what to do by role playing difficult bullying scenarios. Help them identify strategies for dealing with a bully and the positive, appropriate responses for each situation. Confidently handling a bully is not easy and may not come naturally for your children. So provide honest feedback on their responses, actions, body language, tone of voice, etc.

First Stop: Teach Adaptive Coping Strategies

The best protection against unsafe, worrisome behaviors is to teach your children positive, adaptive coping strategies. Research suggests that children who are victimized are better able to self-soothe emotionally and to self-protect if they use adaptive coping skills.[4] These include positive self-talk, reality checking, and deep breathing. When kids possess a variety of healthy coping strategies they are less likely to turn to dangerous quick fixes when stressed and are better prepared to overcome life's challenges.

By using adaptive coping strategies, children can become more competent in the way that they think, feel, and behave in stressful situations. Competence, which is the ability or know-how to handle situations effectively, is acquired through actual experience. Children cannot become competent without first developing a set of skills that allows them to trust their judgments, make responsible choices, and face difficult situations.[5] We undermine competence when we do not allow our children to raise themselves after a fall (i.e., rescue them). On the contrary, when we notice what our children are doing right and give them opportunities to develop important skills, they feel competent.[5]

POINT TO PONDER

In thinking about your children's competence and how to reinforce it, ask yourself the following.[6]

1. Do I help my children focus on their strengths and build on them?
2. Do I notice what they do well or do I focus on their mistakes?
3. When I need to point out a mistake, am I clear and focused or do I communicate that I believe they always mess up?
4. Do I help them recognize what they have going for themselves?
5. Am I helping them build the educational, social, and stress reduction skills necessary to make them competent in the real world?
6. Do I communicate in a way that empowers my children to make their own decisions or do I undermine their sense of competence by giving them information in ways they can't grasp? In other words, do I lecture them or do I facilitate their thinking?
7. Do I let them make safe mistakes so they have the opportunity to right themselves or do I try to protect them from every trip and fall?
8. As I try to protect them, does my interference mistakenly send the message, "I don't think you can handle this?"
9. Do I recognize the competencies of each of my children without comparing them to their siblings?

Use Positive Self-talk

Using positive self-talk can help your children change how they think (cognitive strategies) about certain events or situations. There is an interplay between our thoughts, feelings, and behaviors. Our thoughts can lead us to assume things will automatically happen based on our experiences. For example, if I am kind (belief), then other people will like me (assumption). Furthermore, thoughts that quickly pop into your head affect how we feel (angry, calm, relaxed, tense) and what we do (avoid or confront new challenges, give up or continue to try). Thoughts can be adaptive or maladaptive.[7] Using Beth's example in the case study, her belief that no one likes her leads her to assume that people are out to make fun of her. She feels sad and, subsequently, stays home on her own. In her mind, Beth convinced herself that if she goes out, she'll end up sitting by herself, so why bother. Even though many incidents have proven contrary to her belief, her self-talk and anxiety cause her to think that things will go wrong and to expect bad things to happen.

So how can you help your children avoid this negative trap? Help them identify and challenge their maladaptive, negative self-talk and replace it with more positive thoughts. Positive self-talk is a way of helping us to take more notice of achievements. The following are helpful statements your children can use to help them focus their thinking on more positive, constructive thoughts. Have them write the following on note cards. Then post the cards in their rooms or throughout the house. These will act as reminders that they are strong and they can overcome obstacles.

- I know I can do this.
- In a while these unpleasant feelings will pass. Accept them and calm down.
- Keep breathing—in through my nose and out slowly through my mouth.
- I don't like feelings of panic, but I know I can bear them.
- Nothing bad will happen if I work hard to calm down.
- One step at a time—calm down.
- This is difficult, but each step I take is a step forward.
- Remember to distract myself—think of something calming.
- Focus on a positive object and calm down. Stretch my arms and legs. Feel the tension slowly dissolve.
- I don't like feeling uncomfortable, but I know I can bear it.

TOOLBOX TACTIC

Have your children write down some of their negative thoughts at the end of each day. Then help them change their maladaptive thoughts to positive, coping self-talk using the following template.[7]

- My negative thoughts were...
- Check my thoughts and see if I have missed anything positive.
- The positive things I missed were...
- What would be my positive self-talk?
- Now change to coping self-talk.

CASE STUDY—PART 3

Changing Beth's Self-Talk

1. The situation or event that makes me feel anxious or worried is going to class with the popular group girls and sitting in study hall. They usually comment on my appearance or make fun of me because they think I am weird or nerdy. No one talks to me when I am in there.

2. The thoughts that make me feel anxious are I think I am not worth spending time with anybody. I will never be good enough. I think I am a loser.

3. My positive self-talk is I'm doing well. I am halfway through study hall. I'm almost to the end. Janie just told me "Hi." That was nice. I can do this.

4. My coping self-talk is:
   - I'm feeling relaxed, I'm in charge, and I want to stay to the end.
   - I am strong and intelligent.
   - I am special, unique, and very important.
   - I do not require the approval of anyone, except myself, to be happy.
   - I love myself for my own uniqueness and value.
   - I am beautiful, both inside and out.
   - I am kind, loving, and smart.
   - I am industrious and continue to accomplish great things.

Use Relaxation and Calming Strategies

Reinforce that your kids must not lose their composure. Doing so will only make matters worse. Bullies try to unnerve people. So it is important that your children do not let them. When we get stressed, we get very tense. Relaxation strategies can help us calm our physical reactions, self-regulate more effectively, and cope with and manage our anxiety and stress. These strategies are employed to slow down the heart rate, relax the muscles, and use self-talk and visual cues (imagining pictures in the mind) to prompt better coping.[8] Practice with your kids how to relax physically. Using a series of short exercises, have them tense all of the major muscle groups in the body for about 3–5 seconds and then relax. Tense each muscle group twice, but try not to move the muscle after you have tensed it.

TOOLBOX TACTIC

Quick Relaxation Exercise

Sit in a comfortable chair with your feet flat on the floor, or lie down flat on your bed or floor. Close your eyes. If uncomfortable, just gaze down at the floor.

- Arms and hands: Clench your fists and push your arms straight out in front of you.
- Legs and feet: Push your toes downward, gently raise your legs, and stretch your legs out in front of you.
- Stomach: Push out your tummy muscles, take a breath, and hold it.
- Shoulders: Scrunch up your shoulders.
- Neck: Push your head back against the chair or bed.
- Face: Scrunch up your face, squeeze your eyes tightly, and push your lips together.[8]

When you feel you are ready, open your eyes. How was that? Did you notice any new sensations while you were breathing? How do you feel now? Do you feel more relaxed and calm? Focused? Centered?

For younger children, muscles can be tensed and stretched by playing games like Simon Says or Hokey Pokey.

Practice with your kids how to control breathing. Controlled breathing is a quick way to concentrate and gain control of our breathing.

Have your children slowly take a deep breath in, hold it and count to 4, then breathe out while counting to 5. As you and your kids do this, tell yourselves to relax. Doing this a few times can help your children regain control of their bodies and help to feel calmer.

TOOLBOX TACTIC

Props to Help Teach Controlled Breathing

- Use a pinwheel or dandelions to teach deep breathing.
- Blow bubbles to teach slow, gentle, and controlled breathing.
- Use bubble gum to slow down breathing by blowing a big bubble without popping it.

Another strategy to help your children to relax is to boss back the fear.[8] Encourage your children to boss the fear or anxiety, using a toy or puppet, by shouting out cognitive restructuring statements such as "I am stronger than my fear" or "I am strong and brave" at a chosen object. Doing this may help your children gain power over their fears. It may make the name calling seem less hurtful.

TOOLBOX TACTIC

Focus on the Positives

Help your children discover positive aspects and events that have occurred in their lives to help them overcome their "stinking thinking."

- Have them think about the things that they are GOOD at, anything positive about themselves, or who DOES like them in order to help them keep calm in a difficult situation. Have them list these aspects on an index card to act as a reminder.
- Have them gather little reminders like a favorite photo, an encouraging letter, or tickets from a special trip (i.e., things that they find pleasant). These can help them focus on the good things and feel better by thinking about them.

- Have them compose a love letter to themselves using the following template.[9]

Dear _____ ,

    Have I told you lately how much I value and respect you? Though I have known you for a long time, your _____ still amazes me. To me you are beautiful, especially your _____ and your _____ . I was especially proud of you when _____ . I also admire you when _____ . Remember, you are a truly lovable person. Two of your most lovable traits are your _____ and your _____ . Although there are many wonderful people in the world, there's nobody quite like you!

                                                              I love you.

                                 _____

If someone makes a nasty remark to them, they will need to remember this list of good things. Repeat to themselves, "I am a worthy person. I am a good person. I am a likeable person."

TOOLBOX TACTIC

Visualize and Practice to Be Successful

Option One

When faced with a new or challenging situation, teach your children to visualize calming pictures. Think about some place that makes you happy. It could be somewhere you have been or an imaginary place. Create a picture of it in your head. Make the picture as restful and peaceful as possible. Try to make the picture as real as you can. Think about the following: the noise of the waves crashing on the beach, the wind blowing in the trees, the smell of the sea, the scent of flowers in the air, the warm sun shining on your face, or the wind blowing gently in your hair.

Option Two

Teach your children to visualize how they can meet a challenging situation. Help them talk themselves through what will happen.[6] By doing this, your children can be better prepared to meet the challenge and remain calm.

Have them think about past bullying situations. Were there things that they could have done differently that could have resulted in a different outcome?

Step 1: Imagine the challenge.

Make the picture as real as possible. Describe the challenge in plenty of detail. Think about:

- Who will be there.
- The time of day.
- What you are wearing.
- The colors, smells, and sounds.

Step 2: Now think about what will happen.

- What will you do?
- What will you say?
- What will the other people do?
- What will they say?
- What will happen?

Practice this several times to prepare your children for an encounter with a bully and help them see themselves as successful.

Second Stop: Teach Safety Strategies

The best way to help keep your children safe is to help change what they do (behavior strategies). A confident, positive, and resilient appearance can stop bullying from continuing. Assertive techniques can help kids feel confident, resist peer pressure, and defend themselves and others who are bullied. So help your children make the shift from exhibiting passive behaviors and showing fear to displaying empowerment.

TOOLBOX TACTIC

To practice assertive skills, have your children listen to how other people they know or how people in films or on TV talk. See if your kids can point out if a person's response is assertive, aggressive, or passive. Have them repeat some of the comments using different voice tones—gentle, firm, sarcastic, loud, and monotone. Discuss how the responses can be interpreted differently since the message was delivered in several different ways. Then discuss and rehearse how your children might respond to a bully. Help them come up with a list of responses to verbal aggression.

Verbally Disarm

Name calling and taunting are a bully's weapon. So if your children can find a way not to let the words hurt them, the bully has no power. You can teach your children several verbal strategies to act unimpressed. These strategies will give your kids a quick reply to surprise or disarm the bully and walk off confidently. If accomplished in public, these techniques can elicit laughter from surrounding peers or victims and be aimed at the bully. This is a bully's worst nightmare. He or she is dethroned from a position of power over your children. Given that these techniques are tricky to learn, each of your kids really needs to practice them.

- Use an assertive, not an aggressive, voice when standing up for yourself. For example, placing a "no" or "I" at the beginning of a sentence gives it more emphasis. Instead of saying, "Sorry, but I don't want to do that" a child could say "No, I don't want to do that."
- Use fogging (admit the characteristic) in soft but firm comebacks. For example, when the bully says, "Ian, you sure are fat," your child could say, "You're right, I need to lose weight." If the bully says, "You have a big nose," your child could reply, "Yes, I do, don't I." In both incidences, the child accepts what the bully says, agrees with it, then moves on.
- Admit the obvious (point out that the bully sees the obvious) such as "Wow! You noticed I have zits."
- Use a routine response like "OK" or "whatever" to imply that the child is not bothered by the bully's comment.
- Use a sense of humor. Remember, don't make the bully feel like he or she is being laughed at. For example, if the bully says, "You sure do have a lot of zits on your face," your child could say, "I know. Sometimes I feel like I am a pepperoni pizza."
- Sound like a broken record by repeating "What did you say?" or "That's your opinion," or "So."
- Expose the ignorance of the bully. If the bully is teasing your child because because he or she has a medical problem or disability, counter the comment by telling the bully the facts of the condition. For example, my son has verbal dyspraxia, a neurologically based disorder that impairs the organization of movement. It causes him to have difficulty with tying his shoelaces, handwriting, and producing sounds, syllables, and words. He was being teased and made fun of because of the way he wrote on the board or spoke certain words. So we practiced how he could respond to the bullies' comments. He replied, "I know my writing is not great, and I sometimes sound funny when I speak. This is because I have dyspraxia.

Sometimes my brain doesn't let me make certain movements and say certain sounds. So I guess Daniel Radcliffe, known as Harry Potter, and I are alike. We both can't tie our shoes, and our handwriting stinks."

- Avoid using jokes or making sarcastic comments to try to prove that there is nothing the bully can do to hurt your child's feelings. This will only please the bully. It will actually add to the ridicule and humiliation, lowering your child's self-esteem.
- Avoid insulting a bully, particularly if he or she has a history of physically bullying others. This will more than likely instigate a conflict that your child cannot win. Instead of exacerbating the situation, tell your child to walk away with dignity while saying, "I have better things to do with my time." Remember, it is difficult to talk sense to an irrational person. Therefore, removing oneself from the situation may be a safer option.

Hold Emotional Reactions

Help your children show minimal emotional reactions to the bullying. It is natural to get upset by the bullying. However, that is what bullies thrive on—fear, attention, and things (FAT). They feel more powerful and gain satisfaction from emotional reactions. So reacting to bullies may only encourage them further. Help your children develop strategies to hold hurt feelings or other emotional reactions when in front of the bully. Teach your children to wait until they are in a safe, bully-free place before letting out their emotions. A word of caution—there is a downside to this strategy. Most children who bully enjoy the action in and of itself and feel confident, courageous, protected, and safe in tormenting your children. If they see that your children are not reacting as expected or not suffering from their actions, they may persist even further to get the reaction they seek. Therefore, this withholding tactic may backfire depending on the bully. So read the situation carefully. That being said, you can help your children hold in emotional reactions by teaching them the following.

- Wear a poker face until they are clear of any danger. Smiling or laughing at a bully may provoke the bully to retaliate. The bully may interpret the response to mean your children are making fun of him or her.
- Do not react by crying, looking flustered, or appearing upset.
- Cool down. Over the years, my younger students have told me that it has been helpful to practice cool down strategies such as counting to 10, writing down the bully's angry words, or taking deep breaths.

Look Calm and Act Confidently

Your children must do their best to act bravely and confidently. Encourage them to be confident and believe in themselves. True confidence, which is the solid belief in one's own abilities, is rooted in competence.[5] Children gain confidence by demonstrating their competence in real situations. They need confidence to be able to navigate the world, think outside the box, and recover from challenges.[5] Unfortunately, many victimized children's body language—their posture, face, and body movements—send nonverbal signals that they lack confidence. Stooping, avoiding eye contact, fidgeting, and similar gestures show that your children lack confidence. Bullies feed on the fear that they create in other kids. If your children don't give off that fear, the bully may move on and leave your children alone. So teach your children how to look calm, even if they aren't and to act confidently even when they do not feel it. Relaxation techniques can help. Your children remaining calm at all times will puzzle and frustrate a typical bully as he or she attempts to elicit a negative reaction. So help your children practice the following strategies to help them stand, walk, and talk in a way that appears more calm, assertive, and confident.

- Stand up tall with your head held up. Keep your back straight and your shoulders back. Hold your arms beside your body. Don't hold your arms up like you want to fight.
- Don't cry and run off. Instead, move closer, turn sideways, and make nonthreatening eye contact.
- When making eye contact, don't shift your gaze down and look around. Look straight at the bully. If it is too difficult, then focus on the bully's eyebrows. Looking people straight in the eye helps makes them think you are confident. Word of advice—if you look away, you cannot see the potential nasty sucker punch that may come your way.
- Keep your facial expressions neutral. Don't look sad, and don't look angry.
- Speak up to intimidate the bully. Do not be timid, hesitant, or whiny. Practice speaking firmly, loudly, and with assurance. Watch that your tone of voice is not sarcastic. Use the verbal strategies previously described.[8]
- Walk with a purpose and with a "don't you dare attitude" so as not to appear to be a victim. Walk with a relaxed gait but with energy and confidence.

POINT TO PONDER

When thinking about how confident your children are, consider the following questions.[6]

1. Do I see the best in my children so they can see the best in themselves?

2. Do I clearly express that I expect the best qualities (not achievements but personal qualities such as fairness, integrity, persistence, and kindness) in them?

3. Do I help them recognize what they have done right or well?

4. Do I treat them as incapable children or as youngsters who are learning to navigate the world?

5. Do I praise them often enough? Do I praise them honestly about specific achievements or do I give such diffuse praise that it doesn't seem authentic? (More information about praising effectively is later in this chapter.)

6. Do I catch them being good when they are generous, helpful, and kind or when they do something without being asked or cajoled?

7. Do I encourage them to strive just a little bit further because I believe they can succeed? Do I hold realistically high expectations?

8. Do I unintentionally push them to take on more than they can realistically handle, causing them to stumble and lose confidence?

9. When I need to criticize or correct them, do I focus on only what they're doing wrong or do I remind them that they are capable of doing well?

10. Do I avoid instilling shame in my children?

CASE STUDY—PART 4

Beth's Plan for the Day to Help Keep Her Safe

Help Beth develop a plan for the day to help her deal with challenging situations and keep her safe. This is an example of Beth's action plan to help keep her safe.

Before Going to School

Plan by Getting Ready—Before going to school, I will mentally and emotionally prepare for the day to succeed by repeating the following.

• This is going to be tough, but I can handle it.

- I'll take a few deep breaths beforehand.
- Let me think about what I have to do.
- Here's my plan for how to deal with this.
- Don't take it personally.
- Don't jump to conclusions.
- No matter what other people say or do to me, I am still a good person.

During School

Act Face to Face—To help deal with challenging situations, face my fears, and get in the middle of it, I will tell myself the following:

- If I stay cool, I'll be in control.
- Stick to the issues.
- Don't let the bully rattle me.
- I don't need to prove myself.
- I can handle it.
- I have a right to my point of view.

Cope Before It's Too Much—I will use self-talk when I feel overwhelmed, when my feelings are getting out of control, or when the situation becomes difficult. I can handle the situation without feeling that I am losing control. I have to remember to do the following.

- I'm getting tense, so I better breathe.
- The bully wants me to get angry, but I'm not going to.
- Don't let the bully bother me.
- Let the bully make a fool of himself or herself.
- There's no shame in leaving and coming back later.
- It isn't worth getting all stressed out.
- It won't last much longer.
- I'm not giving the control over to the bully.

After School or Following the Situation

Evaluate Afterwards—When reviewing how I did for the day, I was able to remain calm, not get nervous, tell the bully, "Yes, I have a huge zit on my face. Didn't you know I converted to Hinduism?" and walk away. The strategy worked. The bully did not follow me but left me alone."

Note: for this step, have the child analyze the situation, review what he or she did, and note some positives. After the resolution have the child say the following.

If resolved:

- It worked out pretty well.
- It wasn't as bad as I expected.
- I did it!

If unresolved:

- I'll do better next time.
- I can do it differently next time.
- Forget about it.
- Thinking about it only keeps it alive.
- These are tough situations, and they take time to figure out.

Use Empowering Language

Another strategy for deflecting an insulting comment is to use the word "I" rather than "you." "You" statements imply a negative judgment about a person. "I" statements communicate what a person is experiencing without putting the blame on anyone else. "I" messages can be used when someone's behavior renders us uncomfortable or interferes with our wants, needs, or rights. By using "I" messages to confront a bully's behavior, we avoid attacking and blaming the person, take responsibility for our feelings, and evade any defensiveness. Constructing "I" messages has three components.

- Part 1 tells others how you feel about a situation. This can be helpful to those who may not understand your feelings.
- Part 2 tells others what caused you to feel the way you do.
- In Part 3, you ask others to treat you differently and suggest what they might do to help the situation.

For example, when the child who is bullied says, "You make me mad," he or she allows the bully to have power since the victim blames the bully for the way he or she feels. Instead, the victim needs to take back power by acknowledging that he or she had a reaction to what the bully just said. For example, the victim could say, "I feel confused because you say you are my friend. Then again, I was not invited to your party." The child should gain control over his or her emotions.

TOOLBOX TACTIC

Preparing "I" Messages

Have your children think of a situation where they were in conflict with another person. Have them describe the details of the situation in 3 or 4 sentences.

- Have them write down 3 "you" statements that people might use when they are frustrated or angry about the situation.
- Now have them write down 3 "I" statements that they could have used instead.

Using the three components of "I" message construction, have your kids write three "I" messages that tell the person how they feel, what caused them to feel that way, and what they need from the person to make things right.

- Step 1: "I feel..."
- Step 2: "because..."
- Step 3: "I want or need..."

CASE STUDY—PART 5

Beth's "I" Message

Part 1

"I feel angry."

Part 2

"I feel angry when you call me a tramp."

Part 3

"I feel angry when you throw my hat on the floor. Please don't do that."

Operate Around Hot Zones

Help your children to function around the bully and spot unsafe hot zones so they can find a safe escape route. The goal is to try to avoid the bully in school and social situations as much as possible and to escape as quickly as possible. Keep the bully guessing where your children may be located. If the bully cannot find them, then he or she cannot bully them. Here are some strategies to discuss with your children.

- If you see the bully coming, walk in a different direction but do not show that you are intentionally avoiding him or her. Bullies are usually good at reading your reaction as fear and success. He or she will bully you more as a result. So don't act scared, and don't make eye contact. Slowly turn around and walk the other way. Pretend to be putting books or objects into your locker or talking to a friend to avoid initiating contact.
- Never walk alone. Join others nearby for support.
- If the bully uses the same route as you, try a different way. For example, if you walk to and from school, take an alternate route. If you ride the bus, carpool with a friend or have a parent or trusted adult drive you to and from school.

Defend Oneself

It is very important to learn self-defense. Self-defense is protection from harm. Sometimes it is physical. Sometimes it is running or evading a problem in other ways. Certainly, your children can tell the bully, "STOP IT!" and walk away. They can stick their hands out in front of them and tell the bully to leave them alone. However, these strategies may not always work (and they usually don't). What happens if the bully starts to get physical, like throwing a punch or making any other type of physical contact? How could your children defend themselves? Your children may need to fight to stop themselves from being physically hurt. Learning a martial art can prepare your children to defend themselves in a fight if they are pushed into a corner.

> *As a child, I was small, Asian and lousy at sports which made me an ideal target for the school bullies. Then I discovered martial arts. However, the martial arts training as a youth didn't just teach me about fighting, it also taught me a lot about discipline and actually ways to avoid violence. The news got around the school and by the time I was an intermediate level martial arts student, the bullies never targeted me again. So, I never even had to use the fighting aspect to protect myself from the bullies in a fight as it was more of a deterrent now.*
>
> Clint Cora
> Speaker, Author, & Karate World Champion
> *www.clintcora.com*

If you decide to pursue this course of action, I suggest choosing a fighting style that teaches strikes, hand-to-hand combat, and ground fighting so your children can be effective on their feet and/or on the ground. Of course, fighting should be used as a last resort. However, if they are forced into a confrontation and feel that a fight is going to happen, there are several things they can do to protect themselves. Teach and practice the following.

1. Tighten your stomach in case the bully tries to punch you there.
2. Turn a little sideways so your body is not as big of a target.
3. If the bully's grabbing you or pushing you, use this to your advantage. While trying really hard to keep your balance, grab one of the bully's arms with your left hand and hit his or her elbow with the other. Then use your left hand to push away the remaining arm.
4. Put your hands up by your face, as if you are talking with your hands, to protect against a sucker punch or an unprovoked punch by the bully.
5. Hitting the nose blurs the eyes and causes pain. It just might leave your opponent dazed long enough to get away.
6. Use low kicks if you are at arm's reach. Low kicks should be aimed toward shins, ankles, the insides or back of calves or thighs, and kneecaps (if the bully's legs are straight). Do not aim higher than the knee or waist height because the bully will grab your leg.
7. If the bully is male, quickly kick the groin, which will make him feel dazed and probably embarrassed, may give you the time needed to make a quick escape, get somewhere safe, and get help.
8. If kicking the groin does not work (because the bully can pivot and block your strike), try kicking the solar plexus (right below the ribs). Instead, kick a knee to make the person fall or trip. Run away and get help.
9. Scratching, biting, clawing, spitting, pulling hair, and attacking (i.e., poking) the eyes can also be used. You are defending yourself from a violent aggressor, not fighting in a ring with rules. Do anything you can to ensure your safety.
10. Keep moving so the bully cannot get you on the ground. If you're on the ground, bite, scratch, gouge, and so on to help get away.
11. Head butt your opponent fast and hard. Bring the top of your forehead down across the bully's nose and face. The "Glasgow kiss" has defeated many experienced fighters not prepared for it.

12. If others are ganging up on you, hit with outstretched fingers into the front of the throat, always remembering to keep your fingers closed together. Separated fingers are weaker!

TIP

> If fighting is imminent, tell your children to act and fight like they have nothing to lose and try to do it in public. Your children may think they will look ridiculous by being beat up in front of the entire school. However, this could offer the proof you and they need for the bully to be disciplined and the problem to be solved. Also, once the fight starts, your children should never stop punching, kicking, or whatever else comes to mind until the fight is officially over and they are out of danger. Tell your children, " You can rest, cry, shake, or change your clothes later in private. Remember you are fighting for survival, not for pleasure. So you have no cause for guilt of any kind. I will support you."

Use A Buddy System

When children are bullied at school, encourage them to walk around with a buddy. If their buddy is with them when a bully comes around, it is often easier to stand up to the bully. The bully may even walk away. Remember that the bully prefers your children to be alone. Children who are bullied should ask their friends to stay with them at times when there might be bullying (e.g., study time, break times, or lunchtimes). The buddy could be an older child, a relative, or a friend. Encourage them to be friendly with a lot of different groups of children. This will mean they will have plenty of kids to be with when they are at school. If their school offers clubs at lunchtime or study hall, have them think about inviting some of their friends to attend the events with them. These groups are also good ways of making new friends.

Third Stop: Bolster Self-Esteem

According to the National Association for Self-Esteem (*www.self-esteem-nase.org*), self-esteem is the "experience of being capable of meeting life's challenges and being worthy of happiness." Children with strong self-esteem feel good about themselves and are confident in their abilities.

Children who are confident do not tolerate bullying and refuse to let it get them down. You can bolster your children's self-esteem and confidence by reinforcing their strengths, giving them a chance to feel proud, and encouraging their potential. Showing interest in your children builds the foundation for strong self-esteem.[11] For example, ask about their likes, dislikes, and daily routines. Rather than asking them, "How was your day?" which usually elicits a generic response of "OK," be more specific. Instead, say something like the following. "Tell me about the take-down move you did at wrestling practice the other day." "Tell me, what did you think of the movie?" "Tell me about your new friend Anna." "How was the field trip?" "What was the final score for the game?"

Catch your children doing good deeds and praise accordingly. "I really appreciated that you took the dishes out of the dishwasher. It was very thoughtful." Encourage your children to engage in fun activities such as sports, playing games, dancing, and singing since they increase self-esteem.[12] For more ways to bolster your children's self-esteem, check out *The Self-Esteem Workbook* by Glenn Schiraldi. More important is that children with self-esteem tend to have parents who model self-esteem. How have you modeled good self-esteem today?

TOOLBOX TACTIC

Have your children make an assessment of their self-esteem. What events or experiences in their lives have contributed most to their sense of competence or self-worth? Are there areas your kids actively avoid because they do not feel they can deal with them? In their opinion, what role have you (the parent) played in their development of self-esteem? Have them characterize what it was you did, whether beneficial or hindering. After discussing their findings, in your children's opinion, how and what can you do now to help bolster their self-esteem?

Fourth Stop: Encourage Friendships

Encourage your children to make new friends. Help them meet new friends outside of the school environment. A new environment can provide a new chance for your children because they won't be subjected to the negative stereotype other classmates may have about them. For most bullied children, the relentless loneliness is often hardest to bear. While all the other kids from school are hanging out together, going to parties, and having fun, your children are sitting at home, aching to be a part of the fun, and waiting for invitations that never come. Every child needs friends and a social life, especially children who are bullied. A quality friend can provide a cushion to harassment and prevent victimization. Children with at least one friend are less likely to be bullied. Having a best friend reduces the duration of bullying and both emotional and behavioral problems.[13,14]

Parents play a big role in teaching children how to make friends (*www.parentingscience.com*). You can help your children make and keep friends by fostering good conversational skills, interpersonal skills, emotional self-control, empathic concern, perspective taking, a willingness to compromise and offer help, and a willingness to share, take turns, and follow rules. (I will cover these skills in chapter 8.) How can you foster these skills? The most important influence begins at home with you and their relationship with their siblings. Children who have secure attachments with their parents have better quality friendships.[15] Furthermore, because getting along with other children is an important skill for forming friendships, teachers can help children make friends by organizing a buddy system or creating cooperative learning groups. To learn more about friendships, check out *Phoebe's Best Best Friend* by Barbara Roberts.

Encourage your children to make contact with calm and friendly students in their school, neighborhood, and extracurricular activities. You will probably have to teach your kids how to initiate and maintain friendships. Besides practicing conversational skills with you or with siblings at home, have your children make phone calls to or videochat with other people for practice. To initiate a conversation, children should remember five things.

1. Use body basics. Face the other person. Use eye contact. Use appropriate voice. Your expression should match what you say and your tone of voice. Use the right body posture. For example, sit squarely, with an open stance, lean forward, and relax.
2. Greet the other person. "Hi, I'm Alan. What's your name?" Extend your hand to shake hands.
3. Decide what to say before speaking. "This is my first meeting. How long have you been in the scouts?"

4. Wait for the appropriate time. Read the person's body language to evaluate if the person seems like he or she has time to talk. For example, you don't want to interrupt the person if he or she is already talking to someone else or busy doing something that takes a lot of concentration. However, if you want to join in on a group, ask to join. "Hey, can I join your group?"
5. Start speaking. Find a common topic to discuss. For example, talk about activities included in the scouts program.

When holding or maintaining a conversation, kids should remember six things.

1. Use body basics.
2. Wait your turn.
3. Say what you want to say.
4. Listen to the other person.
5. Say at least two more things to the other person.
6. Make a closing remark.

When joining in a conversation, they should remember the following.

1. Watch others. Check out what the group is doing first, and determine if it's a group that you would like to join.
2. Watch yourself. Make sure you appear friendly and approachable, especially in your tone of voice and your posture.
3. Think before you speak.
4. Think about when to speak. Wait for a break in the conversation or the game before speaking.
5. Look at others straight in the eye when speaking to them.
6. Go with the flow of the group.
7. Find common interests and talk about them.
8. Ask a question that shows interest. This makes the other child or children feel very special.

In their book, *Children's Friendship Training*, Fred Frankel and Robert Myatt of the UCLA Semel Institute offer some tips for children who have trouble making friends and making conversation. They stress that children need to practice the art of "trading information." Tips to pass onto your children include the following.

- When starting a conversation with someone new, trade information about your likes and dislikes. Start with something non-threatening.
- Don't be a conversation hog. When engaged in a conversation, answer only the question at hand. Give your partner a chance to talk or ask a question.
- Don't be an interviewer. Don't just ask others questions, but offer information about yourself.
- Don't tease or criticize others.
- Don't brag about yourself.
- Don't take charge and try to control the behavior of other children.
- Don't stand too close or too far away from other children.

TOOLBOX TACTIC

Friendship Assessment

Have your children complete the My Friendship Mirror checklist below to understand how well or not so well they are doing as friends. A maximum 54 points can be earned on this activity. The higher the score, the better the friendship skills are. Explain that the kind of friend they are is mirrored by the kind of friends they hang out with. When your children are finished, discuss the results. Develop a plan of action to make or maintain friendships. Tell your children to imagine themselves looking into a mirror and asking themselves the following.

- How important is it to have good friends?
- How my friends treat me is a direct reflection of how I treat my friends. What kind of a friend am I?

Tip: Remind your kids that they cannot expect their friends to treat them better than they treat their friends. Periodically, your kids may need to look at what kind of friends they are so they can see where they need to improve in order to maintain good friendships.

Have your children complete the personal friendship assessment, My Friendship Mirror.

My Friendship Mirror

Directions: Rate yourself as a friend by putting an X on the line that best describes you. Be honest with yourself.

Almost   Sometimes   Almost
                                 Never

_____ _____ _____   1. I listen carefully when my friends talk to me.

_____ _____ _____   2. I am modest about my own accomplishments.

_____ _____ _____   3. I do not make fun of others.

_____ _____ _____   4. I give credit to others for their successes.

_____ _____ _____   5. I do what I promise; I am dependable.

_____ _____ _____   6. I can control my temper.

_____ _____ _____   7. I am interested in many different things.

_____ _____ _____   8. I am not rude.

_____ _____ _____   9. I can laugh at myself.

_____ _____ _____   10. I can admit when I am wrong.

_____ _____ _____   11. I am honest regardless of the situation or consequences.

_____ _____ _____   12. I am happy for my friends when they win or excel.

_____ _____ _____   13. I offer to help or share when needed.

_____ _____ _____   14. I can keep secrets when asked.

_____ _____ _____   15. I can share the spotlight easily.

_____ _____ _____   16. I respect what belongs to others.

_____ _____ _____   17. I am patient and kind when others make mistakes.

_____ _____ _____   18. I seldom argue with others.

Scoring Directions

To find your personal score, count the number of items in each column. Record that number in the number line (# _____) at the bottom of the column. Multiply those numbers by the numbers just below the line (× numbers). Record the answers on the next three lines. Add the three answers together for a total score.

_____ _____ _____ Count the number of ×s in each column.

× 3   × 2   × 1   Multiply by the number given at the left.

_____ _____ _____ Add the three scores together to see how your friendship skills are.

My total score _____ . Possible score = 54

Use the following guide to find out what your results mean.

- Scores 41 to 54 = You are doing quite well but must keep working to maintain your friendship skills.
- Scores 21 to 40 = You still have some work to do but are showing progress.
- Scores 1 to 20 = You need to work on developing your friendship skills. (As the parent, you must let a child who scores in this group know that he or she is not hopeless; maybe he or she had a bad day. Help your child look for ways to improve so that this does not serve as a blow to his or her self-esteem.)

Fifth Stop: Strengthen Social Skills

Social skills are an important part of life. Children need to learn these skills in order to get along and work with others in various settings. Social skills are communication, problem-solving, decision-making, self-management, and peer relational skills that allow one to initiate, build, and maintain positive social relationships with others. (These skills will be covered in chapter 8.) Bullied children can be at greater risk than others of being bullied again (even when the bullying has been dealt with) if they do not have the social skills to relate to others. Knowing how to deal with bullying and difficult people, not just at school but throughout life in social situations and at work, is a basic life survival skill. Having good social skills can help children who are bullied take care of themselves by learning to correct deficits in their interpersonal skills. Social skills teach kids how to share, control their emotions, manage their anger, and be a friend to others.

One way to reinforce good behavior is to role-play at home. For example, practice by role-playing how to initiate and maintain a conversation, how to join a group activity, how to be respectful, and how to be assertive. Reverse roles often so that your children have a chance to play not only themselves but also the role of the other person. This gives them the opportunity to see things from another person's perspective—an essential element in children's understanding their behavior and its impact on others. (See Perspective-Taking Skill in chapter 8.) For more information about how you can help your children develop better social skills, read *Raise Your Child's Social I.Q.: Stepping Stones to People Skills for Kids* by Cathi Cohen.

Sixth Stop: Build Supportive Social Networks and Connections

Building a strong family network to support your children through their inevitable disappointments and hurts can increase their sense of belonging to a wider world and feeling safe within it. Social support comes from people in your children's social network such as you—the parent, other family members, teachers, classmates, close friends, neighbors, and the school. Social support can take many forms. Emotional or caring support involves listening. Instrumental support provides time or resources. Informational support provides needed information. Appraisal support gives feedback. Establishing connections with people provides social support and strengthens resilience.

Children who are bullied need to learn successful social survival and communication skills to find true friends and belong to a supportive group. Supportive relationships offer children the security they need, which allows them to stand on their own and develop creative solutions to their problems. If your children are being bullied at school or elsewhere, help your kids build connections and friendships outside of that environment. Encourage your children to become involved in activities, clubs, or other organizations where they can participate with peers in an activity they enjoy and where they can feel successful. If they have a lot of different sets of friends, they won't feel as isolated if their peer group at school begins to leave them out. Local park departments and libraries are wonderful outlets and can be a lifeline for lonely teens. However, reach out to the ones that are located nearest to the next town over from where you live (one that doesn't feed into your children's school). You can ask the park or library to e-mail or fax you their list of organized activities for kids. More than likely, they will offer everything from soccer and cheerleading to dance to computer clubs to chess to reader's theater.

For example, one student told me that her mom enrolled her in a youth community theater program where she finally found other kids her own age that she fit in with. However, it is vital that you go to the next town. If children are being bullied at school and engage in a park activity with those same classmates, it defeats the purpose, which is to start fresh with new kids. You can achieve two objectives by enrolling your children in a park or library activity. On the days school feels especially lonely, your children have something to look forward to. Additionally, this new social outlet will likely boost your children's confidence. The more confident they are, the less of a target they will be at school. You will also have more time to address any bullying issues with the school.

TIP

Given that bullies are predators and look for the easiest victim, you should encourage and support your children's efforts to be good at something. Expertise in any area raises children's social currency among their peers, thereby lowering the odds that they will become victims. You can help alleviate your children's feelings of loneliness by finding them a source for support and friendship. However, you must act swiftly, act definitively, and follow up. Don't just print out the brochures from the park department and leave them on a table. Show them to your children, choose an activity together, and then pick up the phone and make it happen.

POINT TO PONDER

Use the following questions when considering how connected your children are to their family and to the broader world.[6]

1. Do we build a sense of physical safety and emotional security within our home?
2. Do my children know that I am absolutely crazy in love with them?
3. Do I understand that the challenges my children will put me through on their path toward independence are normal developmental phases, or will I take them so personally that our relationship will be harmed?

4. Do I allow my children to have and express all types of emotions or do I suppress unpleasant feelings? Are they learning that going to other people for emotional support during difficult times is productive or that it is shameful?

5. Do we do everything to address conflict within our family and work to resolve problems rather than let them fester?

6. Do we have a television and entertainment center in almost every room or do we create a common space where our family shares time together?

7. Do I encourage my children to take pride in the various ethnic, religious, or cultural groups to which we belong?

8. Do I jealously guard my children from developing close relationships with others or do I foster healthy relationships that I know will reinforce my positive messages?

9. Do I protect my friends' and neighbors' children just as I hope they will protect mine?

Seventh Stop: Inspire to Empower

Children have the ability and power to control the outcomes of their decisions and actions. They are not controlled by external events and people unless they choose to let others take over. Even though they may not be able to control another child's actions, they can control their own. Once they arrive at this realization, children are more likely to know that they have the ability to bounce back from challenging situations. On the other hand, if we as parents make all the decisions, children are denied the opportunities to learn control. Children who understand that privileges and respect are earned through demonstrated responsibility will learn to make wise choices and feel a sense of control. Reinforce that they have the power to seek out ways to change and cope. Keep reminding your kids that they do not have an unchangeable character flaw that leaves them a perpetual target. To help them gain or maintain self-control, reinforce the following five steps for success.

1. Stop, take a deep breath, and count to five.
2. Decide what the problem is and how you can deal with it.
3. Think about your choices and their consequences. You can:
   - Ignore the situation.
   - Tell yourself, "It's OK. I'm OK."

- Tell yourself to relax.
- Speak calmly.
- Compromise
- Say how you feel, using empowering statements (i.e., "I" statements).

4. Decide on your best choice.
5. Do it!

To strengthen your children's ability to remain in control, give them responsibility. For example, have them feed the dog every day. Provide opportunities for success, like becoming a member of a club. Encourage their efforts. For instance, you could say, "Keep up the hard work. I noticed you are a lot quicker." Help build up their strengths. You could say, "I noticed you enjoy writing poems. What do you think about enrolling in a poetry course?" When providing choices, ask your kids where they would like to go for a weekend trip, what movie they would like to see, or what restaurant they would recommend. Let them choose whether or not to spend their allowance on a new CD or new game. Give clear praise for trying new things ("Great job!"), not doing what peers are doing ("I'm so proud of you!"), or taking care of even the smallest of household or school responsibilities. For example, "I noticed you worked really hard at cleaning your room. All of your toys are in the storage bins."

We also need to provide and create opportunities for our children to experience success socially and emotionally *outside* of school by making sure they have opportunities to engage in activities with other like-minded individuals. In other words, they need to meet kids who share their interests and passions. Maybe your children could take a karate class or join a robotics club. Bullies are less likely to pick a target who is socially integrated in a group or who has a strong internal sense of self.

TIP

I'm in Control of My Worries

As children discover that worrying is unproductive, yet continue to worry, encourage them to set aside 5 to 15 minutes each day for worrying. Explain that this is the time for them to worry so they can use the rest of the day for more productive activities.[16]

POINT TO PONDER

Consider the following questions when considering how you have or have not fostered an empowering spirit.[6]

1. Do I help my children understand that life's events are not purely random and most things happen as a direct result of someone's actions and choices?
2. On the other hand, do I help my children understand that they aren't responsible for many of the bad circumstances in their lives (such as parents' separation or divorce)?
3. Do I help them think about the future but take it one step at a time?
4. Do I help them recognize even small successes so they learn that they can succeed?
5. Do I help them understand that no one can control all circumstances but that everyone can shift the odds by choosing positive or protective behaviors?
6. Do I understand that discipline is about teaching, not punishing or controlling? Do I use discipline as a means to help my children understand that their actions produce certain consequences?
7. Do I reward demonstrated responsibility with increased privileges?

Eighth Stop: Encourage Mentoring

Role models can be inspiring and provide valuable coping tips. Research shows that providing youths with consistent support through a well-supervised, long-term mentoring relationship improves grades and family relationships. Mentoring helps prevent children from starting to use drugs or alcohol.[17] Mentoring supports children during times of personal or social stress and provides guidance for decision making. Mentoring programs such as Big Brothers Big Sisters of America or Team-Works can help improve children's self-esteem, behavior, and decision-making ability and reduce high-risk behaviors. These programs also introduce children to social, cultural, and recreational activities that they may not have previously experienced.

You can encourage your children to become mentors. Peer mentoring can be an incredibly effective way for children to increase their self-confidence, build their self-esteem, increase their sense of responsibility, and improve academically.[18] It can also provide friendship, guidance, and support as children navigate new and ever more challenging circumstances.[20]

Ninth Stop: Encourage Altruism

If you wish to experience peace, provide peace for another.

Tenzin Gyatso, 14th Dalai Lama

Encourage and model altruistic behavior. Altruism involves doing for others without the expectation of receiving material rewards or reciprocity. Rather, the reward—feeling good about oneself—is helping to alleviate the pains of other people. Children who understand the importance of personal contribution or altruism gain a sense of purpose that can motivate them and empower them to take action. Nursing homes, community centers, and places of worship can benefit from kids' altruism by leading bingo games, babysitting, or making gift baskets for those in need. Plus, children who contribute to their communities and to the well-being of others receive gratitude rather than condemnation (like being bullied). Because they learn that contributing feels good, they may therefore more easily turn to others for help and do so without guilt or shame. So, involve your children in family charity decisions and encourage community service. Consider their interests. For example, do they like socializing? Helping out at a soup kitchen may be a good fit. Are they outdoor people? They may enjoy cleaning up the park. Kids who love to read may enjoy reading to younger kids at the local library. Finally, sports enthusiasts may enjoy teaching baseball or soccer to children with disabilities.

POINT TO PONDER

Before you can foster a sense of contribution in your children, consider the following.[6]

1. Do I communicate to my children (at appropriate age levels, of course) that many people in the world do not have as much human contact, money, freedom, and security as they need?
2. Do I teach the important value of serving others? Do I model generosity with my time and money?
3. Do I make clear to my children that I believe they can improve the world?
4. Do I create opportunities for each child to contribute in some specific way?
5. Do I search my children's circle for other adults who might serve as role models and who contribute to their communities and the world? Do I use these adults as examples to encourage my children to be the best they can be?

Tenth Stop: Keep the Dialogue Going

As parents, we are often overwhelmed by the responsibilities of daily life. Sometimes we are tired and irritable when we get home from work. The thought of going to one more place and doing one more thing is just too much. Let me just say this. Our own emotions and, most especially, logistics should never get in the way of helping our children. Make it a habit to talk to your children daily about what was good and not so good about their day. Praise what they attempted to handle in a positive way, and help them problem solve the rest. If talking about their day is routine in your house, your children will more likely share with you if they are being bullied. If your children are victims of bullying, never give up. Reinforce that they and other children in school have a right to feel safe and to feel that they belong in school.

POINT TO PONDER

Now that you have discovered a repertoire of coping and stress-reduction skills, ask yourself these basic questions.[6]

1. Do I help my children understand the difference between a real crisis and something that just feels like an emergency?
2. Do I consistently model positive coping strategies?
3. Do I allow my children enough time to use imaginative play? Do I recognize that fantasy and play are childhood tools to solve problems?
4. Do I guide my children to develop positive, effective coping strategies?
5. Do I believe that telling my children just to stop the negative behaviors will do any good?
6. Do I recognize that for many young people, risk behaviors are attempts to alleviate their stress and pain?
7. If my children participate in negative behaviors, do I condemn them for it? Do I recognize that I may only increase my children's sense of shame and therefore drive them toward more negativity?
8. Do I model problem solving step-by-step or do I just react emotionally when I'm overwhelmed?
9. Do I model the response that sometimes the best thing to do is conserve energy and let go of the belief that I can tackle all problems?

10. Do I model the importance of caring for our bodies through exercise, good nutrition, and adequate sleep?
11. Do I model relaxation techniques?
12. Do I encourage creative expression?
13. As I struggle to compose myself so I can make fair, wise decisions under pressure, do I model how I take control rather than respond impulsively or rashly to stressful situations?
14. Do I create a family environment in which talking, listening, and sharing are safe, comfortable, and productive?

Phase 3: Develop a Plan of Action

According to scientific analysis, when parents are more involved, their children are 30% more successful in school.

Parent Institute
www.parentinstitute.com

Now that you have discovered your children's stories and discerned how to help them cope, the third step is to develop an action plan and ways to end the bullying. This includes involving your children, contacting a mental health professional, and weighing the risks and benefits of contacting the school, the authorities, or the bully's parents.

Involving Your Children

Encourage to tell: If your children are the victims of bullying, encourage them to report it to a teacher, school counselor, or other responsible adults both in and outside of school as soon as possible to get it to stop. Teach the three D's for involving adults to help. If something is *dangerous, destructive,* or *disturbing,* tell an adult. Remind them that bullying meets these criteria. Therefore, be courageous and speak out against their own victimization as well as that of others. This is so everyone can stay safe. Reassure them by stating, "Do not worry about the bully taking revenge if you report the incident. He or she will more than likely continue to hurt you anyway, and appeasing the bully will not solve your problem." If your kids are scared to tell an adult on their own, they can ask friends to go with them. If their school has a peer support service, they can use it to report the bullying. If the school has a bullying reporting system, such as Stop.Walk.Talk (*stopwalktalk.org*) or Awareity (*www.awareity.com*), they can anonymously report an incident so school personnel can react accordingly. If they find it difficult to talk to anyone at school or at home, they can anonymously report an incident to one of the several free, anonymous online bully reporting systems found on the Internet such as Sprigeo (*www.sprigeo.com*), Bullystoppers.com (*www.bullystoppers.com*), or Word Bully 3.0 (*www.wordbully.net*). At least 11 states require that schools allow students to report bullying anonymously (*www.cyberbullying.us*).

TIP

According to one assistant principal at a middle school in San Diego, California, in the year since implementing their online anonymous bullying reporting form, school staff have been able to support students better in dealing with a difficult situation with minimal amount of time to investigate. The reports have allowed the school a chance to intervene and stop the cycle of bully behavior, prevent retaliatory fighting or worse, and enact more preventive than punitive action. He stated, "The majority of submissions have been legitimate instances where a student needed support...which included mediation between students who have had a disagreement, increased supervision during lunch periods to deter other students from demanding money, changing the direction of on campus cameras to observe acts of bullying during lunch, or parent contact to notify families that their student has been sending threatening messages via Facebook."

An example of the school's Bully Report form can be found at *http://www.sandi.net//cms/module/selectsurvey/TakeSurvey.aspx?SurveyID=808*

www.cyberbullying.us

If your children are older, you may wish to discuss with them how they would like to proceed and how you will proceed before contacting the school. On the other hand, if you are a parent of children in elementary school, you should contact the school as soon as possible. Regardless of their age, when talking to your children about reporting the situation, explain the difference between tattling and telling (see chapter 2). Remind them that reporting is done not to cause trouble for another child but to protect all children. Finally, validate that it takes courage to report bullying. Show them how the incident could be reported.

I believe that anyone can conquer fear by doing the things he fears to do, provided he keeps doing them until he gets a record of successful experiences behind him.

Eleanor Roosevelt
20th-Century American Stateswoman, First Lady

TOOLBOX TACTIC

A Child's Report of a Bullying Incident

Teach your child how to report bullying incidents to adults in an effective way. Adults are less likely to discount a child's report as tattling if the report includes

1. What is being done to him or her that makes the child fearful or uncomfortable
2. Who is doing the bullying
3. What the child has done to try to resolve the problem or to get the bully to quit
4. A clear explanation of what he or she needs from the adult (or what he or she wants the adult to do) to get the bully to quit

Contacting A Mental Health Professional

If you worry that your children are showing signs of distress, such as those mentioned in chapter 2 (withdrawal, depression, anxiety, and so on), feeling suicidal, or are having other health issues due to bullying, contact a health professional immediately. Seeking professional assistance early can lessen the risk of lasting emotional scars for your children. A child and adolescent psychiatrist or other mental health professional can help you, your children, other family members, and school officials develop a plan to deal with the bullying.

Involving the School

Although it is important to listen and problem solve with your children, it is not enough just to send them back to school to handle the situation alone. The bullying may not stop without adult help at school. Thus establish a partnership with school personnel to stop the bullying and achieve a long-term, positive resolution. By working with the school, you lead by example and send a clear message that bullying is wrong. So request a meeting with school personnel immediately. School personnel cannot help if they are unaware of the bullying. Keep in mind that your primary goal should be to obtain the school's cooperation to get the bullying to stop. Knowing your own children are being victimized can evoke strong feelings. However, you will secure much more cooperation from school personnel if you can stick to the facts without becoming overly emotional and accusing the school of failure. Although you may want assurance that everyone involved is punished severely, try to focus on putting an end to the bullying!

All children are entitled to courteous and respectful treatment by students and staff at school. It is the school's responsibility to ensure that students have a safe learning environment. Fortunately, most educators take their responsibilities to stop bullying very seriously. Recent legislation in the United States has focused on bullying prevention efforts. Both federal and state mandates hold schools accountable to develop antibullying policies and evidenced-based programs (*ed.gov*). In March 2011, the Anti-Bullying and Harassment Act of 2011 was introduced in Congress. To date, 49 states have passed legislation related to harassment, intimidation, and bullying in schools. In addition, 42 states have laws that include electronic harassment and 15 include cyberbullying (*cyberbullying.us; stopbullying.gov*). Ask for a copy of your school's policy or check the student guide to see whether your school has policies that will help resolve the problem.

Once the school learns about the bullying, staff should meet with your children to learn about the bullying that they have experienced. The school should develop a plan to help keep your children safe and should be watchful for any future bullying. School personnel should assure your children that they will work hard to see that the bullying stops. Furthermore, school personnel should meet with the children who are suspected of taking part in the bullying. They should make it clear to these children that bullying is against school rules and will not be tolerated. If appropriate, school personnel should administer consequences (such as revoking recess privileges) to the children who bullied, and notify their parents.

TIP

The child's teacher, school counselor, and/or principal are able to work with you to determine the following:

1. Who will look into your complaint and when
2. When that person will get back to you
3. What information you can expect
4. How will the school, now that it is aware of the problem, keep your child safe while the problem is being investigated (for example, supervise the alleged bully)
5. How your child's identity and privacy will be protected to prevent retaliation
6. What services are available in the school or school district should your child need emotional or psychological support

Requesting a meeting. When a meeting with the school is necessary, I suggest starting with your children's teachers since the teachers spend the most time with your children at school. However, if you are not comfortable talking with the teachers, make an appointment to meet with the school counselor or principal to discuss your concerns. Rather than allowing your emotions to demand an on-the-spot meeting, remain calm (use some of the coping strategies listed above). Then call, e-mail, or write a letter to request a meeting. (See the parent letter to the principal on the facing page). Your children must see you calmly and respectfully problem solve with school personnel. If you contact the school by phone, make notes on who you talk to and when. Document the school personnel's responses word for word whenever possible. Documenting conversations, decisions, and agreed-upon plans of action help keep you and the school on the same page during what can be an emotional time.

If you have reached out to your children's teachers and have received disinterested or downplayed responses, do not be deterred. Continue to contact other school personnel—preferably according to a chain of command (e.g., the school board, the superintendent, state department of education)—to make sure that your voice, and more importantly, your children's voices, are heard.

TOOLBOX TACTIC

Parent Letter to the Principal About Bullying[20]

_____ (your street address)
_____, ____ _____ (city, state, zip code)

_____, 20XX (date)

_____ (name of principal)
_____ (name of school)
_____ (school address)
_____

RE: _____ (first and last name of child)
Dear _____, (name of principal)
My child, _____ (first name of child), is in the _____ (grade level) at _____ (name of school). At school _____ (s/he) has been bullied and harassed by _____ (name of harasser(s)). This has occurred on _____ (date or approximate period of time) when _____ (describe as many details of the incident(s) as can be recalled). When this happened _____ (name of witness(es)) heard or saw it and _____ (their response(s)). We became aware of this incident when _____ (describe how you were notified).

_____ (first name of child), was hurt by this bullying and harassment. _____ (She/He) had _____ (describe physical injuries, emotional suffering, and any medical or psychological treatment required). _____ (Our/My) child has the right to be in a safe environment at school so_____ (s/he) can learn.

_____ (I/We am/are) deeply concerned and would welcome an opportunity to meet with you and _____ (first name of child), teachers. _____ (I/We) would like to consider what we can all do to change the situation. At our meeting, _____ (I/We) would like to raise some questions.

- We are wondering if this bullying incident is unique to our child or is bullying a general problem at your school? How do you presently monitor for bullying?
- In our situation, the bullying occurred at recess (an unsupervised area) and study hall. Are there any ways to improve the playground activities and improve the level of supervision? Are there plans to place a teacher to monitor study hall or have a peer mentor available?

- What are you doing schoolwide and in the classroom to reduce bullying?
- Are your teachers trained to identify bullying incidents and in ways to intervene?
- How can parents help reduce bullying?
- Are there specific school services you provide to victims of bullies, to children who bully, and to children who are both a bully and a victim?

Thank you for arranging a meeting with _____ (me/us) and helping _____ (my/our) _____(son/daughter), _____ (first name of child). _____ (I/We) look forward to the meeting. Please let _____ (me/us) know what would be a convenient time to meet. Please call and leave a message at _____ (phone number).

Thank you for your prompt attention to this serious problem.

Sincerely,

(sign in this area)

_____ (your name)

CC: _____ (name of superintendent of schools), Superintendent
(Sign and keep a copy for your records)

Prior to the meeting. Prior to meeting with the teacher, school counselor, or principal, obtain a copy of the school's antibullying policy to determine if the bully violated a school policy. If you believe the bully has violated the school's antibullying policy, calmy bring this up in the meeting. Also write down yours and your children's goals for the conversation with the teacher, counselor, and/or principal. Encourage your children to come with you to the meeting so they can describe what they experienced and go over the school's policy with them.

The meeting. Go into the meeting with the assumption that school personnel are not aware of what's going on and that they will do their best to fix it. You do not want to alienate those who can help. Before your children attend the meeting, share your concerns about your children and ask the teachers such questions as "How do my children get along with other students in the class? With whom do my children spend free time? Have you noticed or have you ever suspected that my children are being bullied by other students?" Give examples of some ways that children can be bullied to be sure that the teachers are not focusing only on one kind of bullying (e.g., physical bullying). Ask the teachers to talk with other adults who interact with your children at school (such as the music teacher, physical education teacher, or bus driver) to see whether they have observed students bullying your children. These conversations should take place before your children join the meeting.

After your children describe the bullying situation, you should repeat the factual information (who, what, when, where, and how). Keep your emotions in check and express yourself calmly. Next ask how you, the teachers, your children, and the school can all work together to ensure that the bullying does not happen again. Research shows that the most effective method of dealing with bullying is to have the whole school involved.

At the end of the meeting, put in writing any agreed-upon resolutions. Request that all involved parties sign the document to indicate their agreement. Set up a follow-up appointment with the teachers to discuss progress. Ask the school to keep a written record of all offenses committed against your children in case law enforcement officials need the information for further complaints. Establishing a paper trail is not a "gotcha!" process but, rather, an effective way of keeping all involved parties organized, informed, and goal directed.

After the meeting. Send a thank you letter to the teachers, counselor, or principal, recapping what he or she said and agreed to do. This will put the teachers, counselor, or principal on notice that you are watching for a resolution to the problem. If there is no improvement after reporting the bullying to the teacher, speak with the school principal. In your meeting with the principal, explore what the school is doing about bullying. Ask about what types of programs, policies, or culture changes are in place to counteract bullying. Insist that protective measures be put in place. Most of all, stay on course and be persistent. Keep an eye on your children's behavior. Follow up on the steps for ending the bullying that were agreed to at the meeting(s). If bullying remains a persistent problem and has not been resolved, make sure that the school administration is aware that you will report the incidents to the police.

Why can't the school tell me more about the consequences for the bully? School staff are required to deal with the student who is bullying, which will include meeting and discussing the issue with that student's parents to discuss the bully's behavior and impose consequences for bullying. School staff are able to tell you generally the range of behavior management strategies and discipline measures that may be applied. They can also tell you how your child appears to be responding at school and should inform you when your child reports concerns to them, such as being bullied. The school cannot provide personal information about other students due to privacy laws. Schools are also unable to provide specific information about disciplinary measures, as each incident must be assessed on an ongoing and case-by-case basis to take the individual students into consideration.

Involving the Authorities

Although it is the school's responsibility to protect children while at school, you as the parent may need to take further action to ensure that bullying is addressed properly. Therefore, if you think the bullying is continuing or getting worse and are concerned about your children's safety, take additional action by contacting the local police. Consider involving the police or an attorney if another child has physically assaulted your child or is seriously threatening him or her with bodily injury. Contact the police or an attorney if the problem persists or escalates and if school officials are unable to stop the bullying. An attorney can also provide legal advice regarding the filing of a lawsuit on behalf of the children for the harm suffered.

Involving the Office of Civil Rights

Schools that fail to respond appropriately to harassment of students who are members of a protected class may be violating one or more civil rights laws enforced by the Department of Education and the Department of Justice. These laws include the following.

- Title IV and Title VI of the Civil Rights Act of 1964
- Title IX of the Education Amendments of 1972
- Section 504 of the Rehabilitation Act of 1973
- Titles II and III of the Americans with Disabilities Act
- Individuals with Disabilities Education Act (IDEA)

If your children are bullied because of their race, ethnicity, sexual orientation, or disability and the local school district is not working to solve the problem, then you can contact the U.S. Department of Education's Office on Civil Rights at *www2.ed.gov/about/offices/list/ocr*. Visit *Stopbullying.gov* to learn about federal laws that may govern protection (*www.stopbullying.gov/laws/federal/index.html*).

TOOLBOX TACTIC

Bullying Laws

Visit *Bullypolice.org*, *Cyberbullying.us*, and *Stopbullying.gov* to see what bullying, cyberbullying, and sexting laws are enacted in your state.

Involving the Bully's Parents

In some cases, contacting the bully's parent(s) might be beneficial in trying to get the bullying to stop. If, for example, you are friends with the bully's parents, you may consider contacting them before contacting the school. The parents may be surprised to learn that their child has harmed your child and will discipline the child themselves. However, in my experience, you should not contact the bully's parent(s). Parents can often get hostile or defensive when they hear bad things about their child. However, if you feel the need to speak to the bully's parent(s), do so where a school official, such as a school counselor or principal, can mediate.

Conclusion

Telling an adult about bullying can help children of all ages to get the bullying to stop. Children who are being bullied may feel embarrassed or afraid to let adults know about the situation, especially if they feel adults will judge them or fail to protect them. If your children tell you that they are being bullied, be understanding and supportive. Your children need a lot of courage to admit to being bullied. Ask your children what they think can be done to help the situation, and make suggestions yourself. Do not ignore the situation or pretend it is not happening. Talking about bullying can help children feel that they are not going through it alone. You need to make rational decisions about the next steps and ways to end the bullying as soon as possible. Informing a teacher can be helpful for five- and six-year-olds; ignoring the bullying can be more effective for older children. If the bullying continues or increases, write a letter to the school to report the bullying and ask for a meeting and response. Finally, be persistent and never give up.

Chapter 7

If Your Child Bullies Others

This chapter provides a road map to character restoration for children who bully others. It focuses on helping them gain awareness of wrongdoing and harm done to self and others, reconciliation, reparation, and restitution, as well as developing alternatives to aggressive behaviors by enhancing and increasing prosocial ones.

What Can I Do If My Child Is Bullying Others?

Well, the only reason I bullied is because the same person I was doing it to did it to me like a week before. It wasn't the right thing to do, but at the time, it felt like I was getting revenge.

A 15-Year-Old Boy

If you find that your child is bullying others, it can be a big shock. You will probably ask yourself questions such as "Where did I go wrong?" "What could I have done to prevent this?" or "I don't understand why my child is behaving this way because we taught him or her better than that; he or she knows right from wrong." My response to you is this—children make mistakes and make bad decisions. They are still learning and need to learn from their mistakes. So it is imperative you respond immediately in order to help your child change his or her negative attitudes and behavior toward others. Without effective intervention (from you and/or the school system), children who bully are at significantly greater risk for engaging in antisocial and criminal behavior later in life.[1]

Parents are one of the best resources to help their child stop bullying and start interacting positively with his or her classmates. It is critically important, however, that you handle your child's behavior in a way that encourages growth and self-worth rather than shame. Most parents (and the school) are well-versed in common discipline techniques based on punishment. These include time-outs, removal of privileges, and more drastic measures like corporal punishment. This approach falls into the broad category of "retributive" justice, which mandates appropriate punishment for an offense.[2,3,4] On the other hand, "restorative justice" helps children learn how their behavior affects others as well as what they can do to take responsibility and mend fences.[2,3,4] For example, when my older son harasses his younger brother—perhaps by taking a game, calling him names, or hitting him—part of the restoration process is to help my older son understand how his younger brother felt. Is the younger afraid of the older? Does the younger one feel he can trust his older brother? Part of the consequence for my older son involves helping his younger brother feel safe again. If I merely sent my older son to his room for a time-out, the teachable moment would be lost. Instead, I have my older son come up with concrete ideas to right the wrong. It is his job to mend the relationship with his younger brother. This has a different effect than simply requiring my older son to say, "I'm sorry." My older son (the bully) must come up with the solution to restore his relationship with his younger brother. So the solution becomes personal, and my older son takes ownership.

A restorative approach can help you transform your child's bullying behavior by teaching him or her ways to have respectful relationships. Teach your child to have empathy, respect, and compassion. Teach your child how to mend broken relationships (reconciliation), compensate for harmful behavior (reparation), and make amends for harm done (restitution).[2,3,4] This chapter will show you how to restore your child's character and build relationships through a restorative approach, what to expect from the school, and how the authorities may get involved.

 TIP

If your child has bullied, you need to teach him or her how to fix the harm caused to the victim and to the community.
- Make it clear that bullying will not be tolerated and it must be stopped.
- Teach that he or she has wronged and hurt others.
- Hold your child accountable for his or her actions. Do not accept any rationalizations for the bullying.
- Help your child fix the harm he or she has caused using restoration, healing, and forgiveness.

- Help your child learn new ways of interacting with others by developing healthy ways to get his or her needs met that do not impede others' ability to meet theirs.
- Encourage empathy, perspective taking, self-regulation, anger management, and conflict resolution.
- Teach your child that his or her actions may result in legal consequences.

CASE STUDY—PART 1

Jacob

Incident: While in the locker room, Jacob pulled Alex's pants down and pushed him out into the gym. The teacher and other students who were in the gym for P.E. class witnessed the incident. Jacob has been suspended for three days.

Background: Jacob and Alex are in the 9th grade. The boys have gone to the same school since kindergarten. Jacob and Alex are not really friends. Rather, they are acquaintances. Jacob is outgoing, is witty, does well academically, participates in sports, and hangs out with the popular kids. Alex is more shy but is not quiet. He talks and socializes with other kids in school. Overall, he is liked by other kids. Alex doesn't participate in sports. However, he is involved with several clubs at school (e.g., band, academic decathlon, and robotics).

School phone call: You are Jacob's parent. You receive a phone call from the school's principal stating that Jacob has been suspended from school for three days because he was caught bullying Alex. From what the principal reports, Jacob has been picking on Alex for the past three months by making derogatory comments like calling Alex gay or a sissy, throwing paper at his head, and shoving and poking him. The principal states that he talked to Alex, who reported that the boys were horsing and joking around, so Jacob pulled down Alex's pants in good fun. Everybody was playing around and ribbing on each other.

Your reaction: Shocked and in disbelief, you become angry and upset because Jacob is a good kid who has never been in trouble at school previously. It is not like him to be cruel. So he must have meant it as a joke—to be funny and not mean. You believe being suspended for three days is too harsh and don't think his punishment is fair. You end the conversation by making the comment, "Now his school record is tarnished. Thanks."

What do you do now? How do you respond?

Using the case scenario above, you will learn what to do and what not to do to help your child take responsibility for his or her actions. You will help your child understand why the behavior is wrong, how it affected the victim, how it affected others, and how to make amends.

First Stop: Examine Your Attitude and Actions

Your first reaction when learning that your child has bullied is to be defensive or take it personally. However, you should not assume you are the culprit or to blame for your child's misbehavior, especially as the child gets older. Children are responsible for the choices they make. At the same time, ask yourself whether you ever modeled bullying behavior yourself and whether your child is copying this behavior. (Review chapter 2, Recognizing Face-to-Face Bullying). Think about how problems and conflicts are dealt with in your home. Do you talk through issues positively as a family? Remember, if your child sees you gossip about people, ridicule others, or use physical, verbal, or passive aggression to solve problems, he or she is more likely to do the same. More than one-quarter of children (25.3%) have witnessed violence in their homes, schools, and communities during the past year. More than one-third (37.8%) have witnessed violence against another person during their lifetimes.[5] Consequently, you may occasionally need to look in the mirror to ensure that you are not perceived at times as a bully. To check, flip back to chapter 2 and take the quiz Could You Be a Bully? Could Your Child Be a Bully? Are your values helping or hurting?

TIP

An important way for you to discourage bullying is to be a good role model for your child.

1. Communicate your distaste for abuses of power.
2. Show your child how to sort out difficulties without using power or aggression.
3. Reinforce that everyone has rights and value.
4. Avoid making excuses for someone's aggressive behavior.

POINT TO PONDER

Children who bully sometimes do so at home as well as at school. Look and listen within your own household. Are there signs that one of your children is being bullied by a sibling? Research has shown that bullies show the same types of aggression to their siblings that they demonstrate with children at school.[6]

Second Stop: Discover Your Child's Story

Some parents defend and/or make excuses for their child's bullying behavior. Some do this out of shock and disbelief. Some do it because they don't want to seem like a bad parent. All too often I was told, "They are only learning to socialize," "The other child is too sensitive," or "Kids will be kids." Unfortunately, these comments are some of the biggest problems we have with deterring bullying.

Take the Problem Seriously

Many adults, particularly parents, support bullying. Obviously, this is counterproductive to getting the behavior to stop. Research shows that when adults get involved, the bullying stops. We cannot expect our children to do better than us if we do not show them how.

Be Realistic

Resist the tendency to deny the problem or discount it. Be objective and listen carefully to the account. The school or the victim's parents may have documented proof of your child's bullying. Therefore, do not deny your child's involvement if there is evidence to the contrary. Check out the dates and the activities to see if there is a pattern in your child's bullying behavior. Your child may bully if he or she lacks empathy and does not sympathize with others, values aggression, likes to be in charge, is an arrogant winner and a sore loser, often fights often with brothers and sisters, and is impulsive.

Remain Calm

You just learned that your child has bullied. Instinctively, you may want to confront him or her and say, "Why did you do that?" or "How could you be so mean and cruel?" Do not overreact. Try to stay calm, and remain levelheaded before talking with your child. STOP and THINK about the reasons why your child bullied. Has a lack of self-confidence compelled your child to be the center of attention? Does your child need to gain or maintain social status? Is he or she getting bullied? Bear in mind all behavior serves a purpose. There is always a motivating factor as to why your child turned to bullying. (Review chapter 3 for reasons why children bully.) Children often bully when they feel sad, angry, lonely, or insecure. Many times, major changes at home or at school may bring on these feelings. By allowing your child to tell his or her story, you can gain a clearer picture for the reason behind the behavior. Although knowing why your child bullies never excuses the bullying behavior, it can sometimes help you know how to help improve your child's behavior.

Be Supportive

Help your child realize that what he or she is doing is wrong. Remember that your child is not a bad person. Rather, the behavior is unacceptable. Do not think of your child as a bad kid. Instead think of your child as a good person who has done something unacceptable. Also avoid using labels when referring to him or her while speaking to the school or others. Talk about the specific unacceptable behaviors instead.

Be Reassuring

Reassure your child that you still love him or her but you do not like the behavior. Indicate that you will work with him or her to alter this behavior and that you will work with the school personnel to monitor progress. Let your child know that you are disappointed in how he or she behaved, but believe that he or she can change this behavior.

Don't Bully

Don't bully your child when addressing what happened. Help your child appreciate how bullying hurts not only the victim but also the bully and the bystanders. Do not try to give your child "a taste of his or her own medicine." Do not shout. Instead, calmly share your concern for what has been happening to the victim and firmly insist that it must not happen again. Reinforce the following.

- Stop the bullying immediately.
- Bullying will not be tolerated.
- Bullying hurts both the victim and the bully.
- Bullying sets a bad example for other children.
- Bullying may cause you to lose friends.
- Every child deserves to be treated with dignity and respect.
- There are other ways to solve conflicts.

Any discipline must help your child either maintain or enhance self-esteem. Listen to your kid. Acknowledge his or her feelings. Describe your own feelings. Explain why the discipline is occurring. Give your child a say in household affairs. All these techniques preserve your child's dignity and self-worth.

TIP

If your child has bullied someone, do not bully the bully as this generates feelings of hostility and alienation. In other words, instead of threatening your child, shaming him or her for wrongdoing, or making sure your kid gets what he or she deserves, it is critical that you (and the school) teach your child to identify and address harms, needs, and obligations in order to heal and put things as right as possible.[2,3]

Accept No Excuses

Sit down and talk with your child immediately. Give him or her an opportunity to explain the behavior. However, do not accept any excuses or justifications. A child who bullies always has an excuse, a way to justify the behavior. This justification is so powerful that it takes the place of empathy for the other person. So do not believe everything your child tells you. Children who bully are good at manipulating adults and can be very creative at weaving a story that makes them look innocent. If the problem is occurring at school, tell your child you support the school's right to hold him or her accountable for the actions if the behavior persists.

Let your child tell you the excuse and then reiterate, "There is no excuse for abuse. Even if the other child involved did something, you made a choice to do what you did." For example, if your child tries to minimize the behavior (e.g., "I only called him a nerd," or "I shoved him because I was in a hurry and he was in my way."), stress that the behavior is unacceptable. Don't validate the thinking errors that go into justifying abusive actions. Let your child know that he or she had other options and is fully responsible for his or her choices. Teach your child that there are consequences for abusing someone. Later, you can talk about appropriate ways to handle a problem.

Be Curious and Investigative

Calmly explain to your child what he or she is accused of. Ask for an explanation and, moreover, if he or she knows that such bullying is unacceptable. If you or someone close to you has been bullied in the past, sharing the story with your child and discussing the emotional impact may help your kid to open up. Listen with empathy. Listen for feelings and needs. Respond to your child's points of view. Remain calm. Try to find out if there is something in particular that is troubling your child and help him or her devise an acceptable plan to work it out.

Use a restorative inquiry approach to discuss the bullying with your child. This method has several facets.

- Be curious. For example, ask your child, "How do you feel about the bullying?"
- Discuss the problem from your perspective. You could say, "I have a problem that I would like to discuss with you," or "I'd like to tell you about this from my perspective."
- Try to resolve the issue. You could begin a discussion by saying, "Tell me how you see things. I'll do the same. Then we can try to sort out this problem."

When discussing the bullying events (who, what, where, etc.), do not interrogate. Explore the reasons for the negative behavior. Remember that a child who bullies is also a hurt child. So encourage your child to talk about what made him or her begin to bully other children.

Questions to ask: Use the following questions and responses as guidelines when discussing the bullying with your child.

1. Start by asking, "Do you know why I wanted to talk to you?" If your child answers "No," then state how you found out about the bullying. Do not add to the story.
2. Then ask, "What is your side of the story? What happened? What exactly did you say and do?" Listen to your child. After your child has finished, reflect back to let him or her know you heard what was just said. For example, you could say, "So what I heard you say was...."
3. Try to clarify what happened. You could ask any of the following.
   - "What were you thinking at the time?"
   - "How were you feeling at the time?"
   - "How are you feeling now?"
   - "Who, other than you, has been affected by the situation."
   - "How do you think the victim feels about what you said and did?"
   - "Why did you say and do that?"
   - "What have you thought about since the bullying?"
   - "What do you need to do to put things right?

POINT TO PONDER

When your children do the wrong thing, how do you challenge them so they stop and think about what they did, take responsibility for their behavior, and not resent you?

What are you trying to achieve by disciplining them? Do you guilt, shame, blame, or reprimand them in trying to deter and correct their cruel behavior, prevent future transgressions, and teach self-control?

Do these tactics hold them accountable for their behavior? Do these tactics encourage or promote ethical character? How do you hold your children accountable? What does student accountability mean to you? If you ask "why" (i.e., "Why did you do that?"), what answers do you expect to get? What is the problem with the "why" question?

Third Stop: Hold Your Child Accountable

To be accountable means being obliged or willing to accept responsibility or to account for one's actions (*www.merriam-webster.com*). Accountability happens when your child gives an account of what he or she proposes to do to right a wrong. Responsibility occurs when a child upholds the action plan to make things right. Holding your child accountable has three components.

1. Owning the mistakes—accepting responsibility for the harm caused
2. Understanding—being aware of the impact of his or her actions on others
3. Repairing—mending the harm by making it right.

Active vs. Passive Responsibility

Active responsibility means taking responsibility by putting something right. In contrast, passive responsibility means being punished, which requires little or no participation from the child who bullied.[7] For example, use the case study of Jacob. Discipline was administered by the principal (i.e., authority figure) who imposed punishment (i.e., suspended for three days) for his bullying behaviors. This means Jacob was not required to take responsibility for his actions, remains silent, resents the authority figure, feels angry, and perceives himself as the victim.[8] Instead of becoming emotionally aware of Alex's (i.e., the victim's) perspective, thinking about the real victim of his offense, or considering other individuals who have been adversely affected by his aggressive actions (i.e., the other kids in the locker or bystanders), Jacob feels aggrieved when punished, which could lead to further misbehavior. Consequently, instead of being helped, Jacob is further disadvantaged and denied the opportunity to apologize and make amends to his victims. In order for Jacob to learn from his mistakes, he must have opportunities to make them (i.e., make bad decisions).

Using a restorative approach provides Jacob with the opportunity to learn from the bullying to help him create a life that is more meaningful and resilient. Subsequently, the parents(s) and the school must engage all participants involved (i.e., Jacob, Alex, and the bystanders) in an active way that holds them accountable for their actions. The goals are threefold. First, build positive relationships between the bully (i.e., Jacob) and those affected (i.e., Alex and the bystanders). Second, prevent the bullying from recurring. Third, begin to rebuild the sense of community that has been lost within the school culture. Restorative justice approaches offer a proven alternative strategy for student misbehavior (e.g., bullying). It reduces suspensions, expulsions, and disciplinary referrals.[9]

TIP

According to the shame management approach, individuals who acknowledge shame and accept personal responsibility for wrongdoing will refrain from further wrongdoing because they have considered the harmful consequences and made amends to avoid them in the future. In contrast, dismissing shame feelings by blaming others will amplify wrongdoing because personal action and consequences are dissociated.[10]

Fourth Stop: Apply Consequences

Follow through with clear, fair, and appropriate consequences for your child's unacceptable behavior. Enforce the no-bullying rule and other household rules with nonphysical discipline. If you physically punish your child, you will only reinforce your child's mistaken belief that physical aggression is an acceptable way to resolve problems and to bully others who are weaker to get what one wants. When developing consequences, think about approaches that put repairing the harm done to relationships and people over and above the need for assigning blame and dispensing punishment (*www.iirp.edu*).

The best consequences are those that are task oriented and that teach the child something. For example, my older son was disrespectful to his brother. As a consequence, he was told he couldn't use his cell phone until he wrote his younger brother a letter of apology. In the letter, my older son had to tell his brother what he will do differently the next time they argue. Writing the letter of apology teaches my older son and helps him win back his phone. That way, he's not just "doing time." He is completing an act that teaches him something.

Discipline Wisely

When your child does something wrong, require him or her to do the following.

1. Say "I'm sorry."
2. Say why he or she is sorry.
3. Find out how restitution can be made by asking, "What can I do to make up for it?"

TIP

Research findings on restorative approaches and bullying found that acknowledging the wrongdoing, being aware of the harm done, being willing to make amends, and offering an apology are effective ways to change a bully's behaviors.[11]

CASE STUDY—PART 2

Jacob: Information Gathered and Consequences

After listening to Jacob's story, you learned the following information. According to Jacob, he did not bully Alex. Alex was playing and horsing around with everybody in the locker room. Jacob stated, "I pulled Alex's pants down because he was walking out of the locker room and I was dared to, so I did it. I did not think he would get all mad. I know it was probably embarrassing, but I thought he would laugh it off. He didn't have to run into the principal's office like a sissy. He could've said something to me instead. So I got in trouble because Alex is a wimp. He can dish out the ribbing, but he can't take it. It's not fair that I get in trouble but not him. When I see Alex, I'm going to tell him off." Jacob also reported that the name calling and shoving is being blown out of proportion and everyone is overreacting. The boys were just playing around and ribbing each other. "This is what boys do. It's all good and done in fun." Jacob is now angry that he is suspended for three days. He thinks the time does not fit the crime. The principal is blowing everything out of proportion.

As you noticed, Jacob's first response was to deny any culpability for wrongdoing. He failed to take sufficient responsibility for his actions. When this happens, take a break. Talk to your child later after he has had more time to think about why his account is not being accepted.

Then you should meet with all parties involved—Jacob, Alex and his family, and the others in the locker room (the bystanders), and school officials. The others can bring a fresh perspective to the situation. Remain hopeful that once Jacob's consequences have been imposed, he might ultimately come to feel remorse and apologize to Alex (the victim). Alex might ultimately be ready to accept the apology and even forgive Jacob.

Jacob had to do the following.

- Write a letter of apology to Alex accepting responsibility for his actions
- Write a letter of apology to his P.E. classmates accepting responsibility for his actions.
- Prepare and deliver a speech to the P.E. class about how to negotiate with words rather than getting physical.
- Monitor his behavior and report to you, which teaches him self-management and self-control.
- Suggest that Alex come over to play video games with him and his friends. Instead, Jacob could invite Alex to his group when playing a massive multiplayer online role-playing game (MMORPG) with parental supervision. Doing this may mend and build the boys' relationship.
- Become a peer helper at school to help build relationships.
- Volunteer at a hospital, nursing home, or shelter.

Fifth Stop: Letter of Apology

The conference went really well. It was difficult and emotional for everyone. I'm convinced restorative justice works. It made me feel a lot worse [for what I did], getting to know the victim.

A Child Who Bullied

A bully should write a letter of apology to tell those affected that he or she is sorry for being a bully. It is written as an attempt to communicate accountability, remorse, acknowledgement and to help mend the pain caused by the offense. The letter should be in your child's own words. It should tell people how your child feels about the offense now that he or she has met with and listened to what everyone said. Because writing an apology letter can be a hard thing for people to do, I put together some helpful hints as well as an example to follow.

Tips for Writing an Apology Letter:

It will be much easier if the child writes the letter soon after the meeting while everything is still fresh in his or her mind.

- Talk to your child about writing a letter of apology. Ask your child what he or she thinks about having to write the letter. If your kid says, "I think this is crap" accept that. You need your child to be honest with you. Once you know how he or she feels, you can ask, "How do we make this less crappy?"
- Set out a procedure for writing the letter to help your child focus. You could say, "Let's focus for 15 minutes. We'll brainstorm thoughts. Then for 5 minutes, you just write. Then for 5 minutes, I will give you feedback." Speak clearly and specifically. Make sure your child agrees to the agenda before you start.
- Help your child write the letter. A good letter has an introduction, body paragraphs, and a conclusion. Explain the basic letter format. Make sure your child includes a few sentences at the beginning to cover who he or she is and why he or she is writing. The second and third paragraphs should support a few key thoughts. Talk with your child about what ideas he or she wants to convey in each of the paragraphs.

   Make sure the letter of apology is personal. Your child may want to include the following:
   1. Important things said in the meeting
   2. How being in the meeting made your child feel
   3. How your child feels about the offense now
   4. Any changes in your child's life since the meeting
   5. What your child felt when he or she heard about how everyone was affected
- Check in with your child. Ask if this letter is from his or her heart or if it is what he or she thinks the victim wants to hear. Use reflective questioning. Ask how your child would feel hearing the letter. Read the letter back to your child.
- Provide feedback about the letter. Make suggestions on improvements, not judgments. Give options for improvements. Start statements with, "I wonder..." or "here's a thought..." Keep your child encouraged.

- Ask your child to gauge the letter-writing process on a scale of 1 to 10 (1 being terrible and 10 being super). Ask how he or she feels about getting the letter done. Thank your child for staying on task, being respectful, and being honest. Be genuine about your experience. You may say, "I am pleased and relieved that you were committed to doing this" or "I felt sad and frustrated when you kept saying you didn't know what to write."
- Read over the letter before sending it.
- Send the apology letter to the victim(s) in a sealed envelope. Include a cover letter explaining what is in the envelope.
- Remember that the apology letter does not ensure that the children involved will have future contact.

TOOLBOX TACTIC

Example Letter of Apology

What does your child need to put in the letter of apology? Consider using the information below as a guide to structure the letter of apology.[12]

1. Reason for writing—Make a statement about the concerns for everyone's feelings about the offense or offenses. For example:
   - I am writing to you because I am feeling _____ about how I have treated you.
   - I am writing to you because I am feeling _____ about you and _____ about what I have put you through.
2. Statement of apology—Give clear and specific details of the offense and harm caused. For example:
   - I am very sorry for _____.
   - I want to apologize for _____.
3. Statement of responsibility—Make a statement about who is responsible for what happened. For example:
   - I know I am fully responsible for what happened and my actions that day. I should not have _____ because _____.
   - I know _____ (co-bullies names if appropriate) and I are responsible for what happened that day. I know I am accountable for my actions and the choices I made that day. We should not _____ because _____.

4. Understanding the impact on others—Write about what you have learned about how the offense has impacted people. For example:
   • I am starting to realize some of what I have put you through. It must have been _____ when _____.
   • I must have frightened you _____.
   • I betrayed you by _____.

5. What you are doing about changing your behavior—Let the people you are writing to know what you are doing to change your behavior or going to do so you don't get into trouble again. For example:
   • I am seeing a counselor so that I can make sure that nothing like this will happen again. I have learned _____.
   • I am learning to understand what I have put you through and I am working out what I need to do so I don't get into the same situation again. I know I should _____.

6. Statement about distancing—Let people know that you are not coming back to hurt them again. For example:
   • I will stay away from your home/shop and your family/staff as I do not want to cause any of you any further hurt.

7. Recurrences—Write about your readiness and ability to face consequences. For example:
   • I know I must take responsibility for my actions. I know that I have committed a criminal offense (if applicable) as well as betrayed you. I am ready to handle whatever consequences that I will have to face from you, my family, the community, and the police/court (if applicable).

8. Future intentions—Let the people you are writing to know about your goals and plans for the future. For example:
   • I am turning my life around. I am now _____ (list what you are doing, for example getting counseling, looking for a job, got a job or traineeship, back at school, etc.).
   • Since the conference, I have _____.
   • If I see you or your family members, I will be respectful.
   • I believe that you have every right to feel angry and betrayed.
   • I am not asking for you to forgive me. I just want you to know that I am really sorry for what I did to you.

CASE STUDY—PART 3

Jacob's Letter of Apology

Dear Alex,

I am writing to you to apologize for pulling your pants down in front of the class in P.E, calling you mean names, and telling everyone that you are gay. It was wrong, and I shouldn't have done it.

After meeting you at school yesterday and hearing how my behavior affected you and your family, I now know how much it hurt each of you. I am terribly sorry that I embarrassed you in front of everyone. It must have been humiliating to have everyone laugh at and make fun of you. You taught me an important lesson about respecting other people's dignity and treating people with respect. I've learned the difference between playing around and hurting someone.

I now realize that what I did was extremely stupid. I wish I'd thought harder about my actions and how it would affect you and everyone else.

At the moment, I am taking an anger management class to help me control my impulsive behavior and to think before I act. I want to be a better person. I am trying to resist giving in to peer pressure. I do not want to hurt some people just so others will like me.

Again, I am very sorry for the harm I have caused you and your family.

Sincerely yours,

Jacob

TOOLBOX TACTIC

To help children (and adults) devise effective apologies, Ben Furman—a psychiatrist, author, and trainer from Finland—developed the Sorry Program. The Sorry Program, which is based on restorative principles, is an "amazing free apology-letter writing tool" that is available from the Helsinki Brief Therapy Institute's website (*http://www.kidsskills.org/sorry/index.html*). It is accessible in five languages.

Sixth Stop: Help Change Behaviors

I've learned that people will forget what you said, people will forget what you did, but people will never forget how you made them feel.

Maya Angelou
Author, Poet, Civil Rights Activist

Bullying is a social relationship problem. It is a complex interaction based on misusing personal power. So it is important to help a child who is bullying to learn better ways of relating to others. Given that bullying is defined as a "systematic abuse of power" (i.e., domination), it is vital that you work with your child to transform the power imbalance (non-domination) that affects his or her social relationships (i.e., empowerment). Help your child develop social, emotional, and cognitive skills (i.e., life skills) that promote recognizing and managing one's emotions, developing caring and concern for others, establishing positive relationships, perspective taking, interpersonal problem solving, making responsible decisions, and handling challenging situations constructively and ethically (*www.casel.org*). Additional skill-building information is discussed in chapter 8.

Teach Self-Awareness

Self-awareness means accurately assessing one's feelings, interests, values, and strengths and maintaining a sense of self-confidence. Unless your child has, through understanding, reached real conviction of what is good or ill in his or her own behavior, ambitions, etc., he or she will not be secure against reverting to it again at some future date. Consequently, help your child examine his or her values, beliefs, ideas, etc.

 TOOLBOX TACTIC

My Personal Motto[13]

Use the top of this worksheet to make notes about your values. Then put these thoughts together to create your personal motto at the bottom of this page.

Character traits I want to have:

_____   _____

_____   _____

Things I value:

People I value:

Ideas I value:

People I want to be like:

Things I care about:

My Personal Motto:

POINT TO PONDER

Friendships are formed, nurtured, and sustained with energy and commitment. Talk with your child to see what he or she thinks about "what being a friend means."
- What makes a person a good friend?
- What qualities do you look for in a friend?
- Think about a time you have felt let down by friends. What happened? How did it affect your friendships?

Teach Social Awareness

Social awareness skills include teaching your child how to empathize and take the perspective of others and recognizing and appreciating individual and group similarities and differences. Bullies often have trouble empathizing with their targets, so it is important to discuss with your child how bullying feels. How would your child feel if it happened to him or her?

Empathy

To empathize means to understand another person's point of view, emotions, thoughts, feelings, and to understand what the other person is going through (i.e., putting oneself in the other person's shoes). Empathy allows us to listen without judgment to what a person is saying, doing, or feeling. It permits us to imagine what someone else is experiencing without having had the experience. Empathy requires hearing the feelings behind the message. For instance, remember how it felt to be embarrassed by someone or to be made fun of. Without empathy, there is no compassion.

TOOLBOX TACTIC

Exposure to Emotionally Arousing Events and Experiences

Exposure to events or experiences such as portrayals of misfortune, deprivation, or distress on the part of others tends to increase empathetic feelings and responses.[14,15] Thus, watch movies such as *The Blind Side, Marley & Me, The Lion King, Finding Nemo, The Notebook*, or *Dying Young* with your child and/or help him or her generate empathic responses to the person, situation, event, or experience. Encourage your child to think about others and their needs in order to stimulate empathetic feelings and responses.

TIP

Older youth are better able to recognize emotive states in other people, more capable of relating to and sharing others' feelings, able to feel empathy for more diverse kinds of people, and more willing to express their empathetic response in generosity toward others. In contrast, the developmental level of very young children is characterized by greater self-involvement, frequent objectification of others, and a tendency to experience and act on empathetic feelings only toward people very much like themselves in age, ethnicity, and gender.[16]

CASE STUDY—PART 4

Jacob's Empathic Responses

Incident: Alex was ridiculed in front of his classmates in gym class because he could not kick the soccer ball into the net.

To help Jacob be more empathic toward Alex, have him think "What could he say to Alex that shows he understands what Alex is feeling?

In listing three empathic responses to the above scenario, Jacob writes:

1. That must have been embarrassing when you couldn't get the ball into the net.
2. That must have been humiliating to miss the net every time you kicked.
3. That must have been tough and uncomfortable.

Visit *www.psychpage.com* or *eqi.org/fw.htm* for a list of feeling words to use.

Perspective Taking

Perspective taking is understanding another person's point-of-view, having empathy for another person or group, developing tolerance, and gaining acceptance of others or those who are different from your child. Many things can affect your child's point of view—the child's experiences, family, where he or she lives, his or her height or age, and so on. Therefore, when your child has a different idea than another child, both have reasons for his or her opinion. It is important to understand that each child's opinion is not necessarily right or wrong. It's just different. Sometimes when your child has a disagreement with you, another child, or a teacher, he or she stops listening. This is because he or she wants to get a point across, to the point where he or she is not hearing or understanding what the other person is trying to say. By learning how to listen to other people's points of view, your child will become more sensitive to other's needs, thoughts, feelings, and behaviors.

When helping your child learn how to take another's perspective, repeated practice is more effective than one-shot or infrequent efforts.[15,17,18] For children (and many adults), the ability to imagine and gain insight into another person's point of view does not come easily. Thus, sustained practice at perspective-taking is an effective means to increasing levels of empathy.

TOOLBOX TACTIC

When you witness inequality, cruelty, or discrimination, make it a point to discuss with your children that these are all unacceptable acts.

Teach Self-Management Skills

Self-management skills include teaching your children how to control their impulses, regulate their emotions, handle stress, persevere in overcoming obstacles, and set and monitor progress toward goals.

Impulse Control

Impulse control is the ability to maintain self-control. Self-control and reflection skills allow your children to regulate their behavior. Unless they are able to understand their impulses or desire behaviors, self-control cannot be attained. In other words, once your children firmly grasp the thought (I must not hit), the act (hitting behavior) will eventually follow their conviction. To help your child control his or her impulses, teach the 3 R's: relax, reflect, and respond.

- *Stop and Relax.* Stop the emotion that is running through your head or body. Take a deep breath and slowly count to 10. Don't say anything yet. Concentrate on counting so you don't react immediately. Get in touch with your needs and feelings. Take a step back from the situation so you can look at the whole picture. Think about your personal values. What are your beliefs about the way others should be treated? Remember when you let emotions take control, you are more likely to be impulsive.
- *Think and Reflect.* Think about the bullying incident that just happened. Think about your reasons for bullying. What need were you trying to meet? Is what you are about to do or say right or wrong? Is what you are about to do or say going to help or hurt the other person? Hurt yourself? The situation? By asking yourself these questions, you can de-escalate the problem before it begins to escalate. Then tap into the feelings that are stirring inside of you. Think of a word or two that describes how you feel. Think of alternative ways to express your feelings. Name some options that would help you feel better about what just happened. By

thinking and reflecting on the incident before reacting to the situation, you can control your emotions, which will help control the impulse.

- *Plan and Respond.* Choose how you would respond to the bullying incident. Examine the pros and cons of how your actions might affect the victim and others involved. Pick your best option and give it a try. Start by stating the problem. Speak slowly and calmly. Use a quiet, inside voice to tell those involved how you are affected by what just happened. Now listen to what others involved in the bullying incident have to say. Everyone involved should share ideas and try to cooperatively find a workable solution. Remember, if your child makes the wrong choice or if the choice didn't work out, there is always the option of choosing another way to respond.

TOOLBOX TACTIC

Calming strategies to help your child reduce impulsive reactions.
- Hand "C": The child forms his or her hand into the shape of a "C" and traces the "C" with his or her right index finger, all the while repeating the phrases "Calm down. Control yourself."
- B.A.T.S.: Breathe (deep breaths). Ask yourself to count to ten. Think of your favorite place. Say, "I'm okay. I can handle it!"
- Stop, Think, Plan (STP). This technique can help prevent physical violence. Teach your child to STOP when he or she becomes angry instead of acting out immediately, to THINK of several possible actions, and to PLAN a reasonable resolution. Using the STP method can help reinforce positive social habits.

Problem Solving

Everybody encounters challenging situations in life. Instead of running away from the problem or using aggressive behaviors to deal with them, parents need to teach their children how to persevere—to stay with a task even if it is difficult. Children need to learn how to develop good problem solving strategies to help cope with life challenges. Problem-solving coping strategies are attempts to alter stressful situations through action or planning to ameliorate the effects of environmental stressors. It also helps to identify obstacles and barriers your children must overcome in order to solve the problem and reach their goal. Problem solving is the ability to explore and use alternative solutions. However, before your children can think of ways to meet a challenging situation, they must be able to control their impulses and emotions. Strong feelings make it hard to think and solve problems. This is because it keeps them from paying attention to what they are doing. That's why it is important for them to cool off before they act. Teach them the following five steps to recognizing and expressing feelings.

1. Think body language basics.
2. Decide how you feel and how the other person feels.
3. Wait for a good time to explore feelings.
4. Think about your choices and their consequences:
   a. Say how you feel. Start with "I feel..."
   b. Ask the other person if he or she feels that way.
   c. Ask if you can help.
5. Act out your best choice.

Now that your children have cooled off, they are ready to act and solve the problem. Use the following four steps to help your children solve their problems.

1. Identify the problem.
   a. What is the problem?
   b. Who owns the problem?
   c. State the problem in one clear sentence.
2. Think of solutions.
   a. List all of the ways your children could solve the problem.
   b. What help or resources do your children need?
   c. Look at the pros and cons of each possible solution.
3. Try a solution.
   a. Choose the best solution.
   b. Plan to try out that solution.
   c. List the steps of what to do to solve the problem.
   d. Try out the solution.
4. Evaluate the outcome.
   a. Did your children's solution work? Why or why not?
   b. What could your children have done differently?
   c. How can your children avoid a similar problem in the future?

POINT TO PONDER

Think of a soda bottle. When you shake it and pop the cap off, what happens? It EXPLODES. This is what happens when your children become angry. The anger begins to build up inside. Once it is released, it explodes. Once it explodes, it is difficult to place the cap back on until the eruption stops. Hence, help your children **C**ontrol their **A**nger toward **P**eople (CAP) by helping them to put the CAP back on the bottle before it explodes. Teach your children that they can control the intensity of their anger eruption.

Teach Anger Management Skills

Anger management is the ability to deal with frustration and express emotions appropriately without violating the rights of others. But before your children can manage their anger, they must understand it. So what is anger? Anger is a normal, healthy emotion.[20] We all experience it! Although feeling angry cannot be avoided, it is manageable. First, anger is a reaction to an inner emotion. It is not a planned action. It is not a behavior. Rather, it is a response that allows your children to defend themselves when they are in danger (e.g., fight-or-flight). Therefore, a certain amount of anger is necessary for survival. Second, anger is easy to show. Everyone has issues that can cause feelings of anger. It is important not to think of anger as good or bad. Rather, how your children choose to express their anger—either healthily (acceptable) or unhealthily (unacceptable)—determines the consequences of the anger. Third, the underlying feelings of anger cause your children to feel vulnerable and weak. Most of the time their anger makes them feel—at least momentarily—strong and in control. Fourth, anger can be an immediate reaction to an isolated event. It can be a delayed response after many events have occurred. Fifth, the way children express anger is usually a learned behavior. Thus, they can unlearn the behavior. It can be replaced with healthier patterns of coping with anger and disappointment. Finally, do not reprimand your children for being angry. Rather, focus on how your children choose to express their anger. It is an impossible task to believe that we can eliminate anger, but we can learn how to control our anger, how we choose to express it, and how it affects other people.

The Anatomy of Anger

Anger is an emotion characterized by a strong feeling of displeasure. It is the desire for revenge, which is triggered by a real or imagined wrong done to someone.[20] Anger is often called a "second emotion" because we tend to resort to anger in order to protect ourselves from or to cover up other vulnerable feelings. These feelings can be thought of as an "iceberg." Only 10% of an iceberg can be seen above the water's surface. The rest lies hidden beneath the surface. In other words, anger is an outward expression of an underlying, deeper emotion. These underlying emotions include sadness, loneliness, abandonment, humiliation, and so on.

Help your children explore their anger. Teach them that their anger is only the tip of the iceberg, so that they can understand the underlying feelings that impact their anger. It may be difficult for your children to recognize these underlying emotions, especially when they are actively involved in bullying. This is because anger tends to flare up so fast that it overshadows their other feelings. Thus, teach them how to explore the underlying issues that drive their anger. Help them get in touch with the underlying feelings so they will be able to deal with them constructively. When your children are able to recognize their feelings before they explode, they can stop the chain reaction that leads to abuse before it gathers steam. This enables your children to act in ways that don't harm others.

What Triggers Anger?

Do your children have a "long fuse" or "short fuse"? What ignites their fuse? How your children respond to their feelings of anger is their choice. However, in order to help manage anger, they must understand what triggers it or "pushes their buttons." Help your children explore the different types of situations that they run into regularly that cause them to get angry. Once our children are able to identify these situations in advance, they will be able to see them coming. They will be able to take appropriate steps to channel their anger constructively. For example, once your children identify words, situations, and people that trigger their anger—such as dishonesty—they can use positive self-talk (e.g., "I am in charge of my emotions") to help them make good choices (e.g., "I will not pick an argument. Instead, I will use 'I' language to voice my concerns").

Recognizing the Signs of Anger

It is normal to feel angry. It's nature's way of letting us know that we are in a situation that feels threatening to us. Our body gives us physical signals—warning signs—that tell us we are getting angry. This happens even before our mind is aware of it. The key to managing our anger is to figure out what to do with those feelings. Remember, our emotions influence our body (physiological reaction). Our thoughts provoke us to action. Thus, teach your child how to identify the specific emotional and physiological cues that signal they are angry. This will help them to regain control of their anger in order to curb a violent response like bullying. Some internal cues include the following:

- Stomach gets tight or upset
- Heart beats faster
- Fists are clenched
- Face feels flushed or red
- Pressure is felt on the temples
- Palms are sweaty
- You feel a lump in your throat
- Jaw is clenched

Expressing Anger

Children need to know that it's okay to feel angry. They also need to know that it is not okay to express their anger in a way that hurts themselves, others, or possessions. Thus, before they choose a strategy to express their anger, it must meet the following three requirements:

1. It must let off steam.
2. It must not inflict harm on themselves, others, or things.
3. It must not make the situation worse or get anyone in trouble.

There are three ways to express anger:
1. *Aggressive.* This happens when your children's anger is directed toward the bully to hurt him or her emotionally, physically, or psychologically (e.g., yelling, hitting, or putdowns). This is not the best way for your children to react to being bullied. The basic message with an aggressive response style is that my feelings, thoughts, and beliefs are correct and the other person's are wrong. Have you acted aggressively toward another person? Have your children? If so, what was the outcome of the aggressive response? Was the response what you or your children hoped for?
2. *Passive.* This happens when your children hold in their anger. When they stop thinking about what caused the anger. When they do not

acknowledge that they are angry or when they suppress their anger. Some children react this way either to protect themselves from further harm or to protect you, the parent. Thus, if children do not allow their anger to be expressed outwardly, they may turn their anger inwardly by inflicting harm onto themselves, by holding a grudge, by spreading rumors, or by damaging property. The basic message with a passive response style is that the other person's (the bully's) feelings, thoughts, and beliefs are very important, but not mine. Have you acted passively toward another person? Have your children? If so, what was the outcome of the passive response? Was the response what you or your children hoped for?

3. *Assertive.* This is the best way for your children to deal with a person who has violated their rights. Responding assertively involves your children standing up for their right to be treated in a respectful way. When communicating their feelings of anger directly to the other person, the message should be delivered in a nonthreatening way. When they do this, your children make it clear to the other person—without hurting him or her or being pushy or demanding—what their needs are and how to get their needs met. The basic message with an assertive response style is that my feelings, thoughts, and beliefs are equally as important as everyone else's. What are some of the advantages and disadvantages of acting assertively when trying to resolve conflicts? Brainstorm ideas with your children.

Remember, the way your children choose to express their anger is not innate. It is not an unchangeable trait. Your children's responses to anger are learned responses. Thus, use the following questions to help you and your children think about how anger has been expressed in your lives.

- How was anger expressed in your home growing up?
- How did your mother, father, or siblings express anger?
- Were you allowed to show your anger outwardly?
- How do you manage and express your anger?
- How is anger expressed in your home now?

TOOLBOX TACTIC

The purpose of the exercise is for you and your child to become aware of how you both deal with anger. This is so both of you can learn to control your anger and find healthy ways to manage it, so you both can act on it in a healthy manner. The goal of the exercise is for you and your child to discover that people can experience and express anger in different ways. One way is not better than another way. It is just different.

First, complete the exercise by yourself. Then have your child complete the exercise. Finally, compare and discuss answers.

Think of an event that caused you to be angry. Using the chart listed below, identify the following. What triggered your anger? How did you know that you were angry? What did you notice? What were the underlying emotions that drove your anger? What strategies did you use to help calm your anger? Were the strategies effective? How did you express your anger? Would you express it differently? Why or why not?

Identify aggressive acts shown by self:	Call someone names	Throw something
	Give someone a dirty look	Kick someone or something
	Silent treatment	Get in someone's face
	Get others to "gang up"	Shoving, grabbing, hitting
	Spread rumors	Break something
		Other?

Identify thoughts prior to aggressive acts:	You did that on purpose...	You're being unreasonable...
	You wanted to hurt me...	You think you're so good...
	You deserve this...	You started it...
	You never even asked me...	There's no justice...
	I'll show you...	Other?

Identify internal cues prior to aggressive acts:	Stomach gets tight or upset	Sweaty palms
	Heart beats faster	Lump in throat
	Clenching fists	Clenched jaw
	Feel flushed/red in the face	Other?
	Pressure on the temples	

Identify emotional triggers prior to aggressive acts:	Annoyances	Disrespect
	Lying	Disloyalty
	Untrustworthy	Betrayal
	Injustice	Other?

Identify second emotions that influence anger:	Disappointed	Jealous
	Disgusted	Worried
	Hurt	Afraid
	Abandoned	Guilty
	Ashamed	Helpless
	Lonely	Fear
	Embarrassed	Other?
	Heartbroken	

Cage the Rage: Controlling Emotions

Thus far, we examined what triggers our anger or other emotions, how our bodies send signals letting us know that we are angry, and how we let others know that we are angry. Now, I will cover ways we can gain control of our angry feelings before they control us. This does not mean suppressing angry feelings or not allowing your children to feel angry—that too is destructive. Rather, it means expressing angry feelings in appropriate ways. There are five steps to control or tame our emotions or anger:

1. Know what pushes your buttons.
2. Know your body's anger signs.
3. Stop and think before you act.
4. Cage your rage. It's your choice.
5. Decide what to do.

Use assertive statements to tame anger. When your children address their anger assertively, they act on the problem immediately. They ask for a timeout. They acknowledge their feelings. They also ask for alternative ways to respond. Teach your children to express their anger appropriately by giving an assertive response using "I" statements. These statements include "When you... (state fact), I feel... (state feeling), because... (state why). I would like... (state the action)."

Help your children practice constructing assertive statements using events that have led them to become angry. Using the example statement, have your children write a statement that lets the other person know how they are feeling. Then help your children diffuse someone else's anger by using the following tips.

• *Listen*—Let the angry person vent. Don't argue with him or her.

- *Relax*—Deal with your own emotions. Don't get defensive. Own your anger. Say out loud what makes you angry.
- *Paraphrase*—Restate what you heard. Reflect on the content of the message and the feelings behind it. Make sure the other person knows that you understand.
- *Problem Solve*—What can be done to make things better? Reframe the problem. Try to look at situations as both challenges and opportunities.

Use coping self-talk to tame anger. The following is a list of ideas that you can teach your children to use to help control their anger.

- I am in charge of my own feelings.
  1. I own my feelings.
  2. It is okay to feel angry.
  3. Anger is part of being human.
  4. I can learn how to express my anger in helpful ways.
- I don't have to hold onto my anger.
  1. I can find ways to let it go.
  2. I can talk about hurt and angry feelings.
  3. I can look for someone to discuss my anger with.
  4. I can discuss, rather than act on, my words and actions that hurt others.
- I can stop blaming others and myself.
  1. Blaming only keeps people upset.
  2. Blaming is a way of not respecting people.
  3. I can express my feelings and then try to work things out.
- I can take my power.
  1. I can stand up for myself and others without being hurt.
  2. I can learn to defeat negative self-talk.
  3. I can feel good about myself and learn a lot about myself.
  4. I am strong when I use fair and firm words instead of fists.
  5. I can say "no" if I think the demands on my time are unreasonable.
  6. I can remember not to take things personally. I can tell myself, "Consider the source. It's not worth getting upset."
- I can remember that people are important to me.
  1. I can watch my thoughts, words, and actions.
  2. I can stop hurting people with my words and actions.
  3. I can take ownership of the hurtful things I do and say.
  4. Bullying hurts everyone.

Use counter-attack tactics to tame triggers of anger. Avoid "catastrophizing." Catastrophizing is an irrational thought that a lot of children have, believing that something is far worse than it actually is. Things kids tell themselves include: "I can't handle this!" "I'm going to explode!" "This kid is driving me crazy!" The first step to helping children deal with catastrophizing is to help them recognize when they are doing it. The sooner they do this, the quicker they will be able to stop it. It may be helpful to have children record their negative thoughts by writing them on a notepad or saying them into a voice recorder. Have them write down what happened as objectively as possible, what they thought about the situation, what they told themselves, and what their reaction to the situation was. Then, they can begin to notice some of the direct causes and effects of their thoughts so they can begin to work on changing them.

When your children start to catastrophize a situation, tell them to counter-attack with coping self-talk (also see chapter 6). Tell them to say to themselves: *"I am learning to handle this. I may feel like I am going to explode but I can do something about that to calm down. Friends can be annoying, but I am not going crazy. What do they need from me at this time?"* Other tactics they can use to control their anger include:

- Use a calming tone of voice that conveys respect.
- Emphasize that you will hear the other person out when he or she has calmed down.
- Avoid saying "don't" when responding to someone. Instead, say "I prefer" or use "Maybe...and..."
- Preface your statement with an understanding of their point of view, then say, "However, I feel..." or "And I suggest..." or "And I would like..."
- State your request in positive behavioral terms (i.e., "I would like to talk to you when you have more time to discuss how we can handle the situation"). Repeat your statement up to three times. If the negative behavior continues, state the consequence and emphasize that it is their choice to behave in that way.
- Depersonalize the situation: "It's not about me."

Use behavioral tactics to tame anger. Teach your children to control or dissolve their angry feelings using progressive muscle relaxation, controlled breathing, and/or visualization strategies (these were covered in chapter 6). They can engage in vigorous physical exercise to help control their anger. This is just as effective as having them systematically tense and relax their muscles. After all, physical exercise does exactly the same thing—it tenses and then relaxes the muscles. They can also visualize calming pictures, which will help them become more relaxed by thinking about the things that they find enjoyable, pleasant, or restful. Your children can also watch TV, read a book, walk the dog, go to the gym, play games, color, journal, paint, do yoga, keep an anger diary, or give themselves a positive timeout.

TOOLBOX TACTIC

Turtle Technique

The "Turtle Technique" is a strategy for helping young children control their anger.[19] Here are the steps to control feelings and calm down.
- Step 1: Recognize your feeling(s).
- Step 2: Think or say "STOP."
- Step 3: Go inside your "shell." Take a time out. Take 3 deep breaths. Take time to relax and to calm yourself down. Think of a solution.
- Step 4: Come out of your shell when you feel calm. Try out your solution.

Remind your children to practice the steps frequently. Help your children prepare for possible changes or disappointments. Recognize, comment, and praise when your children remain calm when expressing and managing their emotions.

Handling the Outcomes of Anger

Provide ground rules. Provide ground rules for behaviorally expressing anger. For example, tell your children, "When expressing anger, you cannot hurt yourself, others, or property (i.e., throw or break items). However, you can punch a pillow, go for a walk, yell in your room or into a pillow or in the shower, stomp your feet or clap your hands, draw a picture, smash play dough or clay, bounce or kick a ball, beat a drum, write in a diary, listen to music, do an angry dance, dig in the dirt, or talk to a trusted person."

Provide a time-out. Providing a time-out is not considered a punishment. While a brief time-out for young children (one to two minutes) can be useful, poorly planned, overused, or extended stays in time-out can be detrimental. Time-out does provide children with an immediate consequence for dangerous or destructive behaviors and should be reserved for that type of behavior. A time-out should be referred to as a "positive time-out" and should take place in a pleasant, comfortable area. A positive time-out is designed to teach children to take a time-out when they need to cool down so they can eventually take a time-out on their own without being sent there as a consequence.

TIP

Dealing with Your Children's Rage

You should never try to talk to your children in the middle of a rage or tantrum. Any attempt to respond to them at that point will just further "fuel the fire" and reinforce their anger. Plus, your children are not listening very well at that time, so any attempts to reason with them, lecture them, or talk to them about an issue isn't going to sink in if they are in the middle of a rage. Instead, calmly tell them "This is not okay. You need to go to your room to calm down." If your children are screaming at you, calling you names, or saying you are "the worst parent in the world," do not respond. Either give yourself a time-out or give them a time-out. Remove yourself from the situation by going to your room, or send them to their room. Don't yell back, because it will only bring you into their rage and make you the focal point of their anger. Also, avoid using confrontational or blaming comments that begin with:[20]

- "You should..." "You're wrong..." "I demand..." "We can't..." "We won't..." "We never..." "You don't understand..." "That's stupid..." "You must be confused." "I'm too busy for this." "You have to..."

Provide warnings. A warning should always be given for the first offense, and children should not be left alone or given attention during that time. If this initial warning is not effective, a time-out should be implemented, modified, or discontinued. Other approaches, like reasoning or practicing alternative behaviors, should be used for very excited or impulsive children.

TOOLBOX TACTIC

Activities for Managing Anger

- Teach your children the variation of the tune "If you're happy and you know it" to help manage their anger. It can also remind children of positive responses to anger or conflict. Substitute the following words: When you're angry and you know it, stop and think! (verse 1, verse 2, and so forth); When you're angry and you know it, there's a peaceful way to show it, when you're angry and you know it, stop and think! (verse 1, verse 2, and so forth).

    Verse 2: Talk to a friend
    Verse 3: Go for a walk
    Verse 4: Jiggle your body

- Another variation of the song: first verse, "If you're mad and you know it, walk away"; second verse, "If you're mad and you know it, count to ten"; third verse, "If you're mad and you know it, talk it out."

- Help deal with the anger with the ABCD method: (A = ask about the problem; B = brainstorm some solutions; C = choose the best idea; and D = do it).

- A-B-C-D Model—A cognitive restructuring technique that is used to help your children conceptualize their anger. (A = activating event; B = belief about the activating event; C = emotional consequence or feelings experienced as a result of our beliefs concerning this event; and D = dispute with a realistic way of looking at the activating event).

- The Anger Thermometer— Have your children color in a picture of a thermometer to show how upset they are.

- "Peace Table"—This is a table where children are safe from hearing angry words or experiencing physical aggression and can therefore talk about a problem or situation civilly.

- Angry Notes—Children write about their anger or draw a picture that represents how they feel. This will help them to deal with their emotions instead of aggressively acting them out. This is a great activity for kids with verbal disabilities to convey their emotions nonverbally.

- Debug—Used with younger kids, DEBUG is a 5 step process that kids use when someone is "bugging" or irritating them before they get an adult to help. 1) Ignore, 2) Move away, 3) Talk friendly, 4) Talk firmly, and 5) Get adult help.

TOOLBOX TACTIC

Interviewing for Angry Situations

The following questions can be used to inquire about events surrounding a situation that caused your child to become angry.

- What behavior got you in trouble?
- What was the situation that led you to become angry?
- What were the things that made you angry?
- How angry were you on a scale from 1 to 10?

    1 (not angry; feeling calm; relaxed)

    5 (mad; but still in control)

    10 (very angry; not in control; dangerous to self/others)

- When do you lose control?
- What do you look like when you are angry?
- How do people know if you are angry?
- What does your body do when you are angry?
- What feeling is behind your anger? (Hurt, Scared, Sad)
- Have you felt a lot of hurt in your life?
- What were you thinking while you were angry?
- What did you actually do with your anger?
- Did it work? Why or why not? (Help them recognize consequences.)
- Did you get what you wanted?
- What did others want or expect from you?
- What might have worked better?
- What choices did you have?
- What would you need to do differently?
- What would others need to do differently?
- How could you practice?
- What punishments would be really bad?
- Are there times when you get angry and don't get in trouble? (What's the difference?)
- Can you control your anger at all?
- What made you stop?
- Who taught you how to express your anger?
- Who understands your anger most of the time?

Teach Decision-Making Skills

Decision-making is the process of choosing what to do by considering the possible consequences of different choices. Children need skills that enable them to think clearly and make thoughtful decisions by considering the advantages and disadvantages of different options. This leads them to arrive at a feasible solution to the problem at hand. Responsible decision-making includes making decisions based on consideration of right and wrong, safety concerns, appropriate social (peer and family expectations) norms, respect for others, consequences of various actions, and contributing to the well-being of one's school and community.

TOOLBOX TACTIC

How Do You Solve Problems?

It's helpful to recognize how your own problem-solving processes might affect how you work with your children in making decisions. Take a moment to examine your own problem-solving preferences by responding to the following questions.

1. How do you usually solve problems (e.g., deliberate for a long time, talk with someone, give in to others, use a structured process)?

   _____

2. What kinds of decisions are easy for you? _____

3. What kinds of decisions are hard for you? _____

4. How might your own decision-making process influence your work with your children? _____

For example, if you find it easy to solve time-management issues, you may find it difficult to be patient with your children who are having difficulty in understanding the important of prioritizing or organizing.

Decision-Making Model

SODAS are more than just drinks. It is also the name of a decision-making strategy that you can use with your children when teaching them how to make good decisions. By using SODAS, children are more likely to make better choices since they learn how to think through a situation before they impulsively react and create a negative outcome for themselves.[21] Also, the SODAS process can help children better understand how their decisions impact other people. SODAS stands for:

S = *Situation*—Stop. Observe the situation and state the problem. Useful questions to ask:
* "What is the problem?"
    Who, What, Where, When, and How
* "What are the feelings involved with the situation?"
    "What do you feel?"
    "What do family members feel when the problem occurs?"
    "How do others feel, such as friends, employers, teachers, and so on?"
* "What stops you from...?"
* "How do you feel when...?"
* "What happens after you...?"
* "What exactly was said when...?"

O = *Options*—Brainstorm and explore the possible options and consequences when responding to the situation. Useful questions to ask:
* "What could be done to solve the problem?"
* "How can you achieve your goals?"
* "What do you want to do?"
* "What else could you do?"
* "What about...?"
* "We have _____ on the list. Might you want to consider _____?"

D = *Disadvantages*—Examine the cons of the options.

A = *Advantages*—Examine the pros of the options.
* "What are the possible benefits to you related to this option?"
* "Why are those things important to you?"
* "What are the likely drawbacks or disadvantages for you related to this option?"
* "What potential danger or harm for you could result from this option?"
* "Why are those drawbacks or disadvantages important to you?
* "How might family members and other people who support you feel or be affected by this option?"
* "What might happen to you as a result of their feelings or the impact on them?"
* "How about other people (e.g., employers, friends, teachers)?"
* "What might happen right away?"
* "How about a week or a month from now?"
* "What if you changed the option a little?"
* "Might you want to combine the best of these two options?"

S = *Solution*—Select the most appealing option as the solution to the situation. Useful questions to ask:

- "Remember the situation you told me about in the beginning. Will this option resolve that situation?"
- "How feasible is the option?"
- "Can the young person and his or her support system 'pull it off'?"
- "Who, what, when, where, and how?" regarding the actual implementation of the selected option.
- Make sure to follow-up and evaluate. Questions to ask:

    "Did you try implementing the solution as planned?"
    If not, "What prevented the solution from being implemented?"
    If yes, "How did implementation of the solution go?"
    "What happened as a result?"

Tips for Success. I recommend starting with advantages before exploring disadvantages for each option. Also, when asking your children to identify the advantages and disadvantages:

- Do not approve or condone any option.
- Avoid making statements such as "That's a good one." "I don't know about that one." "Do you really think that's a good idea?"
- Do not evaluate any of the options until your children begin to identify the advantages and disadvantages of each option.

TOOLBOX TACTIC

How to Use the SODAS Decision-Making Process

Tell your children that people make a lot of decisions every day. They make decisions about what to wear, what to eat, what they are going to do in the evening, and so on. Some decisions are easier to make than others. Ask your children to name some of the decisions they make every day. Then ask them about some problems or conflicts that they have seen in school. Ask about conflicts with friends or others. Next, explain the SODAS decision-making model. Tell your children to grab some SODAS when they have a problem to solve. Then ask them to think of a situation that they are currently dealing with that needs to be solved. They can also use a previous one. Teach them how to use the SODAS decision-making model to solve their problem.

SODAS

Situation: Describe the problem or situation you are trying to figure out.	
Options: Describe three different things you can really do about the situation you have described.	1. 2. 3.
Disadvantages: Things you don't like about the options you have identified. List at least two disadvantages for each of the options you have identified.	Option #1: a. b.
	Option #2: a. b.
	Option #3: a. b.
Advantages: Things you like about the options you have identified. List at least two advantages for each of the options you have identified.	Option #1: a. b.
	Option #2: a. b.
	Option #3: a. b.
Review the advantages and disadvantages of the options you wrote. Then check the option that gives you the most advantages and least disadvantages.	Option #1: _____ Option #2: _____ Option #3: _____

CASE STUDY—PART 5

How to Use SODAS with Jacob

Using Jacob's case as an example, here is how the SODAS approach works.

S = Ask Jacob to state the Situation.

"I de-panted Alex in PE Class. I gave in to peer pressure."

O= Look at his Options together.

"Do it again and get in trouble" or "Tell my friends no and not get in trouble, get my privileges revoked, not have my parents and friends disappointed in my behavior."

D = Help him consider possible Disadvantages to each option:

"I could get in trouble and get grounded" or "I could miss out on some free time."

A = Brainstorm his possible Advantages.

"Everyone will like me and think I am great" or "I will gain respect from my parents, friends, and teachers because I did not hurt another person."

S = Weigh the pros and cons, and ask Jacob for his Solution.

"Next time I see Alex I will say something nice to him like 'cool shirt.'"

Teach Relationship Skills

Relationship skills include establishing and maintaining healthy and rewarding relationships based on cooperation; resisting inappropriate social pressure; preventing, managing, and resolving interpersonal conflict; and seeking help when needed. "Building a positive relationship with antisocial students is a first step in a strategy for positively influencing their behavior and development."[22]

Encourage Cooperation

Cooperation is an act or instance of working or acting together for a common purpose or benefit. Cooperative play refers to play where children assume assigned and reciprocal roles while pursuing shared goals. It is organized around a theme, with each child taking on a different role that begins at about two years of age. Team sports like football or volleyball can be considered cooperative play. In cooperative play, children learn how to work together, learn empathy, have respect for each other, and share. In playing cooperatively, children should remember five things.

1. Body basics—Attend to body language.
2. Decide who starts—"You can go first since I went first last time."
3. Wait your turn—Allow the person time to finish. Be patient and flexible.
4. Talk and listen to the other person—Don't interrupt the other person who is talking.
5. Say something nice at the end—"Thanks for shooting hoops with me today."

Resist Peer Pressure

Peer pressure is a demand for conformity to group norms and a demonstration of commitment and loyalty. It's not uncommon for us to want to be part of a group and feel like we belong. Our peers influence our lives just by spending time with us. We learn from them, and they learn from us. However, sometimes this desire can affect our decisions and we do something we usually wouldn't do, or not doing something we would like to do. They can have a positive or negative influence. Clearly, as in Jacob's case, he gave in to peer pressure to bully and harass Alex. The idea that "everyone's doing it" can influence some kids to leave their better judgment or common sense behind. On the other hand, positive peer pressure can be used to pressure children who bully into acting better toward other kids. If enough kids get together, peers can pressure each other into doing what's right! Plus, a child's inner strength and self-confidence can help him or her resist peer pressure by standing firm, walking away, and resist doing something when he or she knows better.

 TOOLBOX TACTIC

Exposure to Emotionally Arousing Events and Experiences

You will need a copy of the poem "The Road Not Taken" by Robert Frost. Visit www.poemhunter.com for a copy.

1. View "The Road Not Taken." Ask your child to read it silently or read it together out loud.
2. Ask him or her what the title might mean. Discuss.
3. Then, have him or her discuss the following:
   - Who is the speaker in this poem? How can you tell?
   - Is the poet speaking in the past, present, or future? Explain.
   - What is the speaker facing? Can you think of an example of this kind of dilemma?

- What do you think he will do?
- How does he expect to feel about his choice?
4. Ask: "What are some examples of 'roads traveled' by kids your age?" Responses might include:
   - decisions about friends, styles, etc.
   - dilemmas about members of the opposite sex
   - choices in interests, activities, and ideas
   - decisions about school subjects
   - exposure to peer pressure
5. Ask: "What might taking 'the road less traveled by' mean to kids your age?" (e.g., choosing the less popular option, saying "no" to peer pressure, not always going with the group, etc.)
6. Ask: "Why might taking this road end up 'making all the difference?'" (e.g., the rewards of hard work in the present often end up paying off in the future; a less popular choice may become more popular later on; people often strengthen their identity and self-esteem by acting on their own beliefs, rather than on those of a group; etc.)
7. Have your children brainstorm a list of common dilemmas they have faced that involve choosing one or more "roads." Discuss the list.
   - Ask them to select one dilemma. Explain that they will act out a skit about this problem that shows what might happen in the future as the result of decisions made now. Skits should include:
     - a realistic portrayal of a school situation
     - a logical outcome based on a decision regarding the "road taken"

When the skits are ready, have each child act out his or her skit for you.

Resolve Interpersonal Conflict

Interpersonal conflict is an expressed struggle between at least two interdependent parties who perceive incompatible goals. Many of us experience conflict when we have opposing viewpoints, when our emotions override our thoughts, or when we have a misunderstanding or fail to communicate our needs and wants. Children must learn how to resolve conflict peacefully; therefore, I will cover and explore this topic more fully in chapter 8.

Social Support

Social support is the ability to use community systems for support. Encourage your children to ask adults for help if they feel angry or upset or do not know how to stop bullying. For example, talk with your children to discover whom they would turn to for help. Listen to their reasons for selecting these individuals. From this discussion, create a list of trusted adults they could turn to for advice or help. Tell them to keep this list in a safe place for possible future use.

Seventh Stop: Reward Acceptable Behavior

Never underestimate the power of hearing *"Good job"* or *"I'm proud of you."* Children crave approval at any age. Immediately reinforce and reward positive behaviors with praise. A hug or a smile can be a great incentive for your children to continue their positive behavior. Compliment them whenever you find a genuine opportunity. Don't be tempted to negate the compliment with follow-up comments such as, *"Why can't you always behave this way?"* Whenever possible, tell them what you want them to do, not what you don't want them to do. For example, I remember when I was a kid and my mom used to leave me handwritten notes posted on my bedroom mirror or on my night stand thanking me for helping her around the house (e.g., putting the clothes or dishes away without being asked). It always put a smile to my face knowing that she appreciated my efforts. Consequently, I do the same thing for my children and my husband. It is very rewarding for me to hear that they appreciated the thought and how considerate I was of their efforts. P.S.: Even though I am a grown adult, my mom still leaves me letters of gratitude when she visits—and it still puts a smile on my face. So, it is never too late to start—write a note: send a text, Tweet, Facebook, or Instagram message.

Eighth Stop: Promote the 4 A's.

Attachment (Belonging)

Positive social bonds are prerequisites to prosocial behavior. Help your children participate in local teams and extracurricular activities or have them take classes to build hobbies, but avoid overload. Working in groups and teams builds competency and relationships.

Achievement (Mastery)

Self-satisfaction arises from achievement when internally motivated. Gaining mastery over something (e.g., sports or painting) means setting high expectations and refusing to accept failure. It arises as a natural consequence of striving to do one's best in the world. Help your children to succeed by encouraging effort and following through on tasks. Remember to celebrate their accomplishments.

Autonomy (Independence)

The key to fostering independence is to allow your children to make more decisions about how and when they do things. Obedience implies the power of the few over the many, relies on rewards and punishments, and leads to retaliation and rebellion. In contrast, true discipline lies in demanding responsibility rather than obedience. This means with more freedom comes greater responsibility. For example, as long as your children are completing their tasks or getting their work done, you will try not to impose on or bug them (i.e., respect their freedom). However, if they stop meeting their obligations, then you will have to step in and take over.

Altruism (Generosity)

Through helping others, young people find proof of their own self-worth. Help and encourage your children to find an area of interest, a hobby, a job, or a way to provide service to the community. Encourage them to use their influence in positive ways by leading change in causes or activities they care about. Encourage them to get involved in activities like social clubs, music groups, sports, and/or volunteering so that they have the opportunity to learn the value of compassionately giving back to those less fortunate. Reinforce that power can be experienced through doing good (e.g., through service projects, helping others, correcting wrongs, providing a leadership role in promoting acceptance of others).

Ninth Stop: Working with Professionals

Make sure adults in your children's school and/or extracurricular groups outside the home know that you are committed to ending the bullying, and get them on board to help you.

Working with the School

Work with the school to find out what can be done to ensure that your children will not bully. Meet and work with your children's teachers to help change their behavior. Ask a teacher or a school counselor if your children are facing any problems at school, such as struggling with a particular subject or having difficulty making friends. Ask them for advice on how you and your child can work through the problem. Request that you be kept informed. Find out if your children instigated the bullying or joined in. Discover how your children have bullied and take appropriate steps to curtail the behavior. For a day, go to school with your children—wherever they go, you go with them.

What Can I Expect the School to Do? Schools can use a range of strategies to deal with bullying. The nature of the bullying incidents will help to determine which method is most appropriate. These include:

- Physical or supervisory responses: altering the physical environment where possible to reduce places where bullying can happen and to enhance teachers' ability to supervise students throughout the day, or arranging increased supervision of students at certain times or in certain locations.
- Managing access to technology at school: schools work with students and parents to establish acceptable use of technology, focusing on the use of mobile phones, social networking sites, and websites.
- Teaching and learning programs: implementing programs that promote personal development and address all forms of bullying through the teaching of social-emotional skills, communication skills, social skills, assertiveness, coping strategies, group behavior, understanding the motives for bullying, and being effective bystanders.
- Disciplinary measures: taking action and applying consequences for the bullying to impress upon children who bully others that what they have done is unacceptable, to deter them from repeating that behavior, and to send a message to other students that bullying is unacceptable.
- Restorative approaches: restorative justice approaches put repairing harm done to relationships and people over and above assigning blame and dispensing punishment.
- Mediation: students in conflict are invited to work with a trained teacher or peer-mediator to find a mutually acceptable way of resolving their problem. However, peer mediation is not recommended in bullying situations since it implies equality in power between parties, which by definition does not exist in bullying.

- Counseling: the school counselor can support the students to help them to deal with the bullying.
- Restructure of classes: removing the students from regular contact with each other; using temporary or long-term flexible learning arrangements, such as moving the victim to a different class or lunchtime.

What will I be expected to do in working with the school? As a parent, your role in working with the school includes:

- Focus on teaching your child prosocial behaviors.
- Encourage your child to enact the agreed-upon strategies at school and reinforce them at home.
- Keep the lines of communication open with the school and communicate regularly.
- Seek further outside help (counseling) for your child if needed.
- Employ cyber safety measures at home, such as agreed-upon usage times and parental lock-outs. Install extra security on your computer using blocking, filtering, and key-logging software such as CyberPatrol, Safe Eyes, CyberSitter, NetNanny, or *www.cyberbullyalert.com*.
- Stay informed of school activities and events. Keep a bulletin board at home. Hang the school calendar that schools send home on the refrigerator and post key dates and special events. Post teacher communications such as the Peek of the Week memos, names of key school contact people, weekly meals, and other school-related information.

Working with a Mental Health Professional

Think about seeking professional help from a counselor or therapist, your children's pediatrician, or your family physician if the bullying does not stop or is hard to control. A comprehensive evaluation can help you and your children understand what is causing the bullying and help you develop a plan to stop the destructive behavior. Without intervention, bullying can lead to serious academic, social, emotional, and legal difficulties.

Tenth Stop: More Tips for Success

Model the Behavior You Expect

The values of your family and prosocial behaviors should be demonstrated daily throughout your family interactions. Whatever behaviors you demonstrate and the stand that you take will be taken as expressing the values of the family. Children will judge your values not by what you say but by what you do and what you permit them to do; thus, your family values should encompass a zero tolerance for all forms of harassment and bullying. Children who bully generally come from homes that lack warmth, supervision, or parental involvement and emphasize harsh physical discipline. Be careful and self-conscious about setting a good example in everything you say and do. If you are respectful of people, others in your home will be more likely to adopt that behavior. Also model good self-control. If you are in an irritating situation and your children are present, tell them why you are frustrated and then discuss the potential solutions to the problem. Bullying flourishes because parents tolerate it by either ignoring it, refusing to accept feedback about it, making excuses for the bully (such as "it's just a personality clash"), practicing it themselves, and/or talking about the behavior in humorous ways.

Adopt House Rules That Make Sense

Rules viewed as stupid (in your children's eyes) are the least likely to be followed. Your children need to see how a rule benefits them. They need and deserve an explanation for why things are the way they are, rather than being told "Because I said so." For example, explain to your children that the reason they must be home by 9:00 P.M. on a school night is so they can finish their homework and get a good night's sleep. The exception to the rule is when they are participating in a school event or volunteering. Thus, there should be clear expectations and guidelines about what is expected of your children, what behaviors are encouraged, and what behaviors are unacceptable. Let them know that all forms of harassment—bullying and discrimination—are covered in one policy. Negotiate an online agreement with your children.

Raise Awareness and Understanding

Help your children become aware of harassment and bullying. Let them know how you expect them to treat other people, what the school's policy and expectations state, and what you and the school will do if they bully. Encourage your children to develop their own moral code so they will choose to behave ethically online. Emphasize your expectation that your child will act in accord with the families' values and beliefs at all times and do what is right, regardless of the uncovering and punishment by you or anyone else. Explain that bullying and cyberbullying are harmful and unacceptable behavior.

Be Fair: Don't Treat Everyone the Same

Being fair means giving each person what he or she needs, but not treating everyone exactly alike. Just as children need different approaches to reading or learning, they need different approaches to discipline. Discipline codes that "uniformly" or "consistently" treat all kids the same are doomed to failure. Make sure the consequences are age and developmentally appropriate.

Build a Positive Relationship with Your Child

Your presence matters. Children regard your presence as a sign of care and connectedness. Families who eat meals together, play together, and build traditions together thrive. Does your family eat together at least four times a week? If so, there is a greater chance your kids will perform better in school and be less likely to exhibit negative behavior. Also, increase your supervision of your children's activities and whereabouts, and know who your children are spending time with. Make an effort to observe your children in one-on-one interactions.

Spend time with them. Spend more time with your children and learn about their activities and friends. By spending time with your children, you send the message that they are worthy of your attention. You can play with them, read to them, take a walk, and make positive memories that will last a lifetime. During this quality time, it can be beneficial to talk to your children about the feelings they experienced throughout the day. For example, ask your children what part of the day they felt the saddest? The happiest? Then, share the same about your day. This provides you and your children an opportunity to learn more about each other. It also helps to build a strong foundation for your relationship.

Communicate with them. Keep the lines of communication open. Set up a daily time to check in with your children about their day, what's going on at school, or other activities taking place in their lives. Talking to your children about bullying is an important step in trying to prevent it from happening. A 2010 study reported that 64% of children who were bullied did not report it. Only 36% reported bullying. So opening the lines of communication is critical. Here are five ways to start a conversation with your children:

- How has today been so far on a scale of 1 to 10 (where 1 is terrible and 10 is terrific)?
- What is something you accomplished today (or this week) that you feel good about?
- What is something you are looking forward to?
- What's on your mind these days?
- What is a goal you have been working on lately?

Conclusion

Many children who bully do so as an attempt to meet the basic needs of love and belonging, power, freedom, fun, and survival.[23] If those particular needs go unmet, or conflict arises between needs, the unmet needs drive the children's behavior. Thus, it is critical that we understand the purpose behind their aggressive behavior so they can find healthy, acceptable ways to meet their needs. When children who bully are allowed to engage in aggressive behavior at a young age without effective intervention from parents and/or the school system, they are at significantly greater risk for negative outcomes later in their lives.

Part IV

Preventing Bullying Behaviors

Chapter 8

Building a Strong Foundation to Prevent Bullying

This chapter provides a road map to bully-proof your children by teaching them life skills that build character and reinforce and promote prosocial behaviors. The desired outcome is that they build positive relationships, recognize and manage their emotions, handle challenging situations effectively, and build resilience so they can be buddies and not bullies.

Parents can only give good advice or put their children on the right path.
The final forming of a person's character lies in their own hands.

Anne Frank

Bully-Proofing Your Child

Countless times I've been asked by parents and caregivers, "Is it possible to bully-proof my child?" My answer is always a resounding "Yes. It's possible." But it is challenging, takes time, and requires patience. It means never giving up. However, my other response is that they cannot do it alone; they cannot just protect their children and think they will be safe. Rather, bullying is everyone's business, and the best response to prevent it is a proactive or preventive one from everyone who works with children—school administrators, teachers, counselors, other youths, parents, and the community. Everyone is responsible for addressing bullying; consequently, developing a school-family-community partnership is essential in preventing bullying. When parents partner with their children's school, they help to improve their children's academic performance. When parents and school personnel systematically work together to discourage bullying, respond to incidents when they occur, and teach children the skills they need to treat each other with understanding and respect, we create safe and supportive environments where children develop a sense of belonging, build connections, and work toward creating a caring community.[1] When children feel connected, they are less likely to be bullies or victims of aggression.[2]

Parents are a school's best allies in bullying prevention, so support your children's school in teaching them the skills, knowledge, and attitudes that promote prosocial behaviors. These include character building, relationship fostering, social–emotional learning, and conflict resolution so that children can be a buddy and not a bully. Research shows that the success of any program is 60 percent grounded in whether the same kinds of approaches are used at home.[3] This chapter provides you with a road map on how to bully-proof your children and avert bullying behaviors so they can build and maintain respectful, caring peer relationships in a diverse, multicultural world.

A Roadmap to Preventing Bullying

One of the most important things you can do to help bully-proof your children and reduce the risk for engagement in bullying behaviors is to challenge their positive attitudes towards the use of bullying to resolve conflict. Teach them the "rules of the road" to building and sustaining healthy relationships. Because life is filled with many routes that children can go down, one wrong turn can have disastrous consequences. As such, you are in the driver's seat and can steer them down the path that leads them to prosocial behaviors that build positive relationships (i.e., friendships) which are central to their success in school and life. You ultimately have direct influence on your children's social behavior, beliefs, and treatment of others. Thus it is never too late to teach them good moral values and ethical behavior.

Help Build Character

Children develop character by what they see, what they hear, and what they are repeatedly led to do.

James Stenson
Author

Parents have the greatest influence on children's character development. Abraham Lincoln said, *"Reputation is the shadow. Character is the tree."* Your children's character is much more than just what they try to display for others to see; it is who they are even when no one is watching. Good character is doing the right thing because it is right to do. Thus, their conscience is a big part of character. It is their moral compass that directs their moral values. A person of character encompasses the core universal values that define the qualities of a good person: trustworthiness (includes honesty), respect, responsibility, caring (includes compassion and forgiveness), fairness, and citizenship. The CHARACTER COUNTS! Coalition calls these the six pillars of character (*charactercounts.org*). Of course, there are many other character traits that could be added. Basically, having character is being the best person one can be and is the result of strong integrity. Integrity is an uncompromising commitment to truth, honor, faithfulness, loyalty, and trust. It is standing up for what you believe is right and living by your highest values. No one is born with character. Character must be learned. "We are born with a potential for good character—and for the dispositions and habits that make up bad or weak character."[4]

POINT TO PONDER

You are a person of integrity when your words and actions match. Stephen L. Carter, author of the book *Integrity*, said, "We care more about winning than about playing by the rules." Ask yourself and then your children the following questions.

- What role does integrity play in your relationships and life success?
- How do you show integrity?
- How do they show integrity?

In Carter's book, he outlines three steps for becoming a person with integrity.

1. Discern what is right and wrong. Discernment takes time and emotional energy. It's much easier to follow the crowd than to oppose it.
2. Struggle to live according to the sense of right and wrong you have discerned.
3. Be willing to say what you are doing and why you are doing it.

Building character does not happen overnight. It takes time to practice having good character, so do not give up on your children and tell them not to give up on themselves. Help them build the six pillars of character and reinforce their good character traits by evaluating their own development and the extent that they enact these traits. Tell them that their character counts. Remind them that their success and happiness will depend on who they are inside and not what they have or how they look. Let's take a look at the 6 pillars of character.

TOOLBOX TACTIC

Building good character means developing positive traits that are necessary to build positive relationships with others.[5] First, circle the character traits listed below that you believe you possess. Then have your child do the same.

Exploring Your Character Traits

• Honest	• Bright	• Humble
• Light-hearted	• Courageous	• Friendly
• Leader	• Serious	• Short
• Expert	• Funny	• Adventurous
• Brave	• Humorous	• Hard-working
• Conceited	• Sad	• Timid
• Mischievous	• Poor	• Shy
• Demanding	• Rich	• Bold
• Thoughtful	• Tall	• Daring
• Keen	• Dark	• Dainty
• Happy	• Independent	• Light
• Disagreeable	• Intelligent	• Handsome
• Simple	• Compassionate	• Pretty
• Fancy	• Gentle	• Ugly
• Plain	• Proud	• Selfish
• Excited	• Wild	• Unselfish
• Studious	• Messy	• Self-confident
• Inventive	• Neat	• Respectful
• Creative	• Joyful	• Considerate
• Thrilling	• Strong	• Imaginative

- Busy
- Patriotic
- Fun-loving
- Popular
- Successful
- Responsible
- Lazy
- Dreamer
- Helpful
- Simple-minded

- Pitiful
- Cooperative
- Lovable
- Prim
- Proper
- Ambitious
- Able
- Quiet
- Curious
- Reserved

- Pleasing
- Bossy
- Witty
- Fighter
- Tireless
- Energetic
- Cheerful
- Smart
- Impulsive
- Loyal

Discuss the following questions.
- What traits do you have in common?
- In what traits do you differ?
- What does having good character mean?
- Why is it important to have good character?

TIP

Learning good character will help your children "R.E.A.P." the benefits of developing prosocial behaviors so that they may gain **R**espect for others as well as themselves, show **E**mpathy toward others, gain an **A**cceptance of others, and develop **P**erspective-taking abilities (understanding different points of view).

It is more shameful to distrust one's friends than to be deceived by them.
François duc de la Rochefoucauld
17th-century French memoirist and philosopher

Pillar 1: Trustworthiness

Trustworthy means that a person can be relied upon to do what one says one will do and keep one's promises. A trustworthy person is honest, loyal, and builds a good reputation. Honesty means telling the truth and admitting mistakes even when you know someone might be angry or disappointed. Trustworthy people do not gossip or betray a friend's trust. They don't lie, cheat, or steal. Bear in mind that being wrong is not the same thing as lying, although honest mistakes can still damage trust insofar as it may show poor judgment. But admitting that one was wrong is the first step to mending a relationship. Teach your children ways in which they can build trust in their friendships. Here are some suggestions you may give to them.

- *Fulfill your promises:* When you make promises, take the necessary steps to fulfill them. Think of how and when someone broke a promise to you. How did you feel? If you are unable to keep a promise, make the effort to explain what happened and what prevented you from doing so.
- *Say what you mean:* It is important that people can trust what you say. Home or school can become an untrustworthy environment when people make threats or say things they don't mean. They can become empty words.
- *Encourage others with kind words:* Don't gossip or say things that hurt people. Everyone needs to be built up, especially when you go home. The home is to be a place where you can be refreshed at the end of the day. When homes don't have encouragement, they become a place of dread.
- *Don't take what doesn't belong to you:* This includes material things and liberties. When you respect others' property and space, you create an environment of trust that flourishes.
- *Look for the good in situations:* At times you will face situations that are less than ideal. Sometimes they are unavoidable. However, when these situations occur, it is important that you find at least one positive thing about it (remember the coping self-talk strategies discussed in chapters 6 and 7). If you only see the bad, it will destroy the atmosphere of safety. As a result, trust will go out the window.

POINT TO PONDER

It takes courage to be a trustworthy person. To have courage means to:
- Tell the truth despite the consequences.
- Admit mistakes when you make them.
- Apologize for mistakes and wrongdoing.
- Accept the consequences of your actions.
- Stand up for people who are less fortunate than you.
- Stand up for the beliefs of your faith or religion.
- Resist peer pressure to do the wrong thing.
- Stand up for your beliefs about what is right and wrong.

Have your children think about how they are trustworthy and courageous.[6] Ask them:
- If your friends were here right now, would they say you were trustworthy? What would your parents say? Are you more trustworthy with your friends or with your parents? Do you think your parents should trust you automatically? Why or why not?
- How do you know when you can trust someone?
- How important is trust in your relationships with friends and family? How would these relationships be affected if you found out someone were lying to you?
- What does being trustworthy have to do with the quality of your character?
- Once trust has been broken, what can you do to get it back? Have you ever lost someone's trust? Has someone lost your trust? Explain.
- What are the benefits of being a trustworthy person? How do you benefit from the trustworthiness of others?
- Do you have the courage to be yourself? What do you think that means? How can it require courage to be yourself?
- In what ways have you demonstrated courage in your life?
- What was the hardest stand you ever had to take with your friends? With your family? Did it cost you anything? If so, what? What were the benefits?
- Is peer pressure a very strong influence in your school? Does it take courage to resist peer pressure?
- What do you think stops people from taking a stand against something they know is wrong?

TOOLBOX TACTIC

Trustworthy Friend Kit

Be a trustworthy friend.[7] Help your children make a friendship kit to remind them of what it takes to be a trustworthy friend. Ask them to label an envelope or Ziploc baggie "Friendship Kit" and decorate it. Have them place the things on the list below inside the envelope. Cut out the list and put it in the friendship kit, too. Have them either introduce the kit to a friend or have them give it to a friend. Make sure they know what each thing in the kit stands for.

- Tape—Stick up for your friend.
- Bandage—Never let a friend do anything to harm himself or herself.
- Button—"Button your lips" and keep a secret for a friend.
- Candy heart—Have the courage to do the right thing.
- Word card labeled "Truth"—Remember to always speak the truth. Be honest and sincere with your friends.
- Eraser—Everyone makes mistakes. Forgive a friend's mistakes.
- Mint—A trustworthy friend is worth a mint.

Never look down on anybody unless you're helping him up.

Jesse Jackson
20th-century American political activist, preacher

Pillar 2: Respect

Respect is taking someone's feelings, thoughts, behaviors, and wishes into consideration. It means not gossiping, talking positively about others, and showing consideration for a person's freedom, privacy, and dignity. It also means showing regard for oneself and others. Respect is something that is earned by acknowledging people, listening to them, being truthful with them, and accepting their unique personality. If one does not show respect for other people, then it is hard to gain their respect. If a person wants respect, he or she must understand what it is, practice it, and model it. Respect follows the golden rule: "Do unto others as you would have done to you."

POINT TO PONDER

Respect Is the "Golden Rule"

When we follow the Golden Rule, we are being respectful and considerate of others and ourselves. This reflects a good social attitude. Have your children think about how they would like to be treated.[6] Ask them the following:

- What does the "Golden Rule" mean to you?
- What would things be like if everyone treated everyone else with kindness and respect?
- What are some of your "pet peeves" concerning your treatment by others?
- What type of problems or disagreements are most predominant in your group of friends?
- Why doesn't everyone follow the Golden Rule if it is such a good idea?

TOOLBOX TACTIC

Showing Respect

On the next trip to the grocery store with your children take the opportunity to point out ways to show respect to others. While waiting in line, let someone with fewer items go ahead of you or allow someone who has been waiting longer than you to move over to the check-out lane that just opened. Be polite to the cashier and take your cart back to the corral when you are finished. Explain to your children that actions like these show that we value and respect others and their property. Ask them the following:

- Whom do you respect?
- Is it ever okay to treat another person with disrespect?
- Some say everybody is entitled to be treated with respect. Do you agree?
- Bullies are often trying to make people "respect" them. Is this really respect, or is it fear? What is the difference?
- How is bullying or violent behavior an act of disrespect?
- What are some ways that you feel disrespected?
- What are some ways that you have been disrespectful?
- Describe three things you could do to be a more respectful person. How would that affect your relationships with others?
- How does it benefit you to be a respectful person?

In the long run, we shape our lives, and we shape ourselves. The process never ends until we die. And the choices we make are ultimately our own responsibility.

Eleanor Roosevelt

Pillar 3: Responsibility

Responsibility means taking care of your duties and answering for your actions. Responsible people are accountable for the choices they make, show self-restraint, and pursue excellence. They don't blame others for their mistakes, don't take credit for other people's work or accomplishments, and admit their own mistakes. On the other hand, irresponsible people often go against the rules—often by impulse—without thinking or caring about the possible consequences. They don't follow through with their promises; they make excuses for their behavior. They also do not accept the consequences for the choices they have made (see chapter 7 for further information). When people fail to accept responsibility for their actions, they run the risk of becoming:

- Overly dependent on others for recognition, approval, and acceptance.
- Chronically hostile, angry, or depressed over how unfairly they have been or are being treated.
- Fearful about ever taking a risk or making a decision.
- Overwhelmed by disabling fears.
- Unsuccessful in personal relationships.
- Emotionally or physically unhealthy.
- Unable to develop trust or to feel secure with others.
- Resistant to vulnerablility.

Things that people tell themselves when they have not accepted personal responsibility include:

- It's not my fault I am the way I am.
- I never asked to be born.
- Life is unfair! There is no sense in trying to take control of my life.
- You can't help me; nobody can help me. I'm useless and a failure.
- Life is so depressing. If only I had better luck and had been born into a healthier family or attended a better school.
- How can I ever be happy, seeing how bad my life has been?
- My parents made me what I am today!
- I am who I am; there is no changing me.

This type of negative self-talk is dangerous thinking. Help your children "forget" past failures at being responsible. They cannot change them, but they can make better choices in the future. Now is the time for them to be responsible. Your children need to develop the following behavior traits in order to accept personal responsibility:

- Seek out help and accept it for themselves—go talk to a counselor, community leader, spiritual leader, etc.
- Be open to new ideas.
- Affirm themselves positively ("you are worthy of love, you are a good person"); see chapters 6 & 7 for further examples.
- Recognize that they decide the choices they make.
- Recognize that they choose their responses to the people, actions, and events in their lives. Remind them not to give a bully their power.
- Let go of anger, fear, blame, mistrust, and insecurity.
- Take risks. Become vulnerable to change and growth that take place in their lives.
- Realize that they are in charge of the direction their lives take.

With great power comes great responsibility.

Voltaire
(and Uncle Ben to Peter Parker in *Spider-man!*)

POINT TO PONDER

Have your children think about how they are responsible.[6] Ask them:
- Do you consider yourself to be a responsible person? Why? In what ways?
- Describe something you've done that was really irresponsible. How did you feel afterward? What did you learn from it?
- What responsibilities do you feel you have toward your classmates?
- What are your responsibilities? At home? At school?
- What happens if you are irresponsible?
- What would you do differently the next time?
- What are the rewards of being responsible at home or at school?

TOOLBOX TACTIC

I'll Do That

Oftentimes, our children take things for granted when their meals are on the table or the laundry is always put back in their drawers. To help them to better understand their responsibilities at home, have your children assume a new home responsibility. Have them write a paragraph or discuss with you about the new responsibility and what it involves. A new responsibility could be making supper one night, doing the laundry, cutting the grass, etc.[8]

It is not fair to ask of someone else what you are not willing to do yourself.

Eleanor Roosevelt

Pillar 4: Fairness

Fairness means treating people objectively, listening to their opinions and viewpoints and considering all the facts—*before* making decisions (I will discuss this later in the chapter). It means playing by the rules, taking turns, being open-minded, and not taking advantage of other people. Being fair means equal treatment for everyone, admitting fault, and compromising. But most of all, it is about making sure all are treated with the kindness and respect they deserve.

POINT TO PONDER

Have your children think about how they are fair.[6]
- What does treating people fairly mean?
- Does fairness mean everyone gets the same amount?
- Does fairness mean enforcing the rules for everyone, even if it means losing a game?
- Is it possible to treat everyone fairly?
- Think of a time when you've taken unfair advantage of a person or a situation, or when someone has taken unfair advantage of you. Describe it.
    - What was unfair about it?
    - How did it make you feel?
    - What did you learn from the experience?
    - What would you do differently?

TOOLBOX TACTIC

Fair Cents: Teaching Fairness

Materials needed: ten pennies, two nickels, and one dime.

Stack the pennies on top of one another. Stack the nickels next to them. Place the dime beside the nickels. Begin by discussing the fact that although each set of coins looks different, they all have the same value. This is the same with people. We look different on the outside (short, tall, blonde, etc.), but we are all of equal value and deserve to be treated fairly. When you share, take turns, and treat others equally and with respect, you are showing signs of fairness.[9]

Human kindness has never weakened the stamina or softened the fiber of a free people. A nation does not have to be cruel to be tough.

Franklin Delano Roosevelt
32nd American President (1882–1945)

Pillar 5: Caring & Compassion

A caring person is kind, considerate, compassionate, and generous. Caring means showing understanding of others by treating them with generosity and a forgiving spirit. Caring people always take into account how decisions, words, and actions are likely to affect other people. A caring spirit directs people to identify acts that show compassion, consideration, kindness, and charity. A compassionate person considers the needs of others, not just his or her own, and deeply feels the joy and sadness of others and their situations. Compassion gives a person an emotional bond with his or her world. When people learn compassion for another, they look beyond their own needs and give their time, talents, and resources to helping others. Genuine, selfless concern for others is a sign of ethical maturity.[10] Caring people are not cruel, mean, or insensitive to the feelings of others.

POINT TO PONDER

Have your children think about how they are caring and compassionate.[6] Ask them:

• How do you feel when people show that they really care about you?

• How do you feel when you do something really caring for someone else?

TOOLBOX TACTIC

"Strive for Five!" Campaign

Challenge your children to choose 5 people they can help in some way. For example, they may choose to play with someone new, help a person who has fallen, say thank-you to the cafeteria workers, etc. Then, challenge them to do 5 acts of kindness a day. Don't be surprised when "Strive for Five" becomes a desire to help in more than 5 different ways![11]

Be humble and give more honor to others than to yourself. Do not be interested only in your own life, but be interested in the lives of others.

Saint Paul

Pillar 6: Citizenship

Citizenship means being responsible and respectful to people, animals, and the environment. It means caring about your community and country, being informed about the needs within one's school and community, being a good neighbor, and doing your best to make your home, school, and community a better place. Good citizens get involved in the community by helping others, voting, obeying rules and laws, volunteering, and protecting the environment.

TOOLBOX TACTIC

Raising a Good Citizen

Help your children become good citizens by:
- Knowing and understanding the Pledge of Allegiance.
- Knowing and understanding our national anthem, "The Star-Spangled Banner."
- Knowing and understanding the value of recycling. Have them become involved in a recycling program in your community.
- Bring democracy to your dining room table. Illustrate the power of voting by asking younger kids, "Have you and your friends ever had to

make a decision about something that was hard to agree on? Well, voting is a fair way to make decisions." Then take a vote on something—like what activity to do next. Engage older kids in political debate by talking about issues that interest them—like making college more affordable, raising the minimum wage, or lowering the legal voting age. Then help them turn passion into action by writing a letter to an editor or volunteering for a campaign.[12]

Character Traits of Virtue

Although not included in the six pillars, traits of virtue are the essence of your children's character. It is the sum of the six pillars of character. Thus, virtue is defined by the moral excellence of a person. It means having positive character. Virtues are habits that develop through practice; thus, make sure you provide ample opportunities for your children to practice the virtues and discuss the value with them thereafter. How can you reinforce good character in your children? You can find helpful tips in the book *No More Misbehavin': 38 Difficult Behaviors and How to Stop Them* by parenting expert Michele Borba. In her book, Borba offers parents effective strategies for reducing undesirable behavior in their children. For example, for values such as honesty, Borba suggests seven strategies:

1. Expect and demand honesty.
2. Reinforce honesty.
3. Use moral questioning.
4. Don't overreact.
5. Teach the difference between real and make believe.
6. Explain why dishonesty is wrong.
7. Set a consequence for repeat dishonesty.

> *Cultivate virtue in yourself, and virtue will be real. Cultivate it in the family, and virtue will abound. Cultivate it in the village, and virtue will grow. Cultivate it in the nation, and virtue will be abundant. Cultivate it in the universe, and virtue will be everywhere.*
>
> Lao Tzu

TOOLBOX TACTIC

Help your children remember the six pillars of character by using this creative "Color Scheme" device.[10]
- Trustworthiness: **blue**—Think of "true blue."
- Respect: **gold**—Think of the Golden Rule.
- Responsibility: **green**—Think about being responsible for a garden or finances; or as in being solid and reliable like an oak.
- Fairness: **orange**—Think of dividing an orange into equal sections to share fairly with friends.
- Caring & compassion: **red**—Think of a heart.
- Citizenship: **purple**—Think regal purple as representing the state.

TOOLBOX TACTIC

Visit the following websites for free character education resources that can give you more ideas in helping you teach, model, and foster the six essential virtues of character in your children: *charactercounts.org*; *charactered.net*; *www.character.org*; and *goodcharacter.com*.

Reinforce and Promote Prosocial Behaviors to Build Relationships

> *Remember that the best relationship is one in which your love for each other exceeds your need for each other.*
>
> Dalai Lama

"To have a friend you must be one!"

Children need the personal, social, and life skills needed to become competent, caring, compassionate, considerate, and confident young people in their school, community, and home. Because bullying is a social relationship problem, it makes sense to counteract it by helping children develop prosocial behaviors and attitudes. These behaviors will help enhance their interpersonal competence in order to improve, promote, and strengthen their relationships that are central to their success in school and in life. Research shows that children who lack the ability to make friends, adjust to situations, and cope with life events are more likely to participate in verbal bullying.[13] As a result, children need effective communication skills, social-emotional skills, and conflict resolution skills to establish healthy, trusting friendships.

Six Ingredients Needed for Healthy Friendships

In chapter 6, I discussed the importance of having friends and how children can initiate, hold, and join in a conversation. Now, they need to learn how to build and sustain friendships that could last a lifetime. Friendships are important in reducing and preventing victimization, given that mutual friends are more likely to defend each other if they fall victim to teasing or aggressive behavior.[13,14] So teach your children the six ingredients for building and sustaining healthy friendships as indicated in Figure 8.1.

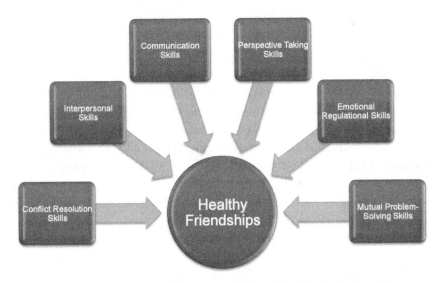

Figure 8.1: Six Ingredients to Building Healthy Relationships

Building healthly relationships includes defining what it means to be a friend, listening when others are talking, recognizing and managing emotions, understanding another person's point of view, being tolerant and accepting of others, disagreeing respectfully, being able to mutually problem solve, and handling interpersonal conflict effectively.

First Ingredient: Interpersonal Relationship Skills

Interpersonal relationship skills help your children relate to others in positive ways. This may mean being able to make and sustain friendly relationships as well as being able to end harmful relationships constructively. Friendships are formed through conversations, seeking things in common with peers (requires perspective taking), showing interest in peer's experiences and thoughts, and creating shared experiences and memories with a peer. In the process of sustaining friendships, children must learn how to evaluate their relationships, to assert one's interests while respecting the rights of others, to resist peer pressure when necessary, to communicate feelings and needs effectively, and to resolve conflicts peacefully—a route that can be daunting for children who have difficulty initiating and maintaining friendships. Unfortunately, many children stop trying to make friends or withdraw from them because of their ineffective social skills or because they can't keep up with the social demands placed upon them.[15,16]

The road leading to becoming someone's friend can be long and filled with many bumps along the way. Children must learn how to navigate—that is, decide—which is the best route to take that will lead to fewer roadblocks that would prevent them from arriving at their final destination: having healthy friendships. But, as you may already know, children do not always make the right choices. Poor decisions can create an undesirable ripple effect. For example, when faced with a challenging situation, quite often children's emotions become so powerful that they cannot access their thinking (remember chapter 3). Soon after, their emotions begin to overshadow their thinking, which causes clouded judgment. Before long, they explode and react in unacceptable ways (remember chapter 7). Consequently, their friendships become strained and begin to break down.

There is a solution to their problem: YOU! You can help your children counteract the devastating ripple effects by teaching them the skills needed to resist engaging in conversations that break down relationships. For example, there are five roadblocks that your children may encounter on their road to building relationships or holding effective conversations. These five roles portray different responses to disagreements and explain how children engage in these roles to manage their emotions and thoughts. By teaching your children these roles, you can help them recognize these behaviors in challenging situations so they can avoid engaging in these behaviors themselves as well as avoid participating in these roles with others.

- *Hider:* Hiders refuse to talk about the conflict and hide their wants and feelings.

- *Pocketer:* Pocketers save up past conflicts, grudges, or hurt feelings and bring them up even though they have nothing to do with the current problem.
- *Wormer:* Wormers blame others for the situation and worm their way out of taking responsibility for their part in the conflict.
- *Blabber:* Blabbers complain about a conflict to someone else instead of facing the problem and solving it with those involved.
- *Pleaser:* Pleasers do not really try to find an acceptable solution. Instead, they settle for any solution—as long as it pleases the other person.

Although friendships take a lot of nurturing, work, and energy, they can be very rewarding. A friend can lift your children's spirits, wipe their tears, and hold their hand through challenging situations. Friendship is a journey, and part of that journey is for you to be your children's tour guide as they explore the meaning of true friendship and discover their own rules and boundaries when it comes to establishing healthy friendships. One thing is for sure—friendships should never make a person feel bad about himself or herself. There are five elements that define healthy friendships or relationships:

1. *Trust:* Trust is the foundation of any relationship.
2. *Mutual respect:* Respect means both parties honor each other's feelings, thoughts, values, and perspectives.
3. *Mutual engagement:* This means sharing similar interests, holding similar values and beliefs, and jointly working together toward a common goal.
4. *Shared experiences:* This means both parties have undergone similar events, situations, or activities; thus, they are better able to identify with and validate each other.
5. *Reciprocity:* This means both parties are equally willing to give and take in the relationship. It means treating others as they treat you.

Being a Friend

Do your children know what is means to be a friend? To find out, ask them the following questions:

- What does it mean to be a friend?
- What makes a person a good friend?
- What qualities do you look for in a friend?
- Think about a time you have felt let down by friends. What happened? How did if affect your friendships?

Here are several points to cover in your discussion with your children about what it means to be a "good friend" and a "bad friend."

- A friend does not put you down. A friend lifts you up.
- A friend does not ignore your needs or your worries. A friend is sensitive and is willing to listen to you if you have an issue you want to address.
- A friend does not try to thwart or sabotage your best efforts at achieving your happiness. A friend wants what is best for you, and is happy when you achieve it.
- A friend does not try to control you or put you in a box just for one's own personal comfort. A friend is open to grow with you as you grow, or at least tries to.
- A friend does not harm you physically, psychologically, emotionally, or verbally. This is abuse, not friendship. In contrast, a friend is your cheerleader who inspires you, reminds you of your best and brightest qualities, and encourages you to keep going forward.
- A friend does not "suck up" or lie to you (which is different from a friend who supports you). A friend gets "real" (i.e., tells you the truth) with you when your ego needs to be checked or when you have done something wrong and you may need to apologize or make amends for any harm done.
- A friend does not blame or make excuses for his or her behavior. A friend is humble and is willing to swallow his or her pride and apologize when he or she has caused you harm.
- A friend does not take your trust for granted. A friend is trustworthy, is someone in whom you can confide, and will stand by you through thick and thin. Trust is the basis of all good relationships and is the cornerstone of good character.

Tip for Being a Friend

When faced with a challenging situation, if your children catch themselves being mean or saying hurtful things to their friends, remind them to stop and think. Coach them on using positive self-talk, such as:

- My friendships are important.
- I can watch my thoughts, words, and actions.
- I can stop hurting people with my words and actions.
- I can take ownership of the hurtful things I do and say.
- "Bullying" hurts everyone.

POINT TO PONDER

Good social skills are needed to build and sustain healthy, trusting friendships. These include:

- Cooperation
- Sharing
- Participation
- Being a friend
- Helping others
- Being patient
- Following directions
- Taking turns
- Remaining on task
- Accepting differences

- Listening
- Praising others and refraining from put downs
- Positive communication and interactions
- Being polite and courteous
- Using good manners
- Respecting ourselves, others, and property
- Being respectful

Which traits are more representative of you? Which are the least?

Second Ingredient: Teach Conflict Resolution Skills

As you have read throughout the book, both bullies and victims often have poor conflict resolution skills. Bullies handle conflict by becoming aggressive or intimidating, and victims often respond by running away or giving in. The way children respond to conflict may have a huge influence on the outcome of their disagreements, as well as on the quality of their social relationships. Conflict resolution teaches children alternative ways to deal with conflict. It helps them identify a problem, express their feelings while controlling behavior, generate and arrive at possible solutions to a conflict, and foster the development of listening skills.[17]

What Is Conflict?

Conflict is a disagreement that results when two or more people have different interests, opinions, beliefs, values, needs, goals, or methods for dealing with a situation. Conflict is a natural part of our lives that is usually inevitable, often unavoidable, but is controllable. It is neither good nor bad, but simply an integral part of life, necessary for growth and change to occur.[18] Figure 8.2 describes the typical progression of conflict.

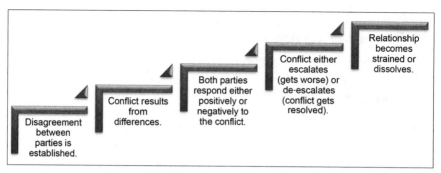

Figure 8.2: The Progression of Conflict

Conflict Response Styles

Conflict response styles are the predominant ways that people deal with conflict. Most people rely on one or two styles that are often defined by emphasis on concern for the self (personal safety) or concern for the other (defense of a victim). Most of us have a favorite style that we use in conflict, but we are all capable of choosing a different conflict style when it is appropriate. Sometimes, depending on the situation, we may choose to adopt a new style in special situations.

POINT TO PONDER

What is your conflict resolution style?

- Procedure—How do you respond to rules set by others?
- People—How do you interact and attempt to influence others?
- Problems—How do you approach conflict and challenges?
- Pace—How do you respond to change and activities?

How do your children approach social conflicts? Using Table 8.1, try to identify which of these five conflict styles your children use.[19]

TABLE 8.1 CONFLICT RESOLUTION STYLES				
Competing: Lion	Avoiding: Turtle	Accommodating: Chameleon	Compromising: Zebra	Cooperative: Dolphin
Win/Lose	Lose/Lose	Lose/Win	Win some/Lose some	Win/Win
Your interest before others. "Do it my way or not at all." Impatient with dialogue, information gathering.	Does not get involved in conflict. "Conflict? What Conflict?" "Just leave me out it." Refuses to dialogue or gather information.	Puts their interest last—let others rule. "Whatever you say." Refuses to dialogue or gather information.	Satisfy some interests but not all of them. "I'll back off if you do the same." Tolerates exchange of views but finds this uncomfortable.	"If we discuss this openly, we can find a solution that benefits everyone."
Strategies	**Strategies**	**Strategies**	**Strategies**	**Strategies**
compete, control, outwit, coerce, fight	flee, deny, ignore, withdraw, delay, wish, hope and pray	agree, appease, flatter	bargain, split the difference, reduce expectations, a little something for everyone	gather information, look for alternatives, dialogue openly, welcome disagreement; examines all options
Prefers others who	**Prefers others who**	**Prefers others who**	**Prefers others who**	**"My preference is... What's your choice?"**
Avoid or Accommodate	Avoid	Force	Compromise or Accommodate	
Leadership Characteristics	**Leadership Characteristics**	**Leadership Characteristics**	**Leadership Characteristics**	**Leadership Characteristics**
authoritarian; threatened by disagreement; maintain status quo; reacts to crisis; power in position	passive, timid; inclined to moralize; aims to weather the storm; discussions and group life seem chaotic, unfocused	ineffective in groups; wishy-washy, easily swayed; needs to please all; discussions drift	cautious but open; urges others not to be too outspoken	cooperative problem-solving style; helps people to work together so everyone can win
Often Appropriate When	**Often Appropriate When**	**Often Appropriate When**	**Often Appropriate When**	**Often Appropriate When**
an emergency looms; you're sure you're right, and being right matters more than preserving relationships; the issue is trivial and others don't really care what happens	the issue is trivial; the relationship is insignificant; time is short and a decision not necessary; you have little power but still wish to block the other	you really don't care about the issue; you're powerless but have no wish to block the other person; when you realize you are wrong	cooperation is important but time or resources are limited; when finding some solution, even less than the best, is better than a complete stalemate; when efforts to collaborate will be misunderstood	the issues and relationship are both significant; cooperation is important; a creative end is important; reasonable hope exists to address all concerns
Often Inappropriate When	**Often Inappropriate When**	**Often Inappropriate When**	**Often Inappropriate When**	**Often Inappropriate When**
collaboration has not yet been attempted; cooperation from others is important; used routinely for most issues; self-respect of others is diminished needlessly	you care about both the relationship and the issues involved; used habitually for most issues; negative feelings may linger; others would benefit from caring confrontation	you are likely to harbor resentment; used habitually in order to gain acceptance (outcome: depression and lack of self-respect); When others wish to collaborate and will feel like enforcers if you accommodate	finding the most creative solutions possible is essential; when you can't live with the consequences	time is short; the issues are unimportant; you're overloaded; the goals of the other person certainly are wrong

When children know their own default patterns, they improve their self-awareness. Once they are aware of their own patterns, they can pay attention to whether or not they are effective, and explore alternatives.

Children often engage in aggressive behaviors because they either do not know how to respond to conflict or they lack the confidence to implement an alternative strategy. Therefore, it is vital that you teach your children effective conflict resolution skills needed to help build and sustain healthy friendships. These skills include:

- Listening when others are talking
- Recognizing and managing emotions

- Understanding another person's point of view
- Being tolerant and accepting of others
- Disagreeing respectfully
- Being able to mutually problem solve
- Handling interpersonal conflict effectively

The ultimate goal of learning conflict resolution strategies is to provide you and your children with the tools to help all of you *MANAGE* and *CONTROL* conflict peacefully. Your children need a lot of practice using these skills, and should be encouraged to practice them regularly.

Third Ingredient: Effective Communication Skills

I know you believe you understand what you think I said, but I am not sure you realize that what you heard is not what I meant.

Author unknown

It is through conversation that we learn about others and develop shared experiences, so help your children improve their relationships with effective communication skills. Communication is the process of transferring signals or messages between a sender and a receiver through spoken words, written words, visual images, or nonverbal cues. When we communicate, we must (1) listen to the other person, (2) interpret what is being said, and (3) respond in an understandable way. Effective communication is much more than being able to talk; it is also the ability to listen and understand others, to "read" and interpret body language, and to know the best ways to get our point across. Since communication is the mechanism we use to establish and modify relationships, having effective communication skills is essential in strengthening relationships, reducing stress, and avoiding engaging in aggressive behaviors.[20]

Active Listening

Active listening, a method of responding to a speaker, is one of the most important aspects of effective communication. Successful listening is not just understanding the words or the information being communicated, but also understanding how the speaker feels about what he or she just communicated. There are verbal and nonverbal behaviors that show they are paying attention or show inattention.[20]

Elements of Active Listening

Attend to Nonverbals. Without saying even a word, your body sends messages to everyone around you—this is called "body language." This wordless, nonverbal communication includes:

- Observing and attending to facial expressions
- Making body movements and gestures
- Making eye contact
- Body posture
- Tone of voice
- Muscle tension and breathing

Smiling, making good eye contact, and nodding show that you are not distracted and you care about what the speaker is saying. Your vocal quality is an instrument that communicates feelings you have toward the speaker and includes three aspects: *Rate*—the speed at which you talk; *Frequency*—the pitch at which you talk; and *Tone*—the quality of the sound. Teach your children to demonstrate positive body language by radiating SOLER energy. SOLER is an acronym to help them remember important non-verbal cues that let the speaker know you are listening:

S—"sit squarely"; **O**—"open stance"; **L**—"lean forward"; **E**—"eye contact"; **R**—"relax"

Restating. Repeat what the speaker said in your own words. This reassures the speaker that he or she has been heard correctly. "So you had to go to the principal's office and were not able to get your work finished." Use initial phrases such as "In other words..."; "I gather that..."; "If I understand what you are saying..."; "What I hear you saying is..."; or "Pardon my interruption, but let me see if I understand you correctly..."

Questioning. Asking questions demonstrates that you are interested and that you care about understanding the speaker. This allows you to clarify details and gather further information. Open questions can be answered with a free response (e.g., "What was it like when you were in elementary school?" or "What can you remember about being hit in the head?"). In contrast, closed questions can be answered with a very short, specific response—usually about some fact—and usually begin with are, is, do, did, who, or when (e.g., "When did you get hit?" or "Are you afraid of going back to school?").

Focusing. Describe what the conversation is about. Put the speaker's thoughts and ideas into a larger context. Say something like, "Although you're recovering on a physical level, I've noticed several issues that continue to worry you, including how you might fit in at school, what your peers will think of you, how they will treat you, and how safe you will be."

Reflecting. Identify what you perceive to be the speaker's underlying feelings. There are four basic feelings—sad, mad, glad, and scared. Say something like, "You're embarrassed about what has happened and a little afraid that people blame you." Have your children try out these reflecting feeling phrases: "I hear you are feeling..."; "It looks like you are feeling..."; "Sounds like you are feeling..."

Validating. Legitimize a person's statements by indicating that what he or she has said makes sense to you: "Your identity has always been tied up with your being a good athlete. Now that you cannot play sports for the rest of the year, it's hard to feel good about yourself. "

Challenging. If your children identify some inconsistency or incongruity between what a speaker is saying and how he or she is acting, or between different statements the speaker has made, they should confront the inconsistent information, saying something like, "You say you are my friend, but you have been spreading rumors about me." Phrases that note incongruity follow this pattern: "On one hand..., but on the other hand..."; or "You say..., but you do ..."

TIP

Importance of Good Communication

Here are some reasons to master the rules and expectations for good communication.

- If you take charge of the way you communicate with people, you'll be more confident.
- If people can understand you easily, they'll pay more attention to what you say.
- Good communication makes a good impression. People will respect you. That makes it easier to get a job and to get along with teachers, friends, and family.
- A good communicator is attractive. People will like being around you.
- Good communication makes it easier to work or learn with other people. Everyone benefits.
- A good communicator can make other people feel good. That makes you feel good, too.
- Good communication can help you avoid trouble. You'll have strategies to deal with problem situations and people who threaten you.

The Don'ts of Active Listening:

Effective communication skills—using active listening and attending to nonverbal behaviors—are needed to build friendships and manage conflict. However, there are certain behaviors your children should avoid when holding a conversation. This is so communication does not break down or stop altogether. The behaviors listed below are what *not* to do when actively listening to the speaker:

- Don't interrupt.
- Don't get defensive.
- Don't change the subject or move in a new direction.
- Don't rehearse in your own head.
- Don't interrogate.
- Don't shrug your shoulders.
- Don't look away from the speaker.
- Don't cross your arms.
- Don't sit slouched over.
- Don't roll your eyes.
- Don't tap your fingers.

What Blocks Communication?

One of the primary reasons for a lack of effective communication is that your children typically—sometimes unknowingly—interject barriers into their conversations. These barriers, or blocks, seriously hamper communication or discontinue it entirely. Blocks to communication are the behaviors that prevent the meaning of a message from being heard and understood.[21,22] In moments of conflict, communication can break down because each person is trying to be right or win the argument. This means each person stops listening, causing blocks to communication. There are several ways in which one can respond that effectively shut down communication. Thus, teach your children how these behaviors can break down communication.

Interrupting. To interrupt means to break in conversations with questions or remarks while another is speaking. There are two reasons your children interrupt others. First, they are reminded of something they want to say and can't wait their turn before saying it. Second, they become impatient when a speaker is slow to transform a thought into a statement. In others words, the speaker has difficulty saying what he or she wants to say. Ask your children, "Have you ever tried to have a conversation with a person who continually interrupts you? How did you feel when that happened?"

Dominating. Your children dominate conversations because they are more interested in their own thoughts and ideas than in those of others. They want to be in control. Ask your children, "Have you ever had a conversation with a person who continually dominated the conversation? How did you feel when that happened?"

Advising. This includes statements like, "Well, if I were you..." or "I think you should..." or "Take my advice and..." By giving unbidden advice, a person immediately takes a position of superiority. Advice giving says, "I know better than you do."

Judging. Forming a negative opinion of someone. Not only does a "communication judge" assume a superior position in conversation, but his or her judgments may be completely wrong. For example, suppose you say to someone, "I have a dog named Charlie." The person responds, "What a good person you are—all dog lovers are fine people. What kind is it?" You answer, "A poodle." Your listener responds, "Oh, that's too bad. Poodles are high strung and hard to train." This sends a message that the other person is stupid or inferior for not thinking, believing, acting, or feeling the same way.

Probing. Asking a lot of questions tends to put the speaker on the defensive. More importantly, questions can lead the speaker away from what he or she wants to say. For example, suppose you are trying to describe your day to a friend. But as soon as you mention the first thing that happened, your friend asks, "What did you do that for?"; "What happened?"; "What did she say?"; etc. Instead of telling your story, you begin to answer your friend's questions.

Criticizing/Name-calling/Putting-down. When someone says something to make us feel put down, frustrated, or angry, we may feel attacked or believe we are wrong. Put-downs cause victims to feel unworthy/less than/inferior to the person. For example, suppose you say, "I have a dog named Charlie." Your listener responds, "You jerk, what did you get a dog for? You can't even take care of that mangy cat of yours!" Few of us want to continue a conversation in which we are being constantly criticized.

Accusing/Contradicting. Contradictions and accusations put the speaker on the spot and cause him or her to get defensive. Suppose while talking to some friends, your child says, "I wrote this paper on my iPad" and a friend jumps in with, "No you didn't. Since when do you have an iPad?" Your child responds, "I bought it with money I saved from cutting grass," to which the friend says, "You never have any money, so how could you save money?" When situations like this occur, your children should know how to respond to the accusations without getting defensive. Here are some ways you can help your children deal with accusations.[23]

- Remind them that the goal of dealing with accusations is to stay in control of their emotions and not make the situation worse. Have them think about why they were accused. What was the accuser thinking?
- Coach them on ways they can talk about the accusation with the accuser. Assist them in finding out what facts the accuser used to make the accusations. Coach them on ways they can calmly share facts the accuser might not know that might change his or her opinion. Remind them to control their emotions and talk calmly. Be a good listener, too.
- Encourage them to take responsibility if they did what they were accused of doing. Coach them on ways they could explain the situation to the accuser.
- Remind them to try to resolve the situation without blaming anyone. They should not let their emotions get out of control.
- Afterward, have them think about the entire situation. Discuss with them what they learned from the situation and how they can avoid further accusations.

Tips for Arguing Fairly in Disagreements

Everyone gets into arguments and has disagreements, but good communicators know how to argue fairly. Understanding empathy, using I-messages, confronting inconsistencies, reframing information, and de-escalating the situation are effective ways your children can deal with people who may be a challenge to communicate with. These strategies will be discussed later in this chapter. Here are some guidelines to teach your children so they can handle difficult conversations and keep their arguments from spiraling out of control.

- Be confident and assertive. Use good listening skills.
- Try the five-second rule. Because we sometimes say things without thinking of the consequences, wait five seconds before you comment on what has just been said. Use this time to exercise control and think about what you should say or do.
- Don't resort to name calling. Use the five-second rule to choose words that are appropriate and relevant to the disagreement.
- Stick to the issue at hand. Talk only about the present point of disagreement. Bringing up or engaging in discussions about past

problems adds the proverbial fuel to the fire. It also shifts the focus from the present problem, which means it probably won't get resolved and will cause trouble again.

- Be self-aware. Recognize emerging feelings in order to control them.
- Manage your anger. Anger is a natural emotion, especially when you are having a disagreement. But don't allow your anger to turn violent. If you feel your anger reaching that point, leave the scene immediately and do something safe to calm yourself down—counting to 20, taking a brisk walk, or exercising.

Hints for Sustaining Friendships in Disagreements

- Explore the relationship from the other person's point of view. Imagine how he or she may experience your behavior. How would this behavior be defined? How would it feel to be the other person?
- Shake off any emotional state that blocks effective communication before continuing to discuss the disagreement (practice the calming strategies in chapters 6 and 7).
- Go outside the relationship and become a detached observer—imagine you are both on a stage. Visualize the other person doing what he does, and see yourself responding. What is being said? What are both individuals doing?
- Shift your question from "How can I change that person's behavior?" to "How am I reinforcing or triggering that person's behavior?" Since you cannot change another person's behavior, think about how you could take control of the situation. Explore how else you could respond that helps you maintain control. See chapters 6 and 7 for specific strategies.
- Speak and act with regard for the other person. Remember with whom you are arguing. It may be a good friend or someone whom you love and care about deeply. Although that is probably the last thing on your mind when having a disagreement, it should be the first.

Fourth Ingredient: Perspective-Taking Skills

"We could learn a lot from crayons...
Some are sharp, some are pretty and some are dull.
Some have weird names, and all are different colors,
but they all have to live in the same box."

Source Unknown

Perspective taking is understanding another person's point of view and develops gradually from infancy until six or seven years of age. It requires inhibitory control, or inhibiting our own thoughts and feelings in order to consider the perspectives of others; cognitive flexibility, or the ability to see a situation in different ways; and reflection, or the ability to consider someone else's thinking alongside our own.[24] This task is what psychologists call Theory of Mind—the ability to understand or anticipate what another person is feeling or thinking. In other words, it is the ability to put oneself in someone else's shoes. There are several types of perspective-taking abilities, including the capacity to understand what another person sees (**perceptual** role-taking), how another person feels (**affective** role-taking), and what another person thinks (**cognitive** role-taking).[24] Perspective taking goes beyond empathy. It involves figuring out what others think and feel, which forms the basis for children's understanding of another person's intentions. (Use chapter 3's discussion of why children say or do the things they do to help your children understand a bully's behavior and the reasons behind the cruelty. Children with better perspective-taking skills are less likely to be involved in conflicts with other children.[25]

POINT TO PONDER

> **"Don't Judge a Book By Its Cover!"**
>
> What does this expression mean? Ask your children what they think, and then ask:
> - Have you ever judged someone before you got to know the person?
> - Has someone ever judged you before getting to know you? How did that make you feel?
> - Have you been made fun of because of a difference?
> - How did it feel when someone did not accept you for who you are?
> - Help your children understand that people can be more than what meets the eye.

Perspective-taking skills also include developing a tolerance and gaining acceptance of others or those who are different from us.[26] Unfortunately, many people judge others by the way they look, how athletic they are, if they have a disability, or the amount of money their family may have. Before we can really know who people are as individuals, we have to know who they are on the inside, not just on the outside. By getting to know others, we can understand and accept their differences. Acceptance is the key to working well with others and making—and keeping—friends. Acceptance is nonjudgmental and simply acknowledges "what is." It doesn't mean that we have to like everyone in our group, class, or work; rather, it means we must acknowledge our differences so we can move past them and get the job done.

Acceptance leads to tolerance. Tolerance is accepting other people's differences and mistakes.[25] Tolerance means being sensitive to all the different races, ethnicities, cultures, and beliefs in the world. Tolerance can be learned. Everyone perceives the world differently and has different values and experiences. By teaching your children to understand those differences and recognize that what may be right for one may not be right for another, you can expand their knowledge and give them a valuable perspective of the world. The world is a brighter place because we all have different colors of skin, hair, eyes, and even teeth. So don't judge the rainbow—celebrate it!

 TOOLBOX TACTIC

A Beautiful World

Help your child break down the walls of prejudice by identifying the joys of living in a multicultural world. Read the following poem to your children, then discuss the poem using the questions provided.[27]

A Beautiful World

What makes the world we live in such a beautiful place to be?
All the colors of the rainbow are so wonderful to see.
The trees are green, the sky is blue, and the ground's a deep dark brown,
There are so many other colors in this bright and cheerful town.
An elephant is gray, the ocean's green and blue,
There's a rainbow of colors in every park and zoo.
A zebra has two colors, a parrot even more,
Colors give our world its beauty, of that we're really sure.
The colors of the rainbow are worn by you and me,
Look around your school and home, what do you see?
Notice all the different colors, there's so much to bring us joy,
We are all so special, look at every girl and boy.

So, why do some people feel their color is the best?
Feels that a person who is different is nothing but a pest?
Sometimes things are said that are really very cruel,
But remember they are being said by a color conscious fool.
Now the question is, can you stand proud and tall?
Can you make your school [home, neighborhood, community]
a place, where colors welcome all?

What makes our world so beautiful?

- What are some things mentioned in the poem? What are their colors?
- Why do you think that some people think their color is the best?
- Why do you think some people say cruel things about someone else's color?
- Has anyone said something cruel to you about your color? How did it feel?
- Has anyone said something nice about your color? How did it feel?
- Why is it better to have a lot of different colors in the world?

Here are some activities you can do at home to reinforce being tolerant of others who are different.[26]

1. Family Chat/Family Album Night: Take the time to share pictures or videos of each member of the family. Look for family resemblances and differences. Look for traits that make each member special.
2. Memory Builder/Family Outing: Before leaving by foot or car, list as many colors as you possibly can. Take a walk around the neighborhood or to your favorite spot. Match items to your color list. On your way home talk about the beauty of the world around you.
3. Refrigerator Art/Handprint Wreath: Make a family handprint page wreath. Cut a paper grocery bag or a piece of cardboard into a circle. On a separate sheet of paper, trace, color, and cut each family member's hand enough to fill the wreath. Now, paste the hands on the wreath and hang it in a prominent spot in your house. Recall your sharing goal, and recall the traffic signal when it becomes difficult to keep your eyes on the road.
4. Look at yourself in a mirror and draw what you see. Color your picture with crayons that match your own skin tones. Write some words that say positive things about you. Discuss the activity.

We live in a multicultural world where we will interact with people who are different from us. Interpersonal conflicts often arise out of misunderstandings about another person's culture and when we perceive things differently—which affects our relationships. To resolve conflicts effectively, we must be *willing* (i.e., be open to doing what is needed to better the relationship) to appreciate, acknowledge, affirm, and accept—but not necessarily agree with—another person's perspective. Acceptance does not mean approval. Approval and disapproval are judgments, whereas acceptance is nonjudgmental and acknowledges "what is."[26]

To show tolerance, we must be willing to put aside our own judgments, assumptions, perceptions, and feelings to accurately hear the perceptions, feelings, and needs of others. This is accomplished when we acknowledge that we perceive things differently than someone else. Tolerance develops when we can consider alternative explanations, yet keep the focus on our own feelings, beliefs, and wants rather than focusing on the other person, and not criticizing, blaming, or judging the other person.[28] When we show a willingness to understand and accept our differences, it may allow us to find common ground, discover similar interest, and work toward resolution.

POINT TO PONDER

If everyone were alike, wouldn't the world be a boring place? To me, color is prettier and more interesting than black and white. What do you think? What can you do to help children recognize biases and reduce prejudices in order to seek understanding?

CASE EXAMPLE

Different Perceptions

Suppose you wanted to arrive at a specific location in New Orleans. A street map of the city would be a great help to you in reaching your destination. But suppose you were given the wrong map. Through a printing error, the map labeled "New Orleans" was actually a map of

Orlando. Can you imagine the frustration of not being able to find your destination?

You might work on your *behavior*—you could try harder, being more diligent and doubling your speed. But your efforts would only succeed in getting you to the wrong place faster.

You might work on your *attitude*—you could think more positively. You still wouldn't get to the right place, but perhaps you wouldn't care. Your attitude would be so positive, you'd be happy wherever you were.

The point is, you'd still be lost. The fundamental problem has nothing to do with your behavior or your attitude. It has everything to do with the wrong map—that is, having incorrect information.

We each have many, many maps in our head, which can be divided into two main categories: maps of the way things are, or realities, and maps of the way things should be, or values. We interpret everything we experience through these mental maps. We seldom question their accuracy; we are usually even unaware that we have them. We simply assume that the way we see things is the way they really are or the way they should be.[29]

TIP

Perspective taking has been shown to improve social relationships by decreasing stereotyping and prejudice toward a victim and the victim's group.[24]

Fifth Ingredient: Emotional Regulation Skills

As the mother of two boys, on any given day I might be faced with verbal complaining, angry stomping, door slamming, or the silent treatment. Thus, helping my children appropriately manage and express their feelings is an important part of my day-to-day parenting. As parents, we can teach our children to handle their emotions in ways that validate their feelings while fostering healthy relationships with others. Children experience a variety of stressors at school and at home. When they are unable to cope with such stressors effectively, their behavioral and emotional well-being can be adversely affected, often leading to further problems in their lives.[30,31] Accompanying these stressors is a range of emotions that can affect their ability to make good choices and decisions. Consequently, children must be taught how to regulate their emotions. That means identifying, understanding, and integrating emotional information, while maintaining control of one's behavior in order to cope with it.

Identifying Emotions

You can help your children get in touch with their feelings by asking questions like "What did you feel when your friend made fun of you in front of the class?" or by stating, "I would have felt angry if my friend had made fun of me that way." Encouraging children to openly discuss the emotionally arousing situation with you can also help them process what they are feeling. Feelings games can help your children name of a range of emotions. Visit the Center on the Social and Emotional Foundations for Early Learning (*csefel.vanderbilt.edu*) or the Collaborative for Academic, Social, and Emotional Learning (*casel.org*) for activities.

Handling Emotions

Conflict occurs when we are not in charge of our emotions. Help your children get a handle on their emotions so they may respond in an acceptable way. This is pivotal since intense emotions (like anger or sorrow) can have negative effects on their health if they do not react appropriately. Over the years, I have found it to be helpful to teach my children the five steps to handling their emotions. They need to name it, claim it, tame it, reframe it, and aim it.

1. *Name the Emotion*—Be specific in how you feel. Body signals can often help define the emotion (e.g., "I feel hurt").
2. *Claim the Emotion*—Your emotions are yours. When your children experience an emotional reaction to something, have them say, "This is my feeling. No one made me feel this way. How I am feeling is my response to this conflict."
3. *Tame the Emotion*—You control your emotions. No one can make you feel an emotion. Only YOU can decide what you feel and how you want to react. Whenever something unpleasant happens, YOU can react in one of these ways: go into a rage, be mildly annoyed, or ignore it. Only YOU can make yourself feel angry, embarrassed, or any other emotion, so don't blame others for the way you feel. You're the boss! ("I am in control of my emotions.") So, if you are uncomfortable with the

intensity of your feelings, do physical or mental activities to lessen the intensity (as suggested in chapters 6 and 7).

4. *Reframe the Emotion*—Think of the emotion in a different way. Have your children say something like: "Although I am hurt that Stacie made fun of me because I tripped and fell on the bleachers, I know she did not mean to. She's my friend. She laughed because I laughed. I know I need to pay attention to where I'm walking instead of playing around and talking." Here are some questions they can ask themselves to help them reframe their emotion: "Is this the first time I've felt this way?" "What are the specific factors in this conflict?" "Is it appropriate for me to reframe my feelings in this situation?"

5. *Aim the Emotion*—Decide whether a situation is serious or not and match the intensity of your emotion appropriately. Emotions must be expressed in a way that does not harm oneself or others. ("Is it really worth throwing a chair because you lost your favorite pen?) Here are some questions to help your children decide how to respond to their emotions: "What am I going to do with this emotion?" "Will I talk with someone?" "Do I need to understand my part of the conflict?" "Will I ask the other party to resolve the conflict?"

Responding to Emotions

Children often react differently to the same situation. For example, a scary movie that grosses out one child might put another child to sleep. One child might be thrilled that the weather is cold and snowy, but another child may be annoyed or depressed about it. Remind your children that they shouldn't judge a person harshly because he or she doesn't feel the same way they do. The way they respond to their emotions may be different than how others respond to theirs. Thus, they need to handle their emotions so they can manage the emotional reactions of others. If your children find themselves on the receiving end of someone's emotional outburst, teach them to manage their emotions by teaching the following:

- *Stay in control.* Don't let what the person is saying or doing get to you. Remember, this is HIS/HER emotion, not yours. You don't need to fight his/her battles or feel his/her feelings.
- *Be quiet and listen.* Sometimes people just need to vent, so just remain quiet and listen. Remember to use good listening skills—make eye contact, nod your head frequently, lean forward, etc.—to let the person know you are with him or her.

- *Offer a gentle touch.* When people are sad, sometimes a hand on the shoulder is all that's needed. However, touching is NOT a good idea when people are angry because it might be perceived as a prompt for a physical fight.
- *Say when you've had enough.* When someone is out of control, you might feel overwhelmed and unable or unwilling to help the person. This can hinder your ability to help the person. You have the right to remove yourself from the situation. You could suggest someone else's help or just excuse yourself politely: "I know this whole divorce thing is getting to you. Maybe you should talk with the school counselor. She's a good listener" or "I know you're upset that Kia dumped you, but I have to get to class."
- *If you think it is serious enough, talk to an adult you trust.* It's tough to know when to consult an adult about someone else's problem. How would you respond to these emotional outbursts?: "I'm so alone since Alex broke up with me, I wish I were dead." or "I can't believe he said that about me. I'm going to kill him!" Said in the heat of the moment, these statements are probably harmless. But if you hear these kinds of comments over and over, you should share them with an adult who can help. There is no harm in enlisting help from an adult you trust. It's hard to know what will push someone to violence, but it's even harder to learn that it's too late to avoid a tragedy.

Sixth Ingredient: Mutual Problem-Solving Skills

When people disagree, it is important to stop and think about what both people in the disagreement can do and are willing to do to resolve the conflict. For most children, "keeping their cool and being willing to compromise are among the most crucial yet challenging aspects of interpersonal effectiveness."[32] To mutually solve a problem, everyone involved must be willing and committed to engage in the resolution process, be rational and clear-headed, and trust that everyone will work together to solve the problem. This process involves cooperation rather than competition and produces a positive solution for all people involved. Sadly, not all people are interested in solving the problem. Rather, they want to be right, have the right answer, and win at any cost.

In most situations, your children's wants and needs will conflict with the wants and needs of others. Therefore, using effective negotiation skills can aid them in the problem-solving process. Negotiation skills include being well prepared, showing patience, maintaining integrity, avoiding argument, controlling their emotions, breaking down bigger issues into smaller ones, avoiding threats and manipulative tactics, focusing on the problem first rather than on the solution, seeking interest-based decisions, and compromising to reach resolution. The aim of effective negotiation is to create a "win-win" situation where a solution is acceptable to everyone involved and leaves everyone feeling that he or she has won in some way. However, for this process to work, everyone must be willing to deal with the problem, get beyond the "I win, you lose" idea, and allow all parties involved to save face. This mean no finger pointing, blaming, or criticizing. They must also be willing to compromise. Compromising means everyone forgoes their ideal outcomes, settling for a solution that is somewhat satisfactory to each participant.

Before entering into the problem-solving process, your children should be prepared and ready to resolve the problem. To help them with this process, they should think and reflect upon the following:

1. *How do they see the problem?* To define the problem, have your children think about:
   - Is the problem really a problem?
   - Whose problem is it? Think of all the people involved in the problem. How is each one affected by the problem? Remind them that if it's not really their problem, they should not act like it's their problem.
   - Do they understand the problem? Have them explain the situation in a way someone not involved could understand. Then tell why it's a problem.
   - How important is this problem? Few everyday problems are life threatening or long lasting. Remind them that if they treat every problem as though it's the end of the world, they will be miserable—so will everyone around them. They should prioritize each problem and rank them in the order of importance: urgent, important, or everyday. Then examine where each problem ranks in importance. Is the problem crucial to their survival or is it just annoying? Remind them to be honest with themselves about how important each problem really is.
   - What do they want to happen? They should think about what they wish would be different. Then think of ways to make that happen.
   - What limits do they need to think about? Before they tackle a problem, they need to be realistic about any limitations. Is what

they want legal? Would you—the parent—allow it? Would it be harmful to them or anyone else? Does it fit with their personal values? The family's values?

2. *How do they and others feel about the problem?* Have them explore everyone's reaction to the problem, how they feel as well as how others feel about the situation. Remind them that a good communicator listens to and empathizes with the other person.

3. *How can they tackle the problem?* When thinking about the problem, your child should examine each person's position and interest. A *position* is *what* someone wants, a tangible outcome that someone argues for. In contrast, an *interest* is *why* someone wants it, the underlying concern about the problem and the reason why that outcome is desired. The ultimate goal of reaching a win-win resolution is to focus on interests, not positions. They should bear in mind that there are usually multiple interests for a given issue. However, remind them that they do not have to share the same common interest to find an agreeable solution. The more your children understand their interests as well as everyone else's, the better they are able to find a solution that will produce mutual and lasting satisfaction.

4. *Are they ready to mutually problem-solve?* Your children need to think about how prepared they are to solve the problem with others. They should only confront conflict with someone if they have the time and are willing to commit to dealing with the issues immediately. They shouldn't try to resolve conflict when they are not in control of their emotions. Being prepared means they analyzed the situation, devised a plan, and formulated their opening remarks.

Once arrangements have been made for a convenient time and place to meet, your children are ready to move to the next step—meeting to solve the problem. Teach them the *TRIBE* method to help them remember what's involved in the problem-solving process. Remind them to pay attention to their tone and attitude during the entire process. The TRIBE method is detailed as follows:

T Tell what's up with you.
- Tell your side of the problem. Speak calmly and clearly in a way that the other person can hear you.
- Remember to "own the problem by using 'I' language."
- No name calling.

- Focus on how you have experienced the problem.
- Describe rather than judge.
- Be brief.

R Reflectively listen to their side of the problem.
- Allow time for the other person to tell his or her story.
- Make sure you understand by asking questions.
- Summarize both feelings and content.
- Understanding is not the same as agreeing.

I Identify what's important to you and the other person.
- State your main concern and the other person's main concern.
- Identify the needs of the other person by asking yourself, "What does he or she want?" "What does he or she need?" "What is his or her interest and how does it differ from my interest in the problem?"
- Ask the other person to summarize your main concern.
- Identify why each of you wants what you want.

B Brainstorm possible solutions:
- Get ideas from both of you about solutions.
- Find common ground. Often during a disagreement, there is something you and the other person can agree on or something you both want, which is called "common ground." If you can discover what you and the other person(s) have in common, that can be a starting point in helping you both to reach a solution to the problem.
- Write all of the ideas down. Get as many ideas as possible.

E Evaluate solutions, pick one, and try it.
- Review all the solutions.
- Choose the ones that will work for both of you.
- Be specific and realistic.
- Repeat the solution back so both of you understand.

Pointers for Success
- In order to create a win-win situation where everyone's needs are met, you must listen to the other person so mutual problem solving can occur.
- Separate people from the problem.
- Keep the focus on the problem rather than the emotion that results.
- Focus on one problem at a time—do not allow old issues to be resurrected as a distraction.
- Assume you do not have all the answers.

- Ask questions so that you understand the other person(s).
- Be prepared to compromise or make a deal.
- Postpone. If tired, sick, or hungry wait until you feel better.
- Enforce. If there are consequences to the behavior, you should follow through with them.
- Compromise. Be willing to give a little.
- Explore. Be willing to find other solutions that have not yet been discussed.

The Role of Peers in Bullying Prevention

Parents can play a role in preventing bullying by encouraging their children to be good bystanders. One of my most proud days was when a parent told me my son stood up for their much smaller son on the playground. She witnessed her child being picked on and before she could get to him to stop it, my son intervened and took care of the bully. I do not advocate my son ever starting a fight, but I always support him when he finishes it. Bystanders hold significant power when it comes to promoting or stopping bullying; hence, parents must help their children understand it is their social responsibility to do something when they know that bullying is taking place.[33] Although your child may not be the bully or the victim, everyone suffers when bullying occurs, and everyone can help to prevent it. In 85% of cases, bullying takes place in front of witnesses.[33] Bystanders usually avoid getting involved because they are afraid they could become a target themselves or make things worse for the person being bullied. You can help your children understand that bullying is not acceptable and that they can help stop it. This way, you encourage and enable your children to care for and take responsibility for each other. Research indicates that bullying is greatly reduced when bystanders stand up for the victim.[34,35] Encourage them to become an "upstander" by helping them develop antibullying attitudes through raising awareness of bullying and providing them opportunities for self-reflection. Help awaken their feelings of responsibility to intervene and support the victim by refusing to participate in bullying behavior, affirming the victim, speaking with the bully about his or her behavior, or telling an adult for help and support. Role-playing or rehearsing what your children would say and do will help build their confidence to intervene in positive ways that stop the bullying immediately. Lastly, create an environment of trust and confidentiality where they feel safe talking to you about bullying or other problems they might have.

The Role of the School in Bullying Prevention

Prevention of bullying is becoming a legal obligation of the schools. In March 2011, the Antibullying and Harassment Act of 2011 was introduced in Congress, and, to date, forty-nine states have passed legislation related to harassment, intimidation, and bullying in schools (*stopbullying.gov*, 2012). Bullying prevention programs are a necessity for schools, given their "in loco parentis" legal responsibility. Thus, advocate that your children's school implement antibullying programs across the school curriculum. You can also advocate for stronger antibullying policies and for increased supervision at the school. Offer your assistance to help make the school a bully-free zone. In her book *The Essential 6 R's of Bullying Prevention*, Michele Borba offers six tips for helping schools create a safe climate:

1. Rules: Establish an antibullying policy.
2. Recognize: Teach stakeholders to identify bullying.
3. Report: Create procedures to report bullying.
4. Respond: Teach witnesses how to respond to bullying.
5. Refuse: Teach bully-proofing strategies to reduce victimization.
6. Replace: Replace a bully's aggression with acceptable skills.

You can also ask the school's principal the following:

- Can parents view a copy of the district's antibullying policy? (A critical section in an antibullying policy would cover the procedure for reporting bullying and how the report is investigated by the school.)
- Has the school completed a staff and student survey to assess the present level of bullying and other aggressive behaviors?
- Does the school have a team identified to review the survey results and to look at evidence-based solutions that will be sustained long-term?
- Who is on the team, and does it include a broad representation of parents?
- Has all staff received training on bullying prevention? This includes every adult who interacts with the children (custodians, bus drivers, secretaries, food service, etc.).
- Is the training focused on giving adults the skills necessary to intervene effectively with aggression and create a positive environment?
- Has a behavioral chart (often called a rubric) been developed that lists the consequences for choosing aggressive or bullying behavior?

- What formal instruction are the children receiving on how to behave? In other words, where, and how, is social-emotional skill development being taught?
- Does the school use a punitive approach or a restorative approach to intervene in bullying, or both?
- How does the school help the bully repair harm done to others?
- Does the school offer workshops or resources to help parents support their children whether they are the target of bullying, the aggressor, or the bystander?

Conclusion

Bullying can be extremely harmful to children—threatening their physical, social, and mental well-being, and affecting their healthy development and feelings of self-worth. As a parent or other caring adult, you have a great impact on your children and how they treat others. Thus, it is important that you instill values of kindness, compassion, and empathy in your children at the earliest stage possible. Your children's moral values and ethical behavior is interwoven with your own. If you want your children to be fair, courageous, and humane, you have to take a close, hard look at whether those values are priorities in your parenting and whether you are modeling those values day to day. It is vital that you consistently speak out in opposition against hatred, cruelty, and prejudice toward others. Remember, children must learn how to get along with others, resolve conflict, solve problems, empathize with others, play fairly, and treat others with kindness. These qualities will be needed throughout their lives. So, when working with your children, reinforce the following: "I know that it is not always easy to build, develop, and sustain a friendship, but with practice, it will become easier over time."

I know that it's not always easy to keep your chin up when dealing with challenging people or situations that hurt or harm your children. I appreciate your reading this book to help your children flourish in school and in life. Your involvement in their lives will have a positive impact on their overall well-being.

Chapter Notes

Chapter 1

[1]See Georgiou, S. (2009). "Parental Style and Child Bullying and Victimization Experiences at School." *Social Psychology of Education.*

[2]See National Coalition for Parent Involvement in Education (2006). Research Review and Resources. *www.ncpie.org/WhatsHappening/researchJanuary2006.cfm.*

[3]See Sells, S. (1998). *Treating the Tough Adolescent. A Family-Based, Step-by-Step Guide.* The Guilford Press.

[4]See Lancaster, Lynne C., & Stillman, David (2003). *When Generations Collide: Who They Are. Why They Clash. How to Solve the Generational Puzzle at Work.*

[5]See Lancaster, L. C., & Stillman, David (2010). *The M-Factor and How the Millennial Generation Is Rocking the Workplace.*

[6]See Howe, N., & Strauss, W. (2000). *Millennials Rising: The Next Great Generation.* Also see McCrindle, M. (2011). "The ABC of XYZ: Understanding the Global Generations." *www.mccrindle.com.au*

[7]See Maccoby, E. E., & Martin, J. A. (1983). *Socialization in the Context of the Family: Parent-Child Interaction.* In P. H. Mussen (Ed.), *Handbook of Child Psychology. Vol. 4: Socialization, Personality, and Social Development* (pp. 1–101).

[8]See Baumrind, D. (1991). "The Influence of Parenting Style on Adolescent Competence and Substance Use." *Journal of Early Adolescence,* 11(1), 56–95.

[9]See Elmore (2010). "Generation iY: Our Last Chance to Save Their Future." *www.savetheirfuturenow.com*

[10]See Henderson, A., & Mapp, K. (2002). *A New Wave of Evidence: The Impact of School, Family, and Community Connections on Student Achievement.* Southwest Educational Development Laboratory.

[11]Georgiou (2008). Bullying and Victimization at School: "The Role of Mothers."

[12]See Thomas, A., & Chess (1977). *Temperament and Development.* New York: Brunner/Mazel.

[13]See Goldsmith, H. H., Lemery, K. S., Aksan, N., & Buss, K. A. (2000). "Temperament Substrates of Personality Development." In V. J. Molfese & D. L. Molfese (Eds.), *Temperament and Personality Development Across the Life-span* (pp. 1–32). New Jersey: Erlbaum.

[14]See Kurcinka, M. S. (2009). *Raising Your Spirited Child: A Guide for Parents Whose Child is More Intense, Sensitive, Perceptive, Persistent, and Energetic.* New York: HarperCollins Publishers.

[15]See Popkin, M. (2007). "Taming the Spirited Child: Strategies for Parenting Challenging Children Without Breaking Their Spirits."

[16]See Greene, R. W. (2010). "The Explosive Child: A New Approach for Understanding and Parenting Easily Frustrated, Chronically Inflexible Children."

[17]See Aron, E. N. (2002). "The Highly Sensitive Child: Helping Our Children Thrive When the World Overwhelms Them."

[18]See Crawford, C. (2009). "The Highly Intuitive Child: A Guide to Understanding and Parenting Unusually Sensitive and Empathic Children."

[19]See Loving Limits Parenting Workshop. Bethany Prescott. *bethany@bethanyprescott.com.*

[20]Summarized from Faber, A., & Mazlish, E. (1999). "How to Talk So Kids Will Listen & Listen So Kids Will Talk."

[21]See Mackenzie, R. (1996). "Setting Limits in the Classroom: How to Move Beyond the Classroom Dance of Discipline."

[22]See Council of Economic Advisers (2000). "Teens and Their Parents in the 21st Century: An Examination of Trends in Teen Behavior and the Role of Parental Involvement. *http://clinton3.nara.gov/WH/EOP/CEA/html/Teens_Paper_Final.pdf*

Chapter 2

[1]See Hawkins, L., Pepler, D., & Craig, W. (2001). "Naturalistic Observations to Peer Interventions in Bullying."

[2]See Hoover, J. H., Oliver, R., & Hazler, R. J. (1992). "Bullying: Perceptions of Adolescent Victims in the Midwestern U.S.A."

[3]See Campbell, W., & Missiuna, C. (2011). "Bullying Risk in Children with Disabilities: A Review of the Literature."

[4]See Cappadocia, C., Weiss, J., & Pepler, D. (2012). "Bullying Experiences Among Children and Youth with Autism Spectrum Disorders."

[5]See Twyman, K., Saylor, C., Saia, D., Macias, M., Taylor, L., & Spratt, E. (2010). "Bullying and Ostracism Experiences in Children with Special Health Care Needs."

[6]See Taylor, L., Salor, C., Twyman, K., & Macias, M. (2010). "Adding Insult to Injury: Bullying Experiences of Youth with Attention Deficit Hyperactivity Disorder."

[7]See Janssen, I., Craig, W. M., Boyce, W. F., & Pickett, W. (2004). "Associations Between Overweight and Obesity Within Bullying Behaviors in School-aged Children."

[8]See Swearer-Napolitano, S. (2011). "Risk Factors and Outcomes of Bullying and Victimization for Further Information." Educational Psychology Papers and Publications. Paper 132.

[9]See LinguiSystems, Inc.

[10]See SunBelt Media.

Chapter 3

[1]See Bowen, J., & Basham, D. Excerpt from "Healing with Language." *SCS Matters, LLC. http://www.scs-matters.com/Download/dramatriangle.pdf.*

[2]See Olweus Bullying Prevention Program. *www.clemson.edu/olweus/history.htm.*

[3]See Sanchez, H. (2008). "A Brain-Based Approach to Closing the Achievement Gap."

[4]See Small, S., & Vorgan, G. (2008). "iBrain: Surviving the Technological Alteration of the Modern Mind."

[5]See Steinberg, L. (2008). "A Social Neuroscience Perspective on Adolescent Risk-taking."

[6]See Phillippi, S. (2011). "Teen Brain Development." 1st Annual Louisiana School Climate Institute. *http://new.dhh.louisiana.gov/assets/docs/BehavioralHealth/publications/ChildMHWeek2012/AdolescentBrainPHILLIPPI.pdf.*

Chapter 4

[1]See Salmivalli, C. (2001). "Feeling Good About Oneself, Being Bad to Others? Remarks on Self-Esteem, Hostility, and Aggressive Behavior."

[2]See Salmivalli C., Kaukiainen A., Kaistaniemi L., & Lagerspetz, K. (1999). "Self-evaluated Self-esteem, Peer-evaluated Self-esteem, and Defensive Egotism as Predictors of Adolescents' Participation in Bullying Situations."

[3]Rigby K., & Slee, P. (2008). "Bullying Among Australian School Children: Reported Behavior and Attitudes Toward Victims."

[4]See Olweus, D. (2003). "A Profile of Bullying at School."

[5]See Schwartz, D. (2000). "Subtypes of Victims and Aggressors in Children's Peer Groups."

[6]See Winsper, C., Lereya, T., Zanarini, M., & Wolke, D. (2012). "Involvement in Bullying in Childhood and Suicide Ideation at 11 Years: A Prospective Birth Cohort Study."

[7]See Atlas, R. S., & Pepler, D. (1998). "Observations of Bullying in the Classroom."

[8]Cross, D., Shaw, T., Hearn, L., Epstein, M., Monks, H., Lester, L., & Thomas, L. (2009). Australian Covert Bullying Prevalence Study (ACBPS). Child Health Promotion Research Centre, Edith Cowan University, Perth. Retrieved from *http://www.deewr.gov.au/schooling/nationalsafeschools/pages/research.aspx.*

[9]See Human Relations Media (2011). "Bully Bystanders: You Can Make a Difference."

[10]See Hawkins, L., Pepler, D., & Craig, W. (2001). "Naturalistic Observations to Peer Interventions in Bullying."

Chapter 5

[1]See Rideout, V., Foehr, U., & Roberts, D. (2010, January). "Generation M^2: Media in the Lives of 8- to 18-Year-Olds. A Kaiser Family Foundation Study."

[2]See Pew Research Center's Internet & American Life Project (2011). "Teens, Kindness and Cruelty on Social Network Sites: How American Teens Navigate the New World of 'Digital Citizenship.'"

[3]See Nielsen (2011). "Q3 2011 Social Media Report. Measuring Top 10 Online Categories for U.S. Internet Users."

[4]See Mason, K. L. (2008). "Cyberbullying: A Preliminary Assessment for School Personnel." *Psychology in the Schools.*

[5]See Schwartz, D. (2000). "Subtypes of Victims and Aggressors in Children's Peer Groups."

[6]See Teen Online & Wireless Safety Survey: Cyberbullying, Sexting, and Parental Controls (2009). "Cox Communications Teen Online and Wireless Safety Survey in Partnership with the National Center for Missing and Exploited Children."

[7]See Robers, S., Zhang, J., & Truman, J. (2012). "Indicators of School Crime and Safety: 2011 (NCES 2012-002/NCJ 236021). "National Center for Education Statistics, U.S. Department of Education, and Bureau of Justice Statistics, Office of Justice Programs, U.S. Department of Justice. Washington, DC."

[8]See U.S. Department of Education's National Center for Education Statistics. (2011). Student Reports of Bullying and Cyber Bullying: Results From the 2009 School Crime Supplement to the National Crime Victimization Survey.

[9]See Survey findings available at *http://www.consumerreports.org/cro/magazine-archive/2011/june/electronics-computers/state-of-the-net/facebook-concerns/index.htm.*

Chapter 6

[1]See Donald Meichenbaum. Research Director of The Melissa Institute for Violence Prevention and Treatment. *www.melissainstitute.org.*

[2]See Zimmerman, M. A., & Arunkumar, R. (1994). "Resiliency Research: Implications for Schools and Policy." Social Policy Report, 8, 1-18.

[3]See Thompson, Rosemary (2012), chapter12, for life-skills psychoeducational model.

[4]See Bogar, C. B., & Hulse-Killacky, D. (2006). "Resiliency Determinants and Resiliency Processes Among Female Adult Survivors of Childhood Sexual Abuse." *Journal of Counseling Development*, 84, 318-327.

[5]See Ginsburg, K. (2011). *Building Resilience in Children and Teens: Giving Your Child Roots and Wings, 2nd Ed.* Elk Grove Village, IL: American Academy of Pediatrics.

[6]See *fosteringresilience.com.*

[7]See Stallard, P. (2002) "Think Good—Feel Good."

[8]See Paris Goodyear-Brown. (2010). "The Worry Wars: An Anxiety Workbook for Kids and Their Helpful Adults."

[9]See Parlay International. *http://www.parlay.com.*

[10]See Beane, A. "Bully Free." *http://www.bullyfree.com.*

[11]See Schmitt, D. P. (1997). "Evolutionary Social Psychology [Review of the book *Evolutionary Social Psychology*]. *Human Ethology Bulletin,* 12, 11–13.

[12]See Gardner, J. (1990). "On Leadership." The Free Press.

[13]See Hodges, E., Malone, M., & Perry, D. (1997). "Individual Risk and Social Risk as Interacting Determinants of Victimization in the Peer Group." *Developmental Psychology,* 33, 1032–1039.

[14]See Hodges, E., Boivin, M., Vitaro, F., & Bukowski, W. (1999). "The Power of Friendship: Protection Against an Escalating Cycle of Peer Victimization." *Developmental Psychology,* 35, 94–101.

[15]See Freitag, M. K., Belsky, J., Grossmann, K., Grossmann, J. E., & Scheurer-Englisch, H. (1996). "Continuity in Child–Parent Relationships from Infancy to Middle Childhood and Relations with Friendship Competence." *Child Development,* 67, 1437–1454.

[16]See Foxman, P. (2004). "The Worried Child: Recognizing Anxiety in Children and Helping Them Heal." 227–228.

[17]See Tierney, J. P., Grossman, J. B., & Resch, N. L. (1995). *Making a Difference: An Impact Study of Big Brothers/Big Sisters.* Philadelphia: Public/Private Ventures.

[18]See Karcher, M. (2005). "The Effects of Developmental Mentoring and High School Mentors' Attendance on Their Younger Mentees' Self-Esteem, Social Skills, and Connectedness." *Psychology in the Schools,* Vol. 42(1), 65–77.

[19]See Brewster, C., & Fager, J. (1998). *Increasing Student Engagement and Motivation: From Time-on Task to Homework.* Northwest Educational Library.

[20]Adapted from PACER (*www.pacer.org*) and *www.teachsafeschools.org.*

Chapter 7

[1]See Olweus, D. (2003). "A Profile of Bullying at School."

[2]See Zehr, H. (2002). *The Little Book of Restorative Justice.* Intercourse, PA: Good Books.

[3]See Morrison, B. (2007). *Restoring Safe School Communities: A Whole School Response to Bullying, Violence, and Alienation.* Annandale, NSW: The Federation Press.

[4]Costello, B., Wachtel, J., & Wachtel, T. (2009). *The Restorative Practices Handbook for Teachers, Disciplinarians, and Administrators.* Bethlehem, PA: International Institute for Restorative Practices.

[5]See Finkelhor, D., Turner, H., Ormrod, R., Hamby, S., & Kracke, K. (2009). "Children's Exposure to Violence: A Comprehensive National Survey." U.S. Department of Justice. *www.ncjrs.gov/pdffiles1/ojjdp/227744.pdf.*

[6]See Thornberg, R., & Knutsen, M. A. (2010). "Teenagers' Explanations of Bullying." *Child and Youth Care Forum,* 40(3), 177–192.

[7]See Wachtel, T. (1999, February). "Restorative Justice in Everyday Life: Beyond the Formal Ritual." Paper presented at Reshaping Australian Institutions Conference: Restorative Justice and Civil Society, The Australian National University, Canberra.

[8]Amstutz, L., & Mullet, J. (2005). *The Little Book of Restorative Discipline for Schools: Teaching Responsibility; Creating Caring Climates.* Intercourse, PA: Good Books.

[9]See National Center for Mental Health Promotion and Youth Violence Prevention (2009). Restorative Justice: Implementation Guidelines. Also see Teske, J. S. C., & Huff, J. J. B. (2010). "The Dichotomy of Judicial Leadership: Working with the Community to Improve Outcomes for Status Youth." *Juvenile and Family Court Journal,* 61, 54–60.

[10]See Ahmed, E., Harris, N., Braithwaite, J., & Braithwaite, V. (2001). "Restorative Justice and a New Criminal Law of Substance Abuse." *Youth & Society,* 33, 227–248.

[11]Ahmed, E., & Braithwaite, J. (2006). "Forgiveness, Reconciliation, and Shame: Three Key Variables in Reducing School Bullying." *Journal of Social Issues,* 62(2), 347–370.

[12]See *www.justice.act.gov.au.*

[13]See LinguiSystems, Inc. (2004). A Social Language Program.

[14]See Barnett, M. A., Matthews, K. A., & Howard, J. A. (1979). "Relationship Between Competitiveness and Empathy in 6- and 7-Year-Olds." *Developmental Psychology*, 15(2), 221–222.

[15]See Pecukonis, E. V. (1990). "A Cognitive/Affective Empathy Training Program as a Function of Ego Development in Aggressive Adolescent Females." *Adolescence*, 25(97), 59–76.

[16]See Cotton, K. "Developing Empathy in Children and Youth." School Improvement Research Series.

[17]See Black, H., & Phillips, S. (1982). "An Intervention Program for the Development of Empathy in Student Teachers." *The Journal of Psychology*, 112, 159–168.

[18]See Kremer, J. F., & Dietzen, L. L. (1991). "Two Approaches to Teaching Accurate Empathy to Undergraduates: Teacher-Intensive and Self-Directed." *Journal of College Student Development*, 32, 69–75.

[19]See Lentini, R., Vaughn, B. J., & Fox, L. (2005). "Teaching Tools for Young Children with Challenging Behavior." Tampa, Florida: University of South Florida, Early Intervention Positive Behavior Support.

[20]See Luhn, R. R., (1992). *Managing Anger.* Crisp Publications.

[21]See Blase, K., Wagner, R., & Clark, H. B. (2004). "The SODAS Framework." The National Center on Youth Transition.

[22]See Walker, H., Colvin, G., & Ramsey, E. (1995). *Antisocial Behavior in School: Strategies and Best Practices.* Pacific Grove, CA: Brooks/Cole Publishing Company.

[23]See Glasser, W. (2000). *Counseling with Choice Theory.* New York: HarperCollins.

Chapter 8

[1]See Blazej, B. (2009). "The Community Circles Model." K–12 Youth Violence Prevention Project, Peace & Reconciliation Studies Program, University of Maine, Orono. *umaine.edu/peace/k-12-conflict-resolution-education/community-circles.*

[2]See Centers for Disease Control and Prevention. *School Connectedness: Strategies for Increasing Protective Factors Among Youth.* Atlanta, GA: U.S. Department of Health and Human Services, 2009.

[3]See Labi, N. "Let Bullies Beware." *Time* online, March 25, 2001.

[4]See Making Ethical Decisions. *www.josephsoninstitute.org.*

[5]See Teacher Vision. Character Traits. *http://www.teachervision.fen.com/writing/resource/2669.html.*

[6]See *www.goodcharacter.com.*

[7]See "Developing Character When It Counts—Grades 2–3."

[8]See *Character Education Informational Handbook & Guide*, 2002.

[9]See *http://schools.cms.k12.nc.us/dilworthES/Documents/Character%20Education/Justice%20and%20Fairness.pdf.*

[10]See Character Counts. *www.charactercounts.org.*

[11]See *ilovethatteachingidea.com.*

[12]See *http://www.education.com/magazine/article/Ed_How_Raise_Citizens/.*

[13]See Lodge, J., & Frydenberg, E. (2004). "The Role of Peer Bystanders in School Bullying: Positive Steps Toward Promoting Peaceful Schools." *Theory into Practice*, 44(4), 329–336.

[14]See Boulton, M. J., Trueman, M., Chau, C., Whitehand, C., & Amtya, K. (1999). "Concurrent Longitudinal Links Between Friendship and Peer Victimization: Implications for Befriending Interventions." *Journal of Adolescence*, 22, 461–466.

[15]See Myles, B. S., & Simpson, R. L. (1998). "Aggression and Violence by School-Age Children and Youth: Understanding the Aggression Cycle and Prevention/Intervention Strategies." *Intervention in School and Clinic*, 33(5), 259–264.

[16]See Nelson, C. M. (1997). "Aggressive and Violent Behavior: A Personal Perspective." *Education and Treatment of Children*, 20(3), 250–262.

[17]See Priest, C. (2007). "Incorporating Character Education into the Early Childhood Degree Program: The Need and One Department's Response." *Journal of Early Childhood Teacher Education*, 28(2), 153–161.

[18]See Dugan, M. "A Nested Theory of Conflict." *A Leadership Journal: Women in Leadership—Sharing a Vision.*

[19]See Thomas-Kilmann Conflict Mode Instrument. Consulting Psychologists Press (CPP). *www.cpp-db.com.*

[20]See Young, M. E. (2012). *Learning the Art of Helping: Building Blocks and Techniques.* (5th ed.). Upper Saddle River, NJ: Merrill Prentice Hall.

[21]See Wood, J. T. (2009). *Gendered Lives: Communication, Gender, and Culture.* Boston: Wadsworth Cengage Learning.

[22]See Schilling, D., & Dunne, G. (1992). *Understanding Me.* Innerchoice Publishing.

[23]See "Dealing with Accusations." A Social Language Program. LinguiSystems, Inc.

[24]See Epley, N., & Caruso, E. M. (2008). "Perspective Taking: Misstepping into Others' Shoes," *In The Handbook of Imagination and Mental Stimulation* (pp. 297–311) K. D. Markman, W. M. P. Klein, & J. A. Suhr (Eds.).

[25]See Galinsky, A. D., Ku, G., & Wang, C. S. (2005). "Smarter and Slower: The Differential Impact of Perspective-Taking on Judgments and Behavior" and "Perspective-Taking and Self-Other Overlap: Fostering Social Bonds and Facilitating Social Coordination." *Group Processes & Intergroup Relations*, 8(2) 109–124.

[26]See Bonner, C. (2002). "Emotion Regulation, Interpersonal Effectiveness, and Distress Tolerance Skills for Adolescents: A Treatment Manual." University of Pittsburgh Services for Teens At Risk (STAR-Center), Pittsburgh, PA.

[27]See The Ohio Commission on Dispute Resolution and Conflict Management (2001).

[28]See Wexler, D. (1991). The PRISM Workbook: A Program for Innovative Self Management. New York: W.W. Norton & Company.

[29]See Covey, S. *7 Habits of Highly Effective People*, pp. 23–24.

[30]See Linehan, M. M. (1993). *Skills Training Manual for Treating Borderline Personality Disorder.* New York: The Guilford Press.

[31]See Frydenberg, E. (2008). *Adolescent Coping: Advances in Theory, Practice, and Research.* New York, NY: Routledge.

[32]See Bonner, C. (2002). "Emotion Regulation, Interpersonal Effectiveness, and Distress Tolerance Skills for Adolescents," p. 36.

[33]See Craig, W. M., Pepler, D. J., & Atlas, R. (2000). "Observations of Bullying on the Playground and in the Classroom." *International Journal of School Psychology*, 21, 22–36.

[34]See Pepler, D., Craig, W., & O'Connell, P. (2010). "Peer Processes in Bullying: Informing Prevention and Intervention Strategies," in *Handbook of Bullying in Schools: An International Perspective* (pp. 469–479), S. R. Jimerson, S. M. Swearer, & D. L. Espelage (Eds.). New York: Routledge.

[35]See Salmivalli, C., Kärnä, A., & Poskiparta, E. (2010). "From Peer Putdowns to Peer Support: A Theoretical Model and How It Translated into a National Anti-Bullying Program," in *Handbook of Bullying in Schools: An International Perspective* (pp. 441–454), S. R. Jimerson, S. M. Swearer, & D. L. Espelage (Eds.). New York: Routledge.